D0782307

MICAH

WISDOM COMMENTARY

Volume 37

Micah

Julia M. O'Brien

Carol J. Dempsey, OP
Volume Editor

Barbara E. Reid, OP
General Editor

REGIS COLLEGE LIBRARY
100 Wellesley Street West
Toronto, Ontario
Canada M5S 2Z5

A Michael Glazier Book

LITURGICAL PRESS
Collegeville, Minnesota

www.litpress.org

BS
1615.53
O27
2015

A Michael Glazier Book published by Liturgical Press

Cover design by Ann Blattner. *Chapter Letter 'W', Acts of the Apostles, Chapter 4*, Donald Jackson, Copyright 2002, *The Saint John's Bible*, Saint John's University, Collegeville, Minnesota USA. Used by permission. All rights reserved.

Scripture texts in this work are taken from the *New Revised Standard Version Bible*, © 1989, Division of Christian Education of the National Council of the Churches of Christ in the United States of America. Used by permission. All rights reserved.

© 2015 by Order of Saint Benedict, Collegeville, Minnesota. All rights reserved. No part of this book may be reproduced in any form, by print, microfilm, microfiche, mechanical recording, photocopying, translation, or by any other means, known or yet unknown, for any purpose except brief quotations in reviews, without the previous written permission of Liturgical Press, Saint John's Abbey, PO Box 7500, Collegeville, Minnesota 56321-7500. Printed in the United States of America.

1   2   3   4   5   6   7   8   9

Library of Congress Cataloging-in-Publication Data

O'Brien, Julia M.
    Micah / Julia M. O'Brien ; Carol Dempsey, volume editor ; Barbara E. Reid, OP, general editor.
        pages   cm. — (Wisdom commentary ; Volume 37)
    "A Michael Glazier book."
    Includes bibliographical references.
    ISBN 978-0-8146-8161-9 — ISBN 978-0-8146-8186-2 (ebook)
    1. Bible. Micah—Commentaries.   I. Title.

BS1615.53.O27   2015
224'.93077—dc23   2015018707

To my mother, Aileen Lipe Myers,
whose dogged determination to live life on her own terms
remains an inspiration

REGIS COLLEGE LIBRARY
100 Wellesley Street West
Toronto, Ontario
Canada M5S 2Z5

Contents

Abbreviations

AB	Anchor Bible
ABRL	Anchor Bible Reference Library
AIL	Ancient Israel and Its Literature
AOTC	Abingdon Old Testament Commentaries
BibInt	*Biblical Interpretation*
BibInt	Biblical Interpretation Series
BRev	*Bible Review*
BZAW	Beihefte zur Zeitschrift für die alttestamentliche Wissenschaft
FCB	Feminist Companion to the Bible
IFT	Introductions in Feminist Theology
Int	*Interpretation*
JBL	*Journal of Biblical Literature*
JETS	*Journal of the Evangelical Theological Society*
JFSR	*Journal of Feminist Studies in Religion*
JPS	Jewish Publication Society
JR	*Journal of Religion*
JSOT	*Journal for the Study of the Old Testament*
JSOTSup	Journal for the Study of the Old Testament Supplement Series

KJV   King James Bible

LHBOTS   Library of Hebrew Bible/Old Testament Studies

MT   Masoretic Text

NRSV   New Revised Standard Version

NIV   New International Version

OBT   Overtures to Biblical Theology

OTG   Old Testament Guides

SBL   Society of Biblical Literature

SBLDS   Society of Biblical Literature Dissertation Series

SemeiaSt   Semeia Studies

VT   *Vetus Testamentum*

Acknowledgments

I thank all those who supported this work:

- Lancaster Theological Seminary for providing a sabbatical during which I completed much of the writing
- my editors Carol Dempsey and Barbara Reid for continuing to encourage my wrestling with Micah
- and Liturgical Press for ably bringing this volume to fruition

I also thank the Contributing Voices, whose work enriched and stretched my own, and Dr. Pippa Salonius, who graciously consulted on the art history that I discuss in my commentary on Micah 4–5.

And, mostly, I thank my husband David for understanding—and sharing—the satisfaction that comes from work, play, and partnership.

Contributors

Rev. Dr. Kharma Amos is the associate director of formation and leadership development for Metropolitan Community Churches (MCC). A thoughtful queer theologian, she is instrumental in preparing MCC candidates for ordination.

Dr. Matthew J. M. Coomber is assistant professor of theology at St. Ambrose University. An ordained priest in the Episcopal Church, he writes widely on the Bible and social justice.

Rev. Tracey Cox is executive minister at Shiloh Baptist Church, York, Pennsylvania. A former elementary school educator, she raises questions of race and class in the biblical text.

Ms. Janet Ruth Falon is an award-winning writer and accomplished author of books, articles, essays, plays, poems, documentary scripts, and more. Her website is www.janetfalon.com.

Ms. Merle Feld is a widely published poet, award-winning playwright, peace activist, and educator. Since 2005 she has served as founding director of the Albin Rabbinic Writing Institute. Her website is www.merlefeld.com.

Rev. Beauty Maenzanise is the dean of the Faculty of Theology at Africa University in Zimbabwe. An ordained elder in the United Methodist Church, she is active in international women's organizations.

Ms. Viola Raheb is an independent consultant on development cooperation and cross-cultural dialogue for various institutions. A native of

Bethlehem, Palestine, she currently works at the University of Vienna, where she is completing a PhD.

Dr. Deborah Weissman served for six years as the president of the International Council of Christians and Jews. A resident of Jerusalem, she is a highly respected educator, speaker, and writer.

Ms. Jennifer Williams holds a PhD in Hebrew Bible from Vanderbilt University. Her work examines the areas of gender, literary analysis, and queer theory.

Dr. Karen Lebacqz is professor emerita of theological ethics at Pacific School of Religion. Her lifelong commitment to issues of social justice has led to extensive work in professional ethics, bioethics, and ethical theory.

Foreword

"Tell It on the Mountain"—or, "And You Shall Tell Your Daughter [as Well]"

Athalya Brenner-Idan
Universiteit van Amsterdam/Tel Aviv University

What can Wisdom Commentary do to help, and for whom? The commentary genre has always been privileged in biblical studies. Traditionally acclaimed commentary series, such as the International Critical Commentary, Old Testament and New Testament Library, Hermeneia, Anchor Bible, Eerdmans, and Word—to name but several—enjoy nearly automatic prestige; and the number of women authors who participate in those is relatively small by comparison to their growing number in the scholarly guild. There certainly are some volumes written by women in them, especially in recent decades. At this time, however, this does not reflect the situation on the ground. Further, size matters. In that sense, the sheer size of the Wisdom Commentary is essential. This also represents a considerable investment and the possibility of reaching a wider audience than those already "converted."

Expecting women scholars to deal especially or only with what is considered strictly "female" matters seems unwarranted. According to Audre Lorde, "The master's tools will never dismantle the master's house."[1] But this maxim is not relevant to our case. The point of this commentary is not to destroy but to attain greater participation in the interpretive dialogue about biblical texts. Women scholars may bring additional questions to the readerly agenda as well as fresh angles to existing issues. To assume that their questions are designed only to topple a certain male hegemony is not convincing.

At first I did ask myself: is this commentary series an addition to calm raw nerves, an embellishment to make upholding the old hierarchy palatable? Or is it indeed about becoming the Master? On second and third thoughts, however, I understood that becoming the Master is not what this is about. Knowledge is power. Since Foucault at the very least, this cannot be in dispute. Writing commentaries for biblical texts by women for women and for men, of confessional as well as non-confessional convictions, will sabotage (hopefully) the established hierarchy but will not topple it. This is about an attempt to integrate more fully, to introduce another viewpoint, to become. What excites me about the Wisdom Commentary is that it is not offered as just an alternative supplanting or substituting for the dominant discourse.

These commentaries on biblical books will retain nonauthoritative, pluralistic viewpoints. And yes, once again, the weight of a dedicated series, to distinguish from collections of standalone volumes, will prove weightier.

That such an approach is especially important in the case of the Hebrew Bible/Old Testament is beyond doubt. Women of Judaism, Christianity, and also Islam have struggled to make it their own for centuries, even more than they have fought for the New Testament and the Qur'an. Every Hebrew Bible/Old Testament volume in this project is evidence that the day has arrived: it is now possible to read *all* the Jewish canonical books as a collection, for a collection they are, with guidance conceived of with the needs of women readers (not only men) as an integral inspiration and part thereof.

In my Jewish tradition, the main motivation for reciting the Haggadah, the ritual text recited yearly on Passover, the festival of liberation from

---

1. Audre Lorde, "The Master's Tools Will Never Dismantle the Master's House," in *Sister Outsider: Essays and Speeches* (Berkeley, CA: Crossing Press, 1984, 2007), 110–14. First delivered in the Second Sex Conference in New York, 1979.

bondage, is given as "And you shall tell your son" (from Exod 13:8). The knowledge and experience of past generations is thus transferred to the next, for constructing the present and the future. The ancient maxim is, literally, limited to a male audience. This series remolds the maxim into a new inclusive shape, which is of the utmost consequence: "And you shall tell your son" is extended to "And you shall tell your daughter [as well as your son]." Or, if you want, "Tell it on the mountain," for all to hear.

This is what it's all about.

Editor's Introduction to Wisdom Commentary

"She Is a Breath of the Power of God" (Wis 7:25)

Barbara E. Reid, OP

General Editor

Wisdom Commentary is the first series to offer detailed feminist interpretation of every book of the Bible. The fruit of collaborative work by an ecumenical and interreligious team of scholars, the volumes provide serious, scholarly engagement with the whole biblical text, not only those texts that explicitly mention women. The series is intended for clergy, teachers, ministers, and all serious students of the Bible. Designed to be both accessible and informed by the various approaches of biblical scholarship, it pays particular attention to the world in front of the text, that is, how the text is heard and appropriated. At the same time, this series aims to be faithful to the ancient text and its earliest audiences; thus the volumes also explicate the worlds behind the text and within it. While issues of gender are primary in this project, the volumes also address the intersecting issues of power, authority, ethnicity, race, class, and religious belief and practice. The fifty-eight volumes include the books regarded as canonical by Jews (i.e., the Tanakh); Protestants (the "Hebrew Bible" and the New Testament); and Roman Catholic, Anglican, and Eastern Orthodox Communions (i.e., Tobit, Judith, 1 and 2 Maccabees, Wisdom of Solomon, Sirach/Ecclesiasticus, Baruch, including the Letter of Jeremiah, the additions to Esther, and Susanna and Bel and the Dragon in Daniel).

A Symphony of Diverse Voices

Included in the Wisdom Commentary series are voices from scholars of many different religious traditions, of diverse ages, differing sexual identities, and varying cultural, racial, ethnic, and social contexts. Some have been pioneers in feminist biblical interpretation; others are newer contributors from a younger generation. A further distinctive feature of this series is that each volume incorporates voices other than that of the lead author(s). These voices appear alongside the commentary of the lead author(s), in the grayscale inserts. At times, a contributor may offer an alternative interpretation or a critique of the position taken by the lead author(s). At other times, she or he may offer a complementary interpretation from a different cultural context or subject position. Occasionally, portions of previously published material bring in other views. The diverse voices are not intended to be contestants in a debate or a cacophony of discordant notes. The multiple voices reflect that there is no single definitive feminist interpretation of a text. In addition, they show the importance of subject position in the process of interpretation. In this regard, the Wisdom Commentary series takes inspiration from the Talmud and from *The Torah: A Women's Commentary* (ed. Tamara Cohn Eskenazi and Andrea L. Weiss; New York: Women of Reform Judaism, Federation of Temple Sisterhood, 2008), in which many voices, even conflicting ones, are included and not harmonized.

Contributors include biblical scholars, theologians, and readers of Scripture from outside the scholarly and religious guilds. At times, their comments pertain to a particular text. In some instances they address a theme or topic that arises from the text.

Another feature that highlights the collaborative nature of feminist biblical interpretation is that a number of the volumes have two lead authors who have worked in tandem from the inception of the project and whose voices interweave throughout the commentary.

Woman Wisdom

The title, Wisdom Commentary, reflects both the importance to feminists of the figure of Woman Wisdom in the Scriptures and the distinct wisdom that feminist women and men bring to the interpretive process. In the Scriptures, Woman Wisdom appears as "a breath of the power of God, and a pure emanation of the glory of the Almighty" (Wis 7:25), who was present and active in fashioning all that exists (Prov 8:22-31; Wis 8:6). She is a spirit who pervades and penetrates all things (Wis 7:22-23), and she provides guidance and nourishment at her all-inclusive table (Prov 9:1-5). In both postexilic biblical and nonbiblical Jewish sources, Woman Wisdom is often equated with Torah, e.g., Sir 24:23-34; Bar 3:9–4:4; 38:2; 46:4-5; 2 Bar 48:33, 36; 4 Ezra 5:9-10; 13:55; 14:40; 1 Enoch 42.

The New Testament frequently portrays Jesus as Wisdom incarnate. He invites his followers, "take my yoke upon you and learn from me" (Matt 11:29), just as Ben Sira advises, "put your neck under her [Wisdom's] yoke and let your souls receive instruction" (Sir 51:26). Just as Wisdom experiences rejection (Prov 1:23-25; Sir 15:7-8; Wis 10:3; Bar 3:12), so too does Jesus (Mark 8:31; John 1:10-11). Only some accept his invitation to his all-inclusive banquet (Matt 22:1-14; Luke 14:15-24; compare Prov 1:20-21; 9:3-5). Yet, "wisdom is vindicated by her deeds" (Matt 11:19, speaking of Jesus and John the Baptist; in the Lucan parallel at 7:35 they are called "wisdom's children"). There are numerous parallels between what is said of Wisdom and of the *Logos* in the Prologue of the Fourth Gospel (John 1:1-18). These are only a few of many examples. This female embodiment of divine presence and power is an apt image to guide the work of this series.

Feminism

There are many different understandings of the term "feminism." The various meanings, aims, and methods have developed exponentially in recent decades. Feminism is a perspective and a movement that springs from a recognition of inequities toward women, and it advocates for changes in whatever structures prevent full human flourishing. Three waves of feminism in the United States are commonly recognized. The first, arising in the mid-nineteenth century and lasting into the early twentieth, was sparked by women's efforts to be involved in the public sphere and to win the right to vote. In the 1960s and 1970s, the second wave focused on civil rights and equality for women. With the third wave, from the 1980s forward, came global feminism and the emphasis on the contextual nature of interpretation. As feminism has matured, it has recognized that inequities based on gender are interwoven with power imbalances based on race, class, ethnicity, religion, sexual identity, physical ability, and a host of other social markers.

Feminist Women and Men

Men who choose to identify with and partner with feminist women in the work of deconstructing systems of domination and building structures of equality are rightly regarded as feminists. Some men readily identify with experiences of women who are discriminated against on the basis of sex/gender, having themselves had comparable experiences; others who may not have faced direct discrimination or stereotyping recognize that inequity and problematic characterization still occur, and they seek correction. This series is pleased to include feminist men both as lead authors and as contributing voices.

Feminist Biblical Interpretation

Women interpreting the Bible from the lenses of their own experience is nothing new. Throughout the ages women have recounted the biblical stories, teaching them to their children and others, all the while interpreting them afresh for their time and circumstances.[1] Following is a very brief sketch of select foremothers who laid the groundwork for contemporary feminist biblical interpretation.

One of the earliest known Christian women who challenged patriarchal interpretations of Scripture was a consecrated virgin named Helie, who lived in the second century CE. When she refused to marry, her parents brought her before a judge, who quoted to her Paul's admonition, "It is better to marry than to be aflame with passion" (1 Cor 7:9). In response, Helie first acknowledges that this is what Scripture says, but then she retorts, "but not for everyone, that is, not for holy virgins."[2] She is one of the first to question the notion that a text has one meaning that is applicable in all situations.

A Jewish woman who also lived in the second century CE, Beruriah, is said to have had "profound knowledge of biblical exegesis and out-

---

1. For fuller treatments of this history, see chap. 7, "One Thousand Years of Feminist Bible Criticism," in Gerda Lerner, *Creation of Feminist Consciousness: From the Middle Ages to Eighteen-Seventy* (New York: Oxford University Press, 1993), 138–66; Susanne Scholz, "From the 'Woman's Bible' to the 'Women's Bible,' The History of Feminist Approaches to the Hebrew Bible," in *Introducing the Women's Hebrew Bible*, IFT 13 (New York: T & T Clark, 2007), 12–32; Marion Ann Taylor and Agnes Choi, eds., *Handbook of Women Biblical Interpreters: A Historical and Biographical Guide* (Grand Rapids, MI: Baker Academic, 2012).

2. Madrid, Escorial MS, a II 9, f. 90 v., as cited in Lerner, *Feminist Consciousness*, 140.

standing intelligence."[3] One story preserved in the Talmud (b. Berachot 10a) tells of how she challenged her husband, Rabbi Meir, when he prayed for the destruction of a sinner. Proffering an alternate interpretation, she argued that Psalm 104:35 advocated praying for the destruction of sin, not the sinner.

In medieval times the first written commentaries on Scripture from a critical feminist point of view emerge. While others may have been produced and passed on orally, they are for the most part lost to us now. Among the earliest preserved feminist writings are those of Hildegard of Bingen (1098–1179), German writer, mystic, and abbess of a Benedictine monastery. She reinterpreted the Genesis narratives in a way that presented women and men as complementary and interdependent. She frequently wrote about feminine aspects of the Divine.[4] Along with other women mystics of the time, such as Julian of Norwich (1342–ca. 1416), she spoke authoritatively from her personal experiences of God's revelation in prayer.

In this era, women were also among the scribes who copied biblical manuscripts. Notable among them is Paula Dei Mansi of Verona, from a distinguished family of Jewish scribes. In 1288, she translated from Hebrew into Italian a collection of Bible commentaries written by her father and added her own explanations.[5]

Another pioneer, Christine de Pizan (1365–ca. 1430), was a French court writer and prolific poet. She used allegory and common sense to subvert misogynist readings of Scripture and celebrated the accomplishments of female biblical figures to argue for women's active roles in building society.[6]

By the seventeenth century, there were women who asserted that the biblical text needs to be understood and interpreted in its historical context. For example, Rachel Speght (1597–ca. 1630), a Calvinist English poet, elaborates on the historical situation in first-century Corinth that prompted Paul to say, "It is well for a man not to touch a woman" (1 Cor

---

3. See Judith R. Baskin, "Women and Post-Biblical Commentary," in *The Torah: A Women's Commentary*, ed. Tamara Cohn Eskenazi and Andrea L. Weiss (New York: Women of Reform Judaism, Federation of Temple Sisterhood, 2008), xlix–lv, here lii.

4. Hildegard of Bingen, *De Operatione Dei*, 1.4.100; PL 197:885bc, as cited in Lerner, *Feminist Consciousness*, 142–43. See also Barbara Newman, *Sister of Wisdom: St. Hildegard's Theology of the Feminine* (Berkeley: University of California Press, 1987).

5. Emily Taitz, Sondra Henry, Cheryl Tallan, eds., *JPS Guide to Jewish Women 600 B.C.E.–1900 C.E.* (Philadelphia: JPS, 2003), 110–11.

6. See further Taylor and Choi, *Handbook of Women Biblical Interpreters*, 127–32.

7:1). Her aim was to show that the biblical texts should not be applied in a literal fashion to all times and circumstances. Similarly, Margaret Fell (1614–1702), one of the founders of the Religious Society of Friends (Quakers) in Britain, addressed the Pauline prohibitions against women speaking in church by insisting that they do not have universal validity. Rather, they need to be understood in their historical context, as addressed to a local church in particular time-bound circumstances.[7]

Along with analyzing the historical context of the biblical writings, women in the eighteenth and nineteenth centuries began to attend to misogynistic interpretations based on faulty translations. One of the first to do so was British feminist Mary Astell (1666–1731).[8] In the United States, the Grimké sisters, Sarah (1792–1873) and Angelina (1805–1879), Quaker women from a slaveholding family in South Carolina, learned biblical Greek and Hebrew so that they could interpret the Bible for themselves. They were prompted to do so after men sought to silence them from speaking out against slavery and for women's rights by claiming that the Bible (e.g., 1 Cor 14:34) prevented women from speaking in public.[9] Another prominent abolitionist, Sojourner Truth (ca. 1797–1883), a former slave, quoted the Bible liberally in her speeches[10] and in so doing challenged cultural assumptions and biblical interpretations that undergird gender inequities.

Another monumental work that emerged in nineteenth-century England was that of Jewish theologian Grace Aguilar (1816–1847), *The Women of Israel*,[11] published in 1845. Aguilar's approach was to make connections between the biblical women and contemporary Jewish women's concerns. She aimed to counter the widespread notion that women were degraded in Jewish law and that only in Christianity were

7. Her major work, *Women's Speaking Justified, Proved and Allowed by the Scriptures*, published in London in 1667, gave a systematic feminist reading of all biblical texts pertaining to women.

8. Mary Astell, *Some Reflections upon Marriage* (New York: Source Book Press, 1970, reprint of the 1730 edition; earliest edition of this work is 1700), 103–4.

9. See further Sarah Grimké, *Letters on the Equality of the Sexes and the Condition of Woman* (Boston: Isaac Knapp, 1838).

10. See, for example, her most famous speech, "Ain't I a Woman?," delivered in 1851 at the Ohio Women's Rights Convention in Akron, OH; http://www.fordham.edu/halsall/mod/sojtruth-woman.asp.

11. The full title is *The Women of Israel or Characters and Sketches from the Holy Scriptures and Jewish History Illustrative of the Past History, Present Duty, and Future Destiny of the Hebrew Females, as Based on the Word of God.*

women's dignity and value upheld. Her intent was to help Jewish women find strength and encouragement by seeing the evidence of God's compassionate love in the history of every woman in the Bible. While not a full commentary on the Bible, Aguilar's work stands out for its comprehensive treatment of every female biblical character, including even the most obscure references.[12]

The first person to produce a full-blown feminist commentary on the Bible was Elizabeth Cady Stanton (1815–1902). A leading proponent in the United States for women's right to vote, she found that whenever women tried to make inroads into politics, education, or the work world the Bible was quoted against them. Along with a team of like-minded women, she produced her own commentary on every text of the Bible that concerned women. Her pioneering two-volume project, *The Woman's Bible*, published in 1895 and 1898, urges women to recognize that texts that degrade women come from the men who wrote the texts, not from God, and to use their common sense to rethink what has been presented to them as sacred.

Nearly a century later, *The Women's Bible Commentary*, edited by Sharon Ringe and Carol Newsom (Westminster John Knox Press, 1992), appeared. This one-volume commentary features North American feminist scholarship on each book of the Protestant canon. Like Cady Stanton's commentary, it does not contain comments on every section of the biblical text but only on those passages deemed relevant to women. It was revised and expanded in 1998 to include the Apocrypha/Deuterocanonical books, and the contributors to this new volume reflect the global face of contemporary feminist scholarship. The revisions made in the third edition, which appeared in 2012, represent the profound advances in feminist biblical scholarship and include newer voices. In both the second and third editions, *The* has been dropped from the title.

Also appearing at the centennial of Cady Stanton's *The Woman's Bible* were two volumes edited by Elisabeth Schüssler Fiorenza with the assistance of Shelly Matthews. The first, *Searching the Scriptures: A Feminist Introduction* (New York: Crossroad, 1993), charts a comprehensive approach to feminist interpretation from ecumenical, interreligious, and multicultural perspectives. The second volume, published in 1994, provides critical feminist commentary on each book of the New Testament

---

12. See further Eskenazi and Weiss, *The Torah: A Women's Commentary*, xxxviii; Taylor and Choi, *Handbook of Women Biblical Interpreters*, 31–37.

as well as on three books of Jewish Pseudepigrapha and eleven other early Christian writings.

In Europe, similar endeavors have been undertaken, such as the one-volume *Kompendium Feministische Bibelauslegung*, edited by Luise Schottroff and Marie-Theres Wacker (Gütersloh, Gütersloher Verlagshaus, 2007), featuring German feminist biblical interpretation of each book of the Bible, along with apocryphal books, and several extrabiblical writings. This work, now in its third edition, has recently been translated into English.[13] A multivolume project, *The Bible and Women: An Encylopaedia of Exegesis and Cultural History*, edited by Irmtraud Fischer, Adriana Valerio, Mercedes Navarro Puerto, and Christiana de Groot, is currently in production. This project presents a history of the reception of the Bible as embedded in Western cultural history and focuses particularly on gender-relevant biblical themes, biblical female characters, and women recipients of the Bible. The volumes are published in English, Spanish, Italian, and German.[14]

Another groundbreaking work is the collection The Feminist Companion to the Bible Series, edited by Athalya Brenner (Sheffield: Sheffield Academic Press, 1993–2001). To date, nineteen volumes of commentaries on the Old Testament have been published, with more in production. The parallel series, Feminist Companion to the New Testament and Early Christian Writings, edited by Amy-Jill Levine with Marianne Blickenstaff and Maria Mayo Robbins (Sheffield: Sheffield Academic Press, 2001–2009), contains thirteen volumes with one more planned. These two series are not full commentaries on the biblical books but comprise collected essays on discrete biblical texts.

Works by individual feminist biblical scholars in all parts of the world abound, and they are now too numerous to list in this introduction. Feminist biblical interpretation has reached a level of maturity that now makes possible a commentary series on every book of the Bible. In recent decades, women have had greater access to formal theological education, have been able to learn critical analytical tools, have put their own in-

13. *Feminist Biblical Interpretation: A Compendium of Critical Commentary on the Books of the Bible and Related Literature,* trans. Lisa E. Dahill, Everett R. Kalin, Nancy Lukens, Linda M. Maloney, Barbara Rumscheidt, Martin Rumscheidt, and Tina Steiner (Grand Rapids, MI: Eerdmans, 2012).

14. The first volume, on the Torah, appeared in Spanish in 2009, in German and Italian in 2010, and in English in 2011 (Atlanta, GA: SBL). For further information, see http://www.bibleandwomen.org.

terpretations into writing, and have developed new methods of biblical interpretation. Until recent decades the work of feminist biblical inter- preters was largely unknown, both to other women and to their brothers in the synagogue, church, and academy. Feminists now have taken their place in the professional world of biblical scholars, where they build on the work of their foremothers and connect with one another across the globe in ways not previously possible. In a few short decades, feminist biblical criticism has become an integral part of the academy.

Methodologies

Feminist biblical scholars use a variety of methods and often employ a number of them together.[15] In the Wisdom Commentary series, the authors will explain their understanding of feminism and the feminist reading strategies used in their commentary. Each volume treats the biblical text in blocks of material, not an analysis verse by verse. The entire text is considered, not only those passages that feature female characters or that speak specifically about women. When women are not apparent in the narrative, feminist lenses are used to analyze the dy- namics in the text between male characters, the models of power, binary ways of thinking, and dynamics of imperialism. Attention is given to how the whole text functions and how it was and is heard, both in its original context and today. Issues of particular concern to women—e.g., poverty, food, health, the environment, water—come to the fore.

One of the approaches used by early feminists and still popular today is to lift up the overlooked and forgotten stories of women in the Bible. Studies of women in each of the Testaments have been done, and there are also studies on women in particular biblical books.[16] Feminists recognize that the examples of biblical characters can be

---

15. See the seventeen essays in Caroline Vander Stichele and Todd Penner, eds., *Her Master's Tools? Feminist and Postcolonial Engagements of Historical-Critical Discourse* (Atlanta, GA: SBL, 2005), which show the complementarity of various approaches.

16. See, e.g., Alice Bach, ed., *Women in the Hebrew Bible: A Reader* (New York: Rout- ledge, 1998); Tikva Frymer-Kensky, *Reading the Women of the Bible* (New York: Schocken, 2002); Carol Meyers, Toni Craven, and Ross S. Kraemer, *Women in Scripture* (Grand Rapids, MI: Eerdmans, 2000); Irene Nowell, *Women in the Old Testament* (Collegeville, MN: Liturgical Press, 1997); Katharine Doob Sakenfeld, *Just Wives? Stories of Power and Survival in the Old Testament and Today* (Louisville, KY: Westminster John Knox, 2003); Mary Ann Getty-Sullivan, *Women in the New Testament* (Collegeville, MN: Liturgical Press, 2001); Bonnie Thurston, *Women in the New Testament* (New York: Crossroad, 1998).

both empowering and problematic. The point of the feminist enterprise is not to serve as an apologetic for women; it is rather, in part, to recover women's history and literary roles in all their complexity and to learn from that recovery.

Retrieving the submerged history of biblical women is a crucial step for constructing the story of the past so as to lead to liberative possibilities for the present and future. There are, however, some pitfalls to this approach. Sometimes depictions of biblical women have been naïve and romantic. Some commentators exalt the virtues of both biblical and contemporary women and paint women as superior to men. Such reverse discrimination inhibits movement toward equality for all. In addition, some feminists challenge the idea that one can "pluck positive images out of an admittedly androcentric text, separating literary characterizations from the androcentric interests they were created to serve."[17] Still other feminists find these images to have enormous value.

One other danger with seeking the submerged history of women is the tendency for Christian feminists to paint Jesus and even Paul as liberators of women in a way that demonizes Judaism.[18] Wisdom Commentary aims to enhance understanding of Jesus as well as Paul as Jews of their day and to forge solidarity among Jewish and Christian feminists.

Feminist scholars who use historical-critical methods analyze the world behind the text; they seek to understand the historical context from which the text emerged and the circumstances of the communities to whom it was addressed. In bringing feminist lenses to this approach, the aim is not to impose modern expectations on ancient cultures but to unmask the ways that ideologically problematic mind-sets that produced the ancient texts are still promulgated through the text. Feminist biblical scholars aim not only to deconstruct but also to reclaim and reconstruct biblical history as women's history, in which women were central and

17. Cheryl Exum, "Second Thoughts about Secondary Characters: Women in Exodus 1.8–2.10," in *A Feminist Companion to Exodus to Deuteronomy*, FCB 6 (Sheffield: Sheffield Academic Press, 1994), 75–97, here 76.

18. See Judith Plaskow, "Anti-Judaism in Feminist Christian Interpretation," in *Searching the Scriptures: A Feminist Introduction* (New York: Crossroad, 1993), 1:117–29; Amy-Jill Levine, "The New Testament and Anti-Judaism," in *The Misunderstood Jew: The Church and the Scandal of the Jewish Jesus* (San Francisco: HarperSanFrancisco, 2006), 87–117.

active agents in creating religious heritage.[19] A further step is to construct meaning for contemporary women and men in a liberative movement toward transformation of social, political, economic, and religious structures.[20] In recent years, some feminists have embraced new historicism, which accents the creative role of the interpreter in any construction of history and exposes the power struggles to which the text witnesses.[21]

Literary critics analyze the world of the text: its form, language patterns, and rhetorical function.[22] They do not attempt to separate layers of tradition and redaction but focus on the text holistically, as it is in its present form. They examine how meaning is created in the interaction between the text and its reader in multiple contexts. Within the arena of literary approaches are reader-oriented approaches, narrative, rhetorical, structuralist, post-structuralist, deconstructive, ideological, autobiographical, and performance criticism.[23] Narrative critics study the interrelation among author, text, and audience through investigation of

---

19. See, for example, Phyllis A. Bird, *Missing Persons and Mistaken Identities: Women and Gender in Ancient Israel* (Minneapolis: Fortress Press, 1997); Elisabeth Schüssler Fiorenza, *In Memory of Her: A Feminist Theological Reconstruction of Christian Origins* (New York: Crossroad, 1984); Ross Shepard Kraemer and Mary Rose D'Angelo, eds., *Women and Christian Origins* (New York: Oxford University Press, 1999).

20. See, e.g., Sandra M. Schneiders, *The Revelatory Text: Interpreting the New Testament as Sacred Scripture*, rev. ed. (Collegeville, MN: Liturgical Press, 1999), whose aim is to engage in biblical interpretation not only for intellectual enlightenment but, even more important, for personal and communal transformation. Elisabeth Schüssler Fiorenza (*Wisdom Ways: Introducing Feminist Biblical Interpretation* [Maryknoll, NY: Orbis Books, 2001]) envisions the work of feminist biblical interpretation as a dance of Wisdom that consists of seven steps that interweave in spiral movements toward liberation, the final one being transformative action for change.

21. See Gina Hens Piazza, *The New Historicism*, Guides to Biblical Scholarship, Old Testament Series (Minneapolis: Fortress Press, 2002).

22. Phyllis Trible was among the first to employ this method with texts from Genesis and Ruth in her groundbreaking book *God and the Rhetoric of Sexuality*, OBT (Philadelphia: Fortress Press, 1978). Another pioneer in feminist literary criticism is Mieke Bal (*Lethal Love: Feminist Literary Readings of Biblical Love Stories* [Bloomington: Indiana University Press, 1987]). For surveys of recent developments in literary methods, see Terry Eagleton, *Literary Theory: An Introduction*, 3rd ed. (Minneapolis: University of Minnesota Press, 2008); Janice Capel Anderson and Stephen D. Moore, eds., *Mark and Method: New Approaches in Biblical Studies*, 2nd ed. (Minneapolis: Fortress Press, 2008).

23. See, e.g., J. Cheryl Exum and David J. A. Clines, eds., *The New Literary Criticism and the Hebrew Bible* (Valley Forge, PA: Trinity Press International, 1993); Edgar V. McKnight and Elizabeth Struthers Malbon, eds., *The New Literary Criticism and the New Testament* (Valley Forge, PA: Trinity Press International, 1994).

settings, both spatial and temporal; characters; plot; and narrative techniques (e.g., irony, parody, intertextual allusions). Reader-response critics attend to the impact that the text has on the reader or hearer. They recognize that when a text is detrimental toward women there is the choice either to affirm the text or to read against the grain toward a liberative end. Rhetorical criticism analyzes the style of argumentation and attends to how the author is attempting to shape the thinking or actions of the hearer. Structuralist critics analyze the complex patterns of binary oppositions in the text to derive its meaning.[24] Post-structuralist approaches challenge the notion that there are fixed meanings to any biblical text or that there is one universal truth. They engage in close readings of the text and often engage in intertextual analysis.[25] Within this approach is deconstructionist criticism, which views the text as a site of conflict, with competing narratives. The interpreter aims to expose the fault lines and overturn and reconfigure binaries by elevating the underling of a pair and foregrounding it.[26] Feminists also use other postmodern approaches, such as ideological and autobiographical criticism. The former analyzes the system of ideas that underlies the power and values concealed in the text as well as that of the interpreter.[27] The latter involves deliberate self-disclosure while reading the text as a critical exegete.[28] Performance criticism attends to how the text was passed on orally, usually in com-

24. See, e.g., David Jobling, *The Sense of Biblical Narrative: Three Structural Analyses in the Old Testament*, JSOTSup 7 (Sheffield: Sheffield University, 1978).

25. See, e.g., Stephen D. Moore, *Poststructuralism and the New Testament: Derrida and Foucault at the Foot of the Cross* (Minneapolis: Fortress Press, 1994); *The Bible in Theory: Critical and Postcritical Essays* (Atlanta, GA: SBL, 2010); Yvonne Sherwood, *A Biblical Text and Its Afterlives: The Survival of Jonah in Western Culture* (Cambridge: Cambridge University Press, 2000).

26. David Penchansky, "Deconstruction," in *The Oxford Encyclopedia of Biblical Interpretation*, ed. Steven McKenzie (New York: Oxford University Press, 2013), 196–205. See, for example, Danna Nolan Fewell and David M. Gunn, *Gender, Power, and Promise: The Subject of the Bible's First Story* (Nashville, TN: Abingdon, 1993); David Rutledge, *Reading Marginally: Feminism, Deconstruction and the Bible*, BibInt 21 (Leiden: Brill, 1996).

27. See Tina Pippin, ed., *Ideological Criticism of Biblical Texts: Semeia* 59 (1992); Terry Eagleton, *Ideology: An Introduction* (London: Verso, 2007).

28. See, e.g., Ingrid Rose Kitzberger, ed., *Autobiographical Biblical Interpretation: Between Text and Self* (Leiden: Deo, 2002); P. J. W. Schutte, "When *They*, *We*, and the Passive Become *I*—Introducing Autobiographical Biblical Criticism," *HTS Teologiese Studies / Theological Studies* vol. 61 (2005): 401–16.

munal settings, and to the verbal and nonverbal interactions between the performer and the audience.[29]

From the beginning, feminists have understood that interpreting the Bible is an act of power. In recent decades, feminist biblical scholars have developed hermeneutical theories of the ethics and politics of biblical interpretation to challenge the claims to value neutrality of most academic biblical scholarship. Feminist biblical scholars have also turned their attention to how some biblical writings were shaped by the power of empire and how this still shapes readers' self-understandings today. They have developed hermeneutical approaches that reveal, critique, and evaluate the interactions depicted in the text against the context of empire, and they consider implications for contemporary contexts.[30] Feminists also analyze the dynamics of colonization and the mentalities of colonized peoples in the exercise of biblical interpretation. As Kwok Pui-lan explains, "A postcolonial feminist interpretation of the Bible needs to investigate the deployment of gender in the narration of identity, the negotiation of power differentials between the colonizers and the colonized, and the reinforcement of patriarchal control over spheres where these elites could exercise control."[31] Methods and models from sociology and cultural anthropology are used by feminists to investigate women's everyday lives, their experiences of marriage, childrearing, labor, money, illness, etc.[32]

---

29. See, e.g., Holly Hearon and Philip Ruge-Jones, eds., *The Bible in Ancient and Modern Media: Story and Performance* (Eugene, OR: Cascade Books, 2009).

30. E.g., Gale Yee, ed., *Judges and Method: New Approaches in Biblical Studies* (Minneapolis: Fortress Press, 1995); Warren Carter, *The Gospel of Matthew in Its Roman Imperial Context* (London: T & T Clark, 2005); *The Roman Empire and the New Testament: An Essential Guide* (Nashville, TN: Abingdon, 2006); Elisabeth Schüssler Fiorenza, *The Power of the Word: Scripture and the Rhetoric of Empire* (Minneapolis: Fortress Press, 2007); Judith E. McKinlay, *Reframing Her: Biblical Women in Postcolonial Focus* (Sheffield: Sheffield Phoenix Press, 2004).

31. Kwok Pui-lan, *Postcolonial Imagination and Feminist Theology* (Louisville, KY: Westminster John Knox, 2005), 9. See also Musa W. Dube, ed., *Postcolonial Feminist Interpretation of the Bible* (St. Louis, MO: Chalice, 2000); Cristl M. Maier and Carolyn J. Sharp, *Prophecy and Power: Jeremiah in Feminist and Postcolonial Perspective* (London: Bloomsbury, 2013).

32. See, for example, Carol Meyers, *Discovering Eve: Ancient Israelite Women in Context* (New York: Oxford University Press, 1991); Luise Schottroff, *Lydia's Impatient Sisters: A Feminist Social History of Early Christianity*, trans. Barbara and Martin Rumscheidt (Louisville, KY: Westminster John Knox, 1995); Susan Niditch, *"My Brother Esau Is a Hairy Man": Hair and Identity in Ancient Israel* (Oxford: Oxford University Press, 2008).

As feminists have examined the construction of gender from varying cultural perspectives, they have become ever more cognizant that the way gender roles are defined within differing cultures varies radically. As Mary Ann Tolbert observes, "Attempts to isolate some universal role that cross-culturally defines 'woman' have run into contradictory evidence at every turn."[33] Some women have coined new terms to highlight the particularities of their socio-cultural context. Many African American feminists, for example, call themselves *womanists* to draw attention to the double oppression of racism and sexism they experience.[34] Similarly, many U.S. Hispanic feminists speak of themselves as *mujeristas* (*mujer* is Spanish for "woman").[35] Others prefer to be called "Latina feminists."[36] Both groups emphasize that the context for their theologizing is *mestizaje* and *mulatez* (racial and cultural mixture), done *en conjunto* (in community), with *lo cotidiano* (everyday lived experience) of Hispanic women as starting points for theological reflection and the encounter with the divine. Intercultural analysis has become an indispensable tool for working toward justice for women at the global level.[37]

Some feminists are among those who have developed lesbian, gay, bisexual, and transgender (LGBT) interpretation. This approach focuses on issues of sexual identity and uses various reading strategies. Some point out the ways in which categories that emerged in recent centuries are applied anachronistically to biblical texts to make modern-day judgments. Others show how the Bible is silent on contemporary issues about

33. Mary Ann Tolbert, "Social, Sociological, and Anthropological Methods," in *Searching the Scriptures*, 1:255–71, here 265.

34. Alice Walker coined the term (*In Search of Our Mothers' Gardens: Womanist Prose* [New York: Harcourt Brace Jovanovich, 1967, 1983]). See also Katie G. Cannon, "The Emergence of Black Feminist Consciousness," in *Feminist Interpretation of the Bible*, ed. Letty M. Russell (Philadelphia: Westminster, 1985), 30–40; Nyasha Junior, "Womanist Biblical Interpretation," in *Engaging the Bible in a Gendered World: An Introduction to Feminist Biblical Interpretation in Honor of Katharine Doob Sakenfeld*, ed. Linda Day and Carolyn Pressler (Louisville, KY: Westminster John Knox, 2006), 37–46; Renita Weems, *Just a Sister Away: A Womanist Vision of Women's Relationships in the Bible* (San Diego: Lura Media, 1988).

35. Ada María Isasi-Díaz (*Mujerista Theology: A Theology for the Twenty-first Century* [Maryknoll, NY: Orbis Books, 1996]) is credited with coining the term.

36. E.g., María Pilar Aquino, Daisy L. Machado, and Jeanette Rodríguez, eds., *A Reader in Latina Feminist Theology* (Austin: University of Texas Press, 2002).

37. See, e.g., María Pilar Aquino and María José Rosado-Nunes, eds., *Feminist Intercultural Theology: Latina Explorations for a Just World*, Studies in Latino/a Catholicism (Maryknoll, NY: Orbis Books, 2007).

sexual identity. Still others examine same-sex relationships in the Bible by figures such as Ruth and Naomi or David and Jonathan. In recent years, queer theory has emerged; it emphasizes the blurriness of boundaries not just of sexual identity but also of gender roles. Queer critics often focus on texts in which figures transgress what is traditionally considered proper gender behavior.[38]

Feminists also recognize that the struggle for women's equality and dignity is intimately connected with the struggle for respect for Earth and for the whole of the cosmos. Ecofeminists interpret Scripture in ways that highlight the link between human domination of nature and male subjugation of women. They show how anthropocentric ways of interpreting the Bible have overlooked or dismissed Earth and Earth community. They invite readers to identify not only with human characters in the biblical narrative but also with other Earth creatures and domains of nature, especially those that are the object of injustice. Some use creative imagination to retrieve the interests of Earth implicit in the narrative and enable Earth to speak.[39]

Biblical Authority

By the late nineteenth century, some feminists, such as Elizabeth Cady Stanton, began to question openly whether the Bible could continue to be regarded as authoritative for women. They viewed the Bible itself as the source of women's oppression, and some rejected its sacred origin and saving claims. Some decided that the Bible and the religious traditions that enshrine it are too thoroughly saturated with androcentrism and patriarchy to be redeemable.[40]

---

38. See, e.g., Bernadette J. Brooten, *Love between Women: Early Christian Responses to Female Homoeroticism* (Chicago and London: University of Chicago Press, 1996); Mary Rose D'Angelo, "Women Partners in the New Testament," *JFSR* 6 (1990): 65–86; Deirdre J. Good, "Reading Strategies for Biblical Passages on Same-Sex Relations," *Theology and Sexuality* 7 (1997): 70–82; Deryn Guest, *When Deborah Met Jael: Lesbian Feminist Hermeneutics* (London: SCM, 2011); Teresa Hornsby and Ken Stone, eds., *Bible Trouble: Queer Readings at the Boundaries of Biblical Scholarship* (Atlanta, GA: SBL, 2011).

39. E.g., Norman C. Habel and Peter Trudinger, *Exploring Ecological Hermeneutics*, SBLSymS 46 (Atlanta, GA: SBL, 2008); Mary Judith Ress, *Ecofeminism in Latin America*, Women from the Margins (Maryknoll, NY: Orbis Books, 2006).

40. E.g., Mary Daly, *Beyond God the Father: A Philosophy of Women's Liberation* (London: The Women's Press, 1986).

In the Wisdom Commentary series, questions such as these may be raised, but the aim of this series is not to lead readers to reject the authority of the biblical text. Rather, the aim is to promote better understanding of the contexts from which the text arose and of the rhetorical effects it has on women and men in contemporary contexts. Such understanding can lead to a deepening of faith, with the Bible serving as an aid to bring flourishing of life.

Language for God

Because of the ways in which the term "God" has been used to symbolize the divine in predominantly male, patriarchal, and monarchical modes, feminists have designed new ways of speaking of the divine. Some have called attention to the inadequacy of the term *God* by trying to visually destabilize our ways of thinking and speaking of the divine. Rosemary Radford Ruether proposed *God/ess*, as an unpronounceable term pointing to the unnameable understanding of the divine that transcends patriarchal limitations.[41] Some have followed traditional Jewish practice, writing *G-d*. Elisabeth Schüssler Fiorenza has adopted *G*d*.[42] Others draw on the biblical tradition to mine female and non-gender-specific metaphors and symbols.[43] In Wisdom Commentary, there is not one standard way of expressing the divine; each author will use her or his preferred ways. The one exception is that when the tetragrammaton, YHWH, the name revealed to Moses in Exodus 3:14, is used, it will be without vowels, respecting the Jewish custom of avoiding pronouncing the divine name out of reverence.

Nomenclature for the Two Testaments

In recent decades, some biblical scholars have begun to call the two Testaments of the Bible by names other than the traditional nomencla-

---

41. Rosemary Radford Ruether, *Sexism and God-Talk: Toward a Feminist Theology* (Boston: Beacon, 1983).

42. Elisabeth Schüssler Fiorenza, *Jesus: Miriam's Child, Sophia's Prophet; Critical Issues in Feminist Christology* (New York: Continuum, 1994), 191 n. 3.

43. E.g., Sallie McFague, *Models of God: Theology for an Ecological, Nuclear Age* (Philadelphia: Fortress Press, 1987); Catherine LaCugna, *God for Us: The Trinity and Christian Life* (San Francisco: Harper Collins, 1991); Elizabeth A. Johnson, *She Who Is: The Mystery of God in Feminist Theological Discourse* (New York: Crossroad, 1992). See further Elizabeth A. Johnson, "God," in *Dictionary of Feminist Theologies*, 128–30.

ture: Old and New Testament. Some regard "Old" as derogatory, implying that it is no longer relevant or that it has been superseded. Consequently, terms like Hebrew Bible, First Testament, and Jewish Scriptures and, correspondingly, Christian Scriptures or Second Testament have come into use. There are a number of difficulties with these designations. The term "Hebrew Bible" does not take into account that parts of the Old Testament are written not in Hebrew but in Aramaic.[44] Moreover, for Roman Catholics, Anglicans, and Eastern Orthodox believers, the Old Testament includes books written in Greek—the Deuterocanonical books, considered Apocrypha by Protestants. The term "Jewish Scriptures" is inadequate because these books are also sacred to Christians. Conversely, "Christian Scriptures" is not an accurate designation for the New Testament, since the Old Testament is also part of the Christian Scriptures. Using "First and Second Testament" also has difficulties, in that it can imply a hierarchy and a value judgment.[45] Jews generally use the term Tanakh, an acronym for Torah (Pentateuch), Nevi'im (Prophets), and Ketuvim (Writings).

In Wisdom Commentary, if authors choose to use a designation other than Tanakh, Old Testament, and New Testament, they will explain how they mean the term.

Translation

Modern feminist scholars recognize the complexities connected with biblical translation, as they have delved into questions about philosophy of language, how meanings are produced, and how they are culturally situated. Today it is evident that simply translating into gender-neutral formulations cannot address all the challenges presented by androcentric texts. Efforts at feminist translation must also deal with issues around authority and canonicity.[46]

Because of these complexities, the editors of Wisdom Commentary series have chosen to use an existing translation, the New Revised Standard Version (NRSV), which is provided for easy reference at the top of each page of commentary. The NRSV was produced by a team of ecumenical and interreligious scholars, is a fairly literal translation, and uses

44. Gen 31:47; Jer 10:11; Ezra 4:7–6:18; 7:12-26; Dan 2:4–7:28.

45. See Levine, *The Misunderstood Jew*, 193–99.

46. Elizabeth Castelli, *"Les Belles Infidèles*/Fidelity or Feminism? The Meanings of Feminist Biblical Translation," in *Searching the Scriptures*, 1:189–204, here 190.

inclusive language for human beings. Brief discussions about problematic translations appear in the inserts labeled "Translation Matters." When more detailed discussions are available, these will be indicated in footnotes. In the commentary, wherever Hebrew or Greek words are used, English translation is provided. In cases where a wordplay is involved, transliteration is provided to enable understanding.

Art and Poetry

Artistic expression in poetry, music, sculpture, painting, and various other modes is very important to feminist interpretation. Where possible, art and poetry are included in the print volumes of the series. In a number of instances, these are original works created for this project. Regrettably, copyright and production costs prohibit the inclusion of color photographs and other artistic work. It is our hope that the web version will allow a greater collection of such resources.

Glossary

Because there are a number of excellent readily-available resources that provide definitions and concise explanations of terms used in feminist theological and biblical studies, this series will not include a glossary. We refer you to works such as *Dictionary of Feminist Theologies*, edited by Letty M. Russell with J. Shannon Clarkson (Louisville: Westminster John Knox, 1996), and volume 1 of *Searching the Scriptures*, edited by Elisabeth Schüssler Fiorenza with the assistance of Shelly Matthews (New York: Crossroad, 1992). Individual authors in the Wisdom Commentary series will define the way they are using terms that may be unfamiliar.

Bibliography

Because bibliographies are quickly outdated and because the space is limited, only a list of Works Cited is included in the print volumes. A comprehensive bibliography for each volume is posted on a dedicated website and is updated regularly.

The link for this volume is: wisdomcommentary.org.

A Concluding Word

In just a few short decades, feminist biblical studies has grown exponentially, both in the methods that have been developed and in the number of scholars who have embraced it. We realize that this series is limited and will soon need to be revised and updated. It is our hope that Wisdom Commentary, by making the best of current feminist biblical scholarship available in an accessible format to ministers, preachers, teachers, scholars, and students, will aid all readers in their advancement toward God's vision of dignity, equality, and justice for all.

Author's Introduction

Putting Micah in Context

Advocates for social justice love to quote the book of Micah. Its scathing critique of the wealthy who "covet fields, and seize them; houses, and take them away" (2:2), its radical vision of a day in which "nation shall not lift up sword against nation, neither shall they learn war any more" (4:3), and its plaintive insistence that what YHWH requires is to "do justice, and to love kindness, and to walk humbly with your God" (6:8) have been rallying cries for those who seek a more just world. Often paired with quotes from Amos, verses from Micah adorn the banners under which agents of change march forward.

Even those who seek justice in our world, however, disagree on what justice looks like in the flesh. Does justice entail giving people equal opportunity or ensuring relatively equal outcomes? Does it look the same for women as for men? Should social justice advocates focus on individual rights or institutional structures? How will we know justice when we see it? Who gets to define justice?

This commentary approaches the book of Micah with these questions in mind. It asks what the *details* of the book of Micah mean for the causes of justice. It goes beyond the famous quotes of Micah to explore the book as a whole, paying close attention to its language, its imagery, what it says, and what it does not say. Its guiding interest is what Micah's claims mean for real people's lives. Who in the past and in the present benefits from *all* of Micah's powerful words? Who does not? Is Micah good for women? For persons of color? For the poor? Is Micah's vision of justice one that we should emulate?

While the questions I pose are straightforward, the route by which I will explore them is not. Assessing the effect of words on real human lives requires paying close attention to at least two contexts of the book of Micah: the past and the present. I believe that responsible interpretation of the Bible requires both a deep understanding of the ancient world reflected in its pages and also a deep self-awareness of the lenses through which we read and the commitments that guide our choice of texts and our determination of their meaning.

With regard to the past, I will trace possible resonances of Micah's language within the Persian period community in which I believe this book was composed, drawing on reconstructions of that setting from archaeology and economic records; I will consider not only recent historical information about when the book was written, by whom, and in what social situation, but also the dynamics of power (gendered and otherwise) at work in our sources.

With regard to both the past and the present, I will explore some ways in which Micah's words resonate in a world in which oppression takes on particular shapes depending on one's gender, race, sexual orientation, ethnic identity, and political status. Rather than simply pose the question, "What did/does Micah say about women?" I understand gender construction as an exercise of power and turn to the interdisciplinary field of Gender Studies for guidance.

Gender Studies considers the ways in which cultures create and reinforce definitions of and rules for gender, looking not only at how a culture treats women and men but also at how it defines "man" and "woman"—where those labels come from, what they mean in the culture, and what is at stake in making sure everyone has the right label. In this understanding, gender is not simply recognition of biological facts but a way to control bodies: when you know who you are, then you know how you have to behave. The power inherent in gender is particularly evident in cultures in which men control the public arena and property is passed through the male line. For patriarchy and patrilinear descent to remain in place, male-female partnering for the sake of procreation must remain the only acceptable form of sexual relations and a woman's importance must rely on childbearing. For these rules about procreation, partnering, and male hierarchy to function, humans in turn must be sorted into male or female and the rules for their behavior must be normalized—made into "the way women are" and "the way men are." Gender is *made* but it must look *natural*.

Reading with a gender-critical lens poses important questions to Micah. How does gender work in this book? How does gender intersect with class and other forms of privilege?[1] How might those intersections have functioned in the ancient world? How do they function today? Do Micah's words "work" differently for white women in the United States than for women of color and in other global contexts? Do they affect in different ways persons who fit heterosexual norms and those who do not? What does Micah mean for women living in cities as opposed to those living in rural settings?

In these explorations, I offer not only my own insights but also those of others around the world. As in other volumes of the Wisdom Commentary, contributing voices join—and challenge—my own voice and each other.

As a commentary, this study also joins the scholarly conversation about interpretative cruxes in the book Micah. In addition to grounding Micah in a particular historical context, the commentary focuses on the text as it appears in the Masoretic Text (MT). When the text is not clear, I stop to wrestle with its ambiguity rather than seeking to "repair" the text with emendations. Acknowledging Micah's ambiguity allows us to interpret the text honestly and to notice the ways in which interpreters who claim certainty about the prophet Micah and his message go beyond the text in front of them, filling in the gaps with their own values and concerns: those who speak *for* Micah often commit "biblical ventriloquism," using the Bible's assumed authority to advance their own agenda.

By bringing both the ancient and modern contexts of Micah into view, I hope to spur readers to reflect on the significance of Micah's construction of the world. The way in which this book envisions sin, salvation, the human condition, and the nature of YHWH[2] affects the way people

---

1. This focus on the intersecting nature of oppressions is sometimes known as Intersectional Studies, a term coined in 1989 by Kimberlé Crenshaw. A clear introduction to this approach can be found in Marianne Kartzow, "Intersectional Studies," in *The Oxford Encyclopedia of the Bible and Gender Studies*, ed. Julia M. O'Brien, 2 vols. (New York: Oxford University Press, 2014), 1:383–89.

2. In order to maintain some distinction between Micah's descriptions of the deity and my own understandings, I will attempt consistently to use different language for each. When describing Micah's views, I will speak of YHWH, who in the book is characterized with masculine pronouns and often in masculine imagery; hence, when referring to the book's perspective, I will utilize masculine pronouns. When reflecting my own understandings, my language for the divine will be non-gendered, and labels will include God and the Divine One.

live—in part by shaping their own thoughts and in part by shaping the power structures in which they live. Paying attention to the everyday significance of Micah's meaning-making, I hope, might help us become more attentive to the way in which our own constructions of meaning affect us, one another, and our world. Ideas about God, human nature, and the reality of the world are not abstract concepts but rather interconnected with how we organize our common life and what we think counts as appropriate behavior. Thought translates into action, just as action shapes thought. To challenge the sexism, racism, and heterosexism at work in our world, we need to challenge not only overt acts of oppression but also the ways in which people see one another and themselves.

Seeking Micah's Context

The book's opening verse introduces us to a character named Micah of Moresheth who spoke during the reigns of the Judean kings Jotham, Ahaz, and Hezekiah. According to 2 Kings, these kings ruled over Judah in the eighth century BCE, during the tumultuous years of Assyrian hegemony of the ancient Near East. References later in the book to the Assyrians further locate this figure in the eighth century, as does Jer 26:18, which reports that during the reign of Hezekiah Micah predicted that Jerusalem would be "plowed as a field" (Mic 3:12).

Based on this scant information, many interpreters have imagined what the "real Micah" was like. Identifying Moresheth with Moresheth-Gath, a village in the agriculturally rich Shephelah region, scholars such as George A. Smith have heard Micah's voice as a rural critique of Israelite and Judean urban centers: "We see him on his housetop pouring forth his words before the hills. . . . So some of the greatest poets have caught their music from the nameless brooklets of their boyhood's fields."[3] Similarly, Marvin Sweeney suggests that, from Micah's position in the Shephelah, the prophet would have witnessed the devastating effects of the military campaign of the Assyrian king Sennacherib in 701 BCE.[4]

3. George Adam Smith, "Micah," in *The Twelve Minor Prophets* (New York: George H. Doran, 1929), 382.

4. Marvin Sweeney, *The Twelve Prophets*, vol. 2 (Collegeville, MN: Liturgical Press, 2000).

The *character* of Micah, however, is not necessarily the *author of the book* of Micah.[5] For centuries, interpreters have recognized that not all of the book's contents fit easily within the eighth-century context. Some content refers to the Babylonian exile (Mic 4:10) and shares with later literature the hope for the restoration of the monarchy and Jerusalem's return to world prominence. Like the Persian-era book of Zechariah, the book of Micah accepts the justice of YHWH's punishment of Judah but antici-pates the reversal of the nation's fate. Redaction critics such as James Nogalski have pointed to numerous similarities between Micah and biblical texts written long after the eighth century, including the reference to Pentateuchal narratives, the parallel between Mic 4 and Isa 2, and the theological claim that the fate of Samaria was a warning for Judah (as in 2 Kings).[6]

Scholars have addressed the historical unevenness in Micah in the following ways:

1. Focusing on the Prophet Micah

Some interpreters assume that the book faithfully records the speeches of the eighth-century prophet for whom it is named, either arguing from a confessional perspective that the superscription is sufficient proof that Micah's own words have been faithfully reproduced[7] or utilizing the methods of critical biblical scholarship to locate the book squarely within the eighth-century context.[8] In these interpretations, references to events later than the eighth century are either understood as predictions of the future or as minimally important glosses.

2. Distinguishing between the Original Speeches and Later Additions

Since the nineteenth century, most scholarly interpreters have dis-cerned at least two layers of the book: a base composition written close

5. For this reason, I use the name "Micah" to mean the book of the Micah or the literary character of Micah described within the book. I do not use this name for a supposed eighth-century prophet.

6. James Nogalski, *The Book of the Twelve: Hosea through Jonah* (Macon, GA: Smith and Helwys, 2011), 511.

7. For example, Benjamin A. Copass and Ernest L. Carlson, *A Study of the Prophet Micah: Power by the Spirit* (Grand Rapids, MI: Baker Book House, 1950).

8. For example, Bruce K. Waltke, *A Commentary on Micah* (Grand Rapids, MI: Eerdmans, 2007).

to Sennacherib's siege of Jerusalem in 701 BCE and an edited version of
the book crafted after the Babylonian destruction of Jerusalem in 587
BCE.[9] Such scholars claim that Mic 1–3, which anticipates Assyrian
destruction of Jerusalem, was expanded by the addition of Mic 4–5 to
reflect the reality that Jerusalem's destruction had come at the hand of
the Babylonians and to offer promises of return from exile. In this interpretative approach, Mic 6–7 is usually understood as a miscellany of
preexilic and exilic announcements of both judgment and salvation.
Annotations in various editions of the *New Oxford Annotated Bible* adopt
the two-stage approach, noting which parts of Micah reflect the Assyrian
period and which reflect an exilic setting.

While interpretive details vary depending on how much attention the
interpreter pays to redaction, both of these first two approaches prioritize
the eighth-century context of the book and appeal to Assyrian period
information for background materials. Given the wealth of our knowledge about the Assyrian period, setting Micah within the eighth-century
context is clearly an attractive option. Devadasan N. Premnath[10] and
Matthew Coomber,[11] for example, offer intriguing studies of the way in
which Micah's concerns with land reflect the crises provoked by the
Assyrian imperial taxation system.

Interpreting Micah only in its eighth-century context, however, requires us to ignore the actual book before us. Such an approach forces
us to determine which words were original and which were redactions,
and thus to pull apart threads that an author/redactor intentionally
interwove for a purpose. The book becomes an archaeological dig instead
of a coherent piece of literature. In reaction to such approaches, a growing number of scholars is now less interested in the hypothetical stages
of the book's composition than with the book as its stands—usually
called its "final form," even though no literature is every truly finished
as long as readers continue to find their own meaning in it.

9. Georg H. von Ewald, *Commentary on the Prophets of the Old Testament*, trans. J.
F. Smith (London: Williams & Norgate, 1876).

10. Devadasan N. Premnath, *Eighth Century Prophets: A Social Analysis* (St. Louis,
MO: Chalice, 2003).

11. Matthew J. M. Coomber, "Caught in the Crossfire? Economic Injustice and
Prophetic Motivation in Eighth-Century Judah," *BibInt* 19 (2011): 396–432.

3. Reading the Book within the Exilic or Postexilic Context of Its Final Form

In this approach, interpretation focuses on what the character Micah meant to the era in which the book was compiled. For example, while James Nogalski concurs with other scholars that the book has gone through multiple stages of editing, he places most attention on its final form, which he situates in the exilic period.[12] Rex Mason places the editing later, in the postexilic "return" of Judeans in the Persian period: "The prophet's words furnished the material for preaching and worship in the post-exilic period."[13]

Ehud Ben Zvi places the composition of Micah as well as other prophetic books squarely in the Persian period. Without denying the possibility that the Persian period scribes had some source material at their disposal, he nonetheless views the Persian period writer of Micah as actually composing the book rather than just supplementing it. "The emphasis on explanations of the catastrophe that befell monarchic Jerusalem, the explicit reference to the exile in Babylon (4:10), other references to exile and loss of the land (e.g., 2:4, 10), to the gathering of the exiles (e.g., 2:12-13; 7:12), and salvation after exile (e.g., 4:10; 7:11-13) point to a postmonarchic setting for the book as a whole."[14] Everything in the book of Micah, Ben Zvi insists, reflects the intentions and the interests of literati—the well-educated, privileged scribal class living in Jerusalem in the Persian period. By crafting a book that claimed to preserve faithfully the words of a past prophet who had predicted the fall of Judah as well as its future restoration, these literati communicated to their own community a theological explanation of the exile and hope for a better future. Their ability to read and interpret the words of past prophets also served to bolster their own power within a largely illiterate society.

4. Focusing on the Text Itself and Its Modern Readers Rather Than Hypothetical Ancient Contexts

Many scholars, as well as many average readers, care far more about how the text resonates today than about its disputed original contexts. For some, this approach invites the reader to find resonances between

12. Nogalski, *The Book of the Twelve*.

13. Rex Mason, *Micah, Nahum, and Obadiah*, OTC (Sheffield: JSOT Press, 1991), 53.

14. Ehud Ben Zvi, *Micah*, The Forms of the Old Testament Literature, vol. 21B (Grand Rapids, MI: Eerdmans, 2000), 9–10.

the text and her own context. Elelwani Farisani's entry on Micah in the *Africana Bible*, for example, uses Micah "as a new paradigm in a quest for an African theology of renewal, transformation, reconciliation, and reconstruction. . . . His message of hope, that his nation would ultimately be restored to prominence and prosperity, is relevant in our context today as it stresses the very messages recently conveyed in our own history by advocates of both Pan-Africanism and African Renaissance."[15]

For others, reader-focused interpretation entails exploring the ideological effects of Micah's text and its readers—the power dynamics reflected in and constructed by the book's discourse and those who interpret it. Erin Runions focuses squarely on the ideological interests of readers. Her study underscores the indeterminate, unstable language of Micah: pronouns and imagery shifts abruptly, as does what the book of Micah is "about." To find coherence, readers import their own assumptions, their own ideologies. According to Runions, the reader's ideology "acts as a strategy of containment to limit the production of meaning. . . . What Micah 'means' is limited to 'what I believe in.'"[16]

My own approach to Micah combines the last options described here. As noted above, I share with reader-centered approaches a deep interest in the ways that real people engage the book of Micah and the ideological dimensions of that engagement. How does this book shape our thinking about what is good and who matters and what future to hope for? What is the role of gender, race, class, and empire in meaning that readers create from this book? Does Micah call us to change the world or conform to it? How might a modern Palestinian woman living in Bethlehem or a Jewish woman living in Jerusalem help me see in this text what I do not see from my vantage point as a white middle-class academic living in the United States?

My interest in real people, however, also includes a historical dimension. Believing that authors write books that are intended to cohere and that their words and ideas both reflect and influence the cultures in which they live, I want to imagine what function the book may have played in the fifth century when it was compiled. While we cannot determine who wrote this book, knowing something about the world from which it comes may allow us to be more attentive to the assumptions that it brings

15. Elelwani B. Farisani, "Micah," in *The Africana Bible*, ed. Hugh R. Page Jr. (Minneapolis, MN: Fortress, 2010), 191–92.

16. Erin Runions, *Changing Subjects: Gender, Nation, and Future in Micah* (London and New York: Sheffield Academic Press, 2001), 33.

to its formulations. Knowing what gender relations may have been like in the ancient world prevents us from anachronistically assuming that the past is just like the present, or even that the present is necessarily superior to the ancient world. As the commentary will explore, the author's understanding of who benefits from the wages of a harlot (Mic 1:7), whose future allows sitting in peace (Mic 4:4), and whose interests are served by the return of a Davidic king (Mic 5) are not shared by all gender-sensitive interpreters.

Micah as a Persian-Period Book

A primary clue to the author's intention for the composition of Micah is the book's closing affirmation of and appeal to YHWH's mercy:

> Who is a God like you, pardoning iniquity
>   and passing over the transgression
>   of the remnant of your possession?
> He does not retain his anger forever,
>   because he delights in showing clemency.
> He will again have compassion upon us;
>   he will tread our iniquities under foot.
> You will cast all our sins
>   into the depths of the sea.
> You will show faithfulness to Jacob
>   and unswerving loyalty to Abraham,
> as you have sworn to our ancestors
>   from the days of old. (Mic 7:18-20)

The writer attributes the destruction of Israel and Judah to YHWH's justifiable anger against their sins and presents YHWH's faithfulness in the past as reason to believe YHWH will be gracious in the future.

In this way, Micah's message parallels the way in which the voice of the book of Zechariah addressed those who had returned from the Babylonian exile:

> Do not be like your ancestors, to whom the former prophets proclaimed, "Thus says the LORD of hosts, Return from your evil ways and from your evil deeds." But they did not hear or heed me, says the LORD. (Zech 1:4)

> Were not these the words that the LORD proclaimed by the former prophets, when Jerusalem was inhabited and in prosperity, along with the towns around it, and when the Negeb and the Shephelah were inhabited?

The word of the LORD came to Zechariah, saying: Thus says the LORD of hosts: Render true judgments, show kindness and mercy to one another; do not oppress the widow, the orphan, the alien, or the poor; and do not devise evil in your hearts against one another. But they refused to listen, and turned a stubborn shoulder, and stopped their ears in order not to hear. They made their hearts adamant in order not to hear the law and the words that the LORD of hosts had sent by his spirit through the former prophets. Therefore great wrath came from the LORD of hosts. Just as, when I called, they would not hear, so, when they called, I would not hear, says the LORD of hosts, and I scattered them with a whirlwind among all the nations that they had not known. Thus the land they left was desolate, so that no one went to and fro, and a pleasant land was made desolate. (Zech 7:7-14)

When read alongside other prophetic books, Micah becomes a "voice from the past" that confirms Zechariah's thesis: both Israel and Judah fell as YHWH's punishment for their sin (Mic 1:5; Zech 7:14).[17] This voice also insists that YHWH has promised to exalt Jerusalem (Mic 4; Zech 14), to assemble those to whom the deity did evil (Mic 4:6; Zech 8:14-15), to allow men to sit under vine and fig tree (Mic 4:4; Zech 3:10), and to gather the nations to himself (Mic 4:2; Zech 2:11). Micah 4:8 points forward to a time when kingship will return to Judah, a kingship portrayed as materializing in Zechariah's own day (Zech 9:9). Indeed, as Zech 1:17 insists, earlier prophets such as Micah testified to YHWH's promise to return and show compassion (Mic 7:18-20).

My understanding of Micah's historical context, then, is similar to that of Ben Zvi, who discerns in Micah the desire of Persian period literati to justify Judah's prior destruction and envision its future exaltation. I differ from Ben Zvi, however, in seeking the real life consequences of this theology. Ben Zvi suggests that the author is describing the sins of the past in generic terms;[18] similarly, Nogalski suggests Micah's description of social injustice may have been derived not from the author's own reality but from literary parallels in Kings, especially the story of Naboth's vineyard in 1 Kings 21 in which the evil king Ahab and his foreign wife Jezebel orchestrated the murder of a man who refused to part with his ancestral land holding.[19] Differently from Ben Zvi and Nogalski, I want

17. For further explanation, see Julia M. O'Brien, "Nahum—Habakkuk—Zephaniah: Reading the 'Former Prophets' in the Persian Period," *Int* 61 (2007): 168–83.

18. Ben Zvi, *Micah*, 64–65.

19. Nogalski, *The Book of the Twelve*, 511.

to know how the specifically named sins of the past might have found parallels in the perceived sins of the author's own present. What did this writer believe was unjust in his own day? What injustices did this writer erase from our view through his rhetoric? Along with other feminist, womanist, and mujerista scholars, I believe that words have power in all contexts in which they are employed. No speech is innocent of power.

My desire to explore the daily realities of the Persian period community, however, faces complications. While study of the Persian period has widely expanded in the past decade, much about the era remains unclear, including issues of land tenure which are so central in the book of Micah. Focusing on the lives of those within Micah's original context, however, is worth the trouble, since it provides much insight into this book and its purposes and serves as a window into the real-life consequences of its speech.

The Details of the Context

Given the book's strong interest in the sins and future exaltation of Jerusalem, it was likely composed in the environs of Jerusalem. Its precise date within the Persian period is unclear. As Ben Zvi notes, the book reflects a time in which: "(1) Israel/Jerusalem (i.e., the speaker) is in a situation of distress; (2) the 'city' has neither 'fence' nor security; (3) Israel/Jerusalem expects a gathering of exiles; (4) the nations fare much better than Israel/Jerusalem; (5) Israel/Jerusalem has sinned against YHWH but now trusts in YHWH, its patron, and in YHWH's justice and salvific acts; (6) Israel/Jerusalem is hoping for a reversal of its status vis-à-vis the nations; and (7) Israel/Jerusalem hopes for a territorial expansion that will include areas that were associated with northern Israel."[20] This scenario fits well Lipschits's description of Jerusalem between 539 and 400 BCE, when it was a sparsely settled and relatively insignificant settlement within the Persian province of Yehud.[21] The book expresses no urgency for the rebuilding of the temple as do the books of Haggai and Zechariah; apart from a reference to "the house of the wicked" in Mic 6:10 in language similar to descriptions of the temple

20. Ben Zvi, *Micah*, 182.

21. Oded Lipshits, "Achaemenid Imperial Policy, Settlement Processes in Palestine, and the Status of Jerusalem in the Middle of the Fifth Century B.C.E.," in *Judah and the Judeans in the Persian Period*, ed. Oded Lipshits and Manfred Oeming (Winona Lake, IN: Eisenbrauns, 2006), 19–52.

storehouses, the book does not focus on regulating temple practices as do the books of Ezra and Nehemiah. Micah 7:11 suggests a time before the building of the city walls, generally dated to 445 BCE.

The sins that the book of Micah decries are primarily economic: the confiscation of others' ancestral land holdings (2:1-9); dishonest business practices (6:10-12); and a willingness to do anything for economic gain (3:5-12; 7:3). The book envisions a time in which implements of war will become tools of agriculture (4:4-5) and laments the disintegration of proper relationships within the family and the community (7:5-6). As noted above, Coomber and Premnath locate such practices in the Assyrian period when population growth, trade opportunities, and the market demand for olive precipitated the shift from subsistence farming to administratively controlled agriculture. They maintain that the prophet Micah criticized the new system, including the large estates that disadvantaged traditional modes of farming.[22]

Reading the book within a fifth-century Persian-period context, however, directs our attention to a different economy: that of Yehud, the Aramaic name for the Persian province located in the area formerly called Judah. While archaeologists and historians do not agree on all details of the Persian administration of Yehud—including its population size, provincial borders, the degree of imperial control—I here sketch the broad contours of the period.

Between 539 and 400 BCE, Yehud in general and Jerusalem in particular were sparsely populated and relatively poor, reflecting their lack of strategic importance to the Persian authorities. According to Alexander Fantalkin and Oren Tal, during this period the Persians showed little interest in the region's urban centers, focusing their interests on the agricultural bounty of the coastal areas to Yehud's west.[23] Samaria may have been relatively more prosperous than Jerusalem. According to Gary Knoppers, "At the end of the fifth and during the fourth centuries there were local social and economic elites in this region, as the finds from Shechem and Wadi ed-Daliya and the Samarian coins may attest."[24]

---

22. Premnath, *Eighth Century Prophets*; Coomber, "Caught in the Crossfire?"

23. Alexander Fantalkin and Oren Tal, "Redating Lachish Level I: Identifying Achaemenid Imperial Policy at the Southern Frontier of the Fifth Satrapy," in Lipschits and Oeming, *Judah and the Judeans in the Persian Period*, 167–97.

24. Gary Knoppers, "Revisiting the Samarian Question in the Persian Period," in Lipschits and Oeming, *Judah and the Judeans in the Persian Period*, 31.

Micah's Date

I see the book of Micah as finalized, if not largely written, in the Persian period: but I also believe that the text has roots in the earlier Assyrian period in which the text is set. However, when it comes to exploring Micah's attacks on corruption among Judah's rulers, religious elites, and the populace-at-large, the actual time-scape of its prophecies may not be as important as some might think. Whether the authors addressed corruption under Assyrian or Persian rule—since later authors might have used earlier Judean rulers as targets so as to not have directly challenged and incurred the wrath of contemporary rulers who were guilty of the same offenses—the issue of corruption is not limited to a particular era but affects people across time and culture.

Matthew Coomber

Operated with the structure of the Persian Empire, Yehud was neither politically nor economically independent. While some historians such as Lester Grabbe portray Persian control of Yehud as relatively benign,[25] no occupation is without consequences. Under occupation, a community is not autonomous; the empire pervades every aspect of life and is the context in which decisions are made. Jeremiah Cataldo notes that, "rather than the formation of an 'essentially new political structure,' the society within Yehud operated within and under the infrastructure of the political institution established by the Persian Empire."[26] The Persians controlled Yehud's governors and required the paying of tribute to the imperial treasury. This "tributary mode of production" supported not only the Persian Empire but also the local elite connected to the imperial infrastructure. Documents such as the Murashu Archives indicate that these "tithes" were sometimes collected by family "businesses."

These economic realities are reflected in Nehemiah, a key biblical text describing the situation in Yehud. Nehemiah 5 suggests that imperial demands coupled with crop failures provoked conflict between subgroups. As interpreted by Zipporah Glass, famine and "the king's tax" forced struggling farmers to procure loans from local elites; once the loans were in default, those elites confiscated their compatriot's fields and

25. Lester L. Grabbe, *A History of the Jews and Judaism in the Second Second Period*, vol. 1 (London and New York: T & T Clark, 2004).

26. Jeremiah Cataldo, "Persian Policy and the Yehud Community During Nehemiah," *JSOT* 28 (2003): 251.

turned them and their children into debt slaves. The result was severe food insecurity, caused not by a supply shortage but by the stratified exchange of goods. Glass suggests that "the true object of Nehemiah's 'reform' was that the *chōrîm* (NRSV: 'nobles') and *segānîm* (NRSV: 'officials') were also to return foreclosed and repossessed lands, vineyards, olive groves, and homes (Neh 5:11a), the means to and for production and maintenance of livelihood."[27] Nehemiah boasts that, unlike earlier governors, he did not accept the food allowance due to him: they "laid heavy burdens on the people" (Neh 5:15), but he "acquired no land" (Neh 5:16). This passage acknowledges that previous governors had taxed the populace and procured family plots, though it fails to explain from which funds the large number of guests at Nehemiah's table were fed. Other biblical texts depict the tense economic situation of Yehud: crop failures due to famine, drought, and pests (see, e.g., Joel 1:17-20; Hag 1:6-11), and the presence of "a large, tax-exempt clerical bureaucracy" that included temple personnel, governors, and scribes (Ezra 7:24).[28]

The book of Micah emerges from this context of occupation, and its accusations would have resonated strongly in such a system. Its criticism of those who seize fields and houses (Mic 2:2) and leave women and children homeless (2:9) would have been heard as directed against the community's elites. Its concern for the loss of familial landholdings (2:2-4) would have been heard as challenging the ideal of land divided into kinship groups (see Ezra 2). Its charge that political and religious leaders seek only financial gain would have been heard as criticisms of those in power who colluded with and benefitted alongside the elites. The fields whose seizure Micah decries, the rulers whose behaviors he excoriates, and the city whose exaltation it imagines—all function under the auspices of Persian control.

Ben Zvi argues that, given their own privilege, literate scribes would not have challenged other elites but would have served their own interests. He points out, for example, that when in Mic 4 all the nations stream to Jerusalem, they are seen not as going to the temple to be instructed by priests but as seeking instruction in Torah—the written word in which the scribes just so happen to be experts.[29] Their scribal imagi-

27. Zipporah Glass, "Land, Labor, and Law: Viewing Persian Yehud's Economy through Socio-Economic Modeling" (PhD diss., Vanderbilt University, 2010), 42.

28. Joseph Blenkinsopp, *Ezra–Nehemiah* (Philadelphia: Westminster, 1988), 67–68.

29. Ben Zvi, *Micah*, 106.

nation envisions exaltation not only of Jerusalem and its deity but their own profession.

Timothy Sandoval, however, paints a more nuanced portrait of the Persian period scribe. Scribes, he argues, would have been socially well-placed but not of the highest social class; their interests would diverge from "the 80–90 percent of the population that made up the peasant agricultural population" but "would not have been identical to that of the 1–2 percent of the population that constituted the economic and political elite." They might have served the elite, but they were not identical to them.[30] Sandoval also points out that, as the readers and writers of sacred texts, the scribes would have been the conduit by which the social justice traditions of the culture were communicated to the political and economic elite. They would have been the ones passing down the stories of the liberation from bondage in Egypt and the biblical laws protecting the widow, orphan, and alien; they would have been the ones familiar with the laws of surrounding cultures which seem to have influenced Israel's own guidelines. The scribes might not have been on the lowest rungs of society, but their work would have reminded elites that justice was expected. In the past and in the present, a commitment to social injustice is not the exclusive prerogative of the poor, and those employed by an institution can critique that same institution.

The voice of the privileged ally, however, is not the same as the voice of the oppressed. Throughout this work, I will insist on the distinction between the voice of the scribe and the interests of the average person in ancient Yehud and suggest the ways in which empire has shaped the author's imagination. Along with Steed Davidson, I will consider the ways in which this writer's vision of the future attempted to create "new cartographies of power"[31] within the context of empire, and also, drawing on postcolonial theory, consider who is excluded from the imagined future. Along with Davidson, I also will consider how these power maps attempt to erase women from our view.

Additionally, I will insist that *talking about* women is not the same as *speaking for* women. Paying attention to gender in the past and in the present will help us notice who—and what—is missing from Micah. To do so, we will need not only to notice when Micah does mention gender

30. Timothy Sandoval, "Education: Hebrew Bible," in O'Brien, *The Oxford Encyclopedia of the Bible and Gender Studies*, 1:160.

31. Steed Davidson, "Prophets Postcolonially: Initial Insights for a Postcolonial Reading of Prophetic Literature," *The Bible and Critical Theory* 6 (2010): 24.7.

but also what details about gendered existence are missing. For example, Micah describes only men as sitting under their vines and fig trees (4:4), and when the book laments that women and children are cast out from their houses (2:9), it seems to focus more on their status as victim than as fully empowered owners. Recent studies of Yehud's economy, to the contrary, suggest that women may have actively participated in Yehud's economy. According to Christine Yoder, women in Yehud owned land, participated in the textile industry, served as supervisors of work groups, and even ran credit businesses; a woman named Shelomith, mentioned in a Judean seal, may have been an official in the imperial administration. Nehemiah lists women among those who built the walls of Jerusalem (Neh 3:12).[32] If this information is correct, it indicates that women were far more involved in the affairs of the province than biblical literature leads us to suspect.

Evidence from earlier periods, however, suggests that the majority of women likely continued to be far poorer than their male counterparts. Nathan MacDonald's important study, *What Did the Ancient Israelites Eat?*, underscores the inequitable distribution of food in ancient Israel along class and gender lines: "Even in the premonarchic period the best food resources were being diverted toward elite males."[33] Both skeletal remains and the biblical record itself suggest that men may have received more food (especially meat) than women. The average height of an ancient woman was 152 cm (close to five feet), while the height of an ancient man was 171 cm (five feet seven inches). The differing "portions" allotted to Hannah and Peninah in 1 Sam 1:4-5 may refer to food distribution.

In the modern world, food is clearly a feminist issue. Studies distributed by the World Bank underscore that throughout the world, access to land and food varies by gender:

> The report finds that despite women's importance in agricultural production, they usually have weak land rights. Insecurity of land tenure reduces the likelihood that women will adopt environmentally sustainable agricultural practices and compromises women's ability to obtain credit because land is often the only acceptable form of collateral. Under conditions of food insecurity, male power over food is particularly

32. Christine Yoder, "The Woman of Substance: A Socioeconomic Reading of Proverbs 31:10-31," *JBL* 122 (2003): 427–47. On women's property ownership, see also Grabbe, *A History of the Jews*, 1.

33. Nathan MacDonald, *What Did the Ancient Israelites Eat? Diet in Biblical Times* (Grand Rapids, MI: Eerdmans, 2008), 78.

salient, but even under conditions of food security, gender relations play an important role in food production, distribution, and consumption across cultures and time periods.[34]

Seeing the gendered aspects of hunger and poverty in the past and in the present helps us pay more attention to Micah's constructions of reality—who this book is not talking about, what it leaves unnamed. Indeed, Micah never mentions the poor or explains how they benefit from the horrors of the Assyrian and Babylonian military actions that Micah claims were YHWH's justified punishment of the elite. Instead, leaders and the elite take center stage in Micah—in fact, they monopolize the stage. They are condemned, but they are also presented as the only true human agents. Micah's biggest concern is that of theological fairness: because the landowners took others' lands, they will lose their land. In the past and in the present, however, the poor often disproportionately bear the brunt of war and occupation; their own experience offers counter-testimony to Micah's claim that people get what they deserve. Nehemiah 5 at least acknowledges the existence of undernourished and enslaved women, but in Micah women are generic objects of pity rather than individuals in pain.

Gender. Empire. Blame. Land. Fairness. These are the types of ideological and theological dimensions of the book that I aim to explore. What are the contours of Micah's ethical imagination? What kind of world does this book reflect and construct? How do real people—women, men, children, and those who define themselves as "none of the above"—fare in such a world?

The Aesthetics of the Book

Exploring the ideological and theological purposes of the book requires careful attention to its literary style and presentation. As a rhetorical production, Micah follows a particular structure and employs particular poetic techniques. While readers respond to those techniques in various ways, the aesthetics of the text are a key component of the meaning-making process. They help shape our conclusions about what the text means for today.

34. IFPRI News. "Report Finds Severe Gender Inequities," Consultative Group on International Agricultural Reasearch 2, World Bank (1995), http://www-wds .worldbank.org/external/default/WDSContentServer/WDSP/IB/2002/03/29/00 0094946_0203200402053/Rendered/PDF/multi0page.pdf.

As many interpreters have recognized, the book of Micah interweaves declarations of judgment and promises of salvation. The first three chapters explain the reasons for Samaria's and Jerusalem's fall; Mic 4 and 5 promise a better future; and Mic 6 and 7 alternate between judgment and salvation.

The following outline indicates that the book is punctuated not just by theme but also by repeated vocabulary. Lamentation (Mic 1:8, 11), wailing (1:8, 11; 2:4), and expressions of grief (1:16; 2:1; 7:1) pervade the book, as YHWH, the prophet, and others lament the fate of Samaria, Jerusalem, and their inhabitants. Given the strong association of lament with women in the ancient world, this feature of the book will factor strongly into my discussion of the book's gendered dimensions. A summons to judgment (שמעו, "hear!") begins units in 1:2, 3:1 and 6:1.[35]

Outline of Micah

> 1:1 Superscription: What Micah saw about Samaria and Jerusalem
>> 1:2–3:12 Judgment of Samaria and Jerusalem
>>> 1:2-5 YHWH appears and addresses ("hear," 1:2) humans and earth for judgment
>>> 1:6-7 The punishment of Samaria ("therefore I will make Samaria a heap," 1:6)
>>> 1:8–3:12 The Punishment of Jerusalem
>>>> 1:8-16 First lament ("lament," "wail," "mourn," 1:8)
>>>> 2:1-13 Second lament ("alas!," 2:1)
>>>> 3:1-12 Direct address to leaders ("hear," 3:1 and 3:9) ("therefore Jerusalem shall become a heap," 3:12)
>> 4:1–5:15 (4:1–5:14 MT) Announcement of Jerusalem's Future Salvation
>>> 4:1-7 Jerusalem exalted
>>> 4:8-13 Daughter Zion restored to honor and strength
>>> 5:1-6 (4:14–5:5 MT) The promise of a new ruler
>>> 5:7-15 (5:6-14 MT) Hopes for the remnant
>> 6:1-16 YHWH's Suit against Israel ("hear," 6:1, 2, 9)
>>> 6:1-2 Summoning of witnesses
>>> 6:3-5 YHWH's fulfillment of obligations
>>> 6:6-8 The people's obligations
>>> 6:9-12 Accusations of breach of covenant
>>> 6:13-16 Sentencing

---

35. Mignon Jacobs explores in depth the repeated vocabulary and themes of Micah, discerning features of the book's connective fiber: Mignon R. Jacobs, *The Conceptual Coherence of the Book of Micah*, JSOTSup (Sheffield: Sheffield Academic Press, 2001).

7:1-20 Daughter Jerusalem's Response, in Conversation with YHWH
    7:1-10 Daughter Jerusalem's lament ("woe!," 7:1)
        and expression of confidence
    7:11-13 YHWH's promises of deliverance
    7:14-20 Daughter Jerusalem's final appeals

As formatting in the NRSV and other modern English translations indicates, Micah is poetry. Particular features of its poetic style are important to its effect on readers and will be explored below. While poetry persuades, however, it engages imagination as well as rationality, and its playful use of language often subverts attempts to codify its meaning.

Discussing the poetics of Micah requires us to acknowledge the marked differences between translations of the book. Many of these differences reflect the book's complex textual issues. The Masoretic Text (MT), that version of Hebrew from which most modern translations are made, offers a version of Micah that is often nearly impossible to decipher. For that reason, scholars often try to repair the text, comparing it with other ancient versions of the Bible such as the Septuagint or the Syriac Peshitta and using their own best judgment about what the original Hebrew likely said. Readers of English can see some of this by noticing the textual footnotes in the NRSV, those notes keyed with lowercase letters found below a block of text. Micah 5, for example, has five textual notes in the NRSV that indicate where the translators did not follow the MT. Academic commentaries on Micah offer much more detail and speculation about these and other textual conundrums.

Differences between manuscripts also have created a discrepancy in the numbering of verses in Mic 4 and 5. In MT, Mic 4 includes fourteen verses, so that the reference to Bethlehem occurs in 5:1. In some English texts, such as the NRSV, Mic 4 ends with verse 13, so that Mic 5 begins with a reference to the ruler of Israel. Throughout Mic 5, then, Hebrew and English numberings differ by one verse. Since this commentary is based on the NRSV, I will refer to the English system but will include the Hebrew verse equivalents in parentheses.

Other translational differences derive from the art of moving from one language to another and the choices made between the accuracy and the relevancy of a translation. Eugene Peterson's translation of Micah in *The Message*,[36] for example, chooses relevancy and readability over accuracy.

---

36. Eugene Peterson, *The Message: The Bible in Contemporary Language* (Colorado Springs, CO: NAV Press, 2002).

To accomplish his goal, however, Peterson interprets rather than simply translates, "restoring" the complicated puns on city names in Mic 1:10-16 and adding feminine parallels to the text's masculine language, for example: "each man will sit under his own shade tree / each woman in safety will tend her own garden" (4:4); "what YHWH is looking for in men and women" (6:8). Encountering Micah in *The Message* makes it appear far less androcentric than the Hebrew text indicates. Modernizing Micah often makes it sound more egalitarian than the book actually is.

Peterson's interpretation also has a clear social class orientation. He employs idioms based on modern middle-class experience rather than ancient realities, for example:

> "You'll plant grass but never get a lawn
>   you'll make jelly but never spread it on your bread." (Mic 6:15)

When read in Hebrew, however, Micah's language is rarely inclusive. And its message is neither simple nor plain.

Indeed, several of its features complicate rather than clarify our attempt to make sense of its language.

Parallelism

Like other Hebrew poetry, Micah employs the style of parallelism, in which an idea is expressed in sequential, often building, lines or phrases. Some lines follow classic synonymous parallelism, in which one line is echoed in a similarly worded second line:

> Hear, you peoples, all of you
>   listen, o earth, and all that is in it. (1:2)

> He shall judge between many peoples,
>   and shall arbitrate between strong nations far away. (4:3)

Micah's parallelism, however, is uneven, often deviating from the simple two-line scheme seen in the book of Proverbs. At times, three short parallel lines are followed by two parallel lines:

> All her images shall be beaten to pieces,
>   all her wages shall be burned with fire,
>   and all her idols I will lay waste;
> for as the wages of a prostitute she gathered them,
>   and as the wages of a prostitute they shall again be used. (1:7)

At other points, multiple lines of parallelism are strung together:

> you who hate the good and love the evil,
> who tear the skin off my people
>   and the flesh off their bones;
> who eat the flesh of my people,
>   flay their skin off them,
> break their bones in pieces,
>   and chop them up like meat in a kettle,
>   like flesh in a caldron. (3:2-3)

Occasionally, no parallelism is evident:

> But you, O Bethlehem of Ephrathah,
>   who are one of the little clans of Judah,
> from you shall come forth for me
>   one who is to rule in Israel,
> whose origin is from of old,
>   from ancient days. (5:2; 5:1 MT)

Hyperbole

Micah is not unique among the prophetic books in employing an exaggerated style. Its accusation that leaders eat others' flesh and cook their bones in a kettle (3:3) sounds similar to Amos's claim that Israelites "trample the head of the poor into the dust of the earth" (2:7). Micah's frequent hyperboles deserve particular attention because they render difficult the determination of the exact practices being targeted. Interpreters often distinguish between metaphorical and realistic descriptions based on "common sense," convinced, for example, that the book's accusations of cannibalism are not meant to be taken literally but that accusations of land seizure are.

One interpreter's "common sense," however, does not always agree with another's. Does Mic 6:6-8 deny the validity of the temple cult or use exaggeration to show its relative importance to morality? Is the desire in 4:1-7 for the domination of other nations or does it speak in hyperbole about a desire to be restored from obscurity?

Gendered Language

Micah employs gendered language typical of the prophetic books. The city of Samaria is personified as a woman and compared to a prostitute (1:7); Jerusalem is addressed as Daughter Zion (4:10) and depicted as a woman writhing in labor (4:9) and shamefully stripped in public (4:11).

Most of the cities listed in 1:10-16 are characterized as feminine, and Hebrew forms for the "lame" (הצלעה), "driven away" (הנדחה), and "af-flicted" (הרעתי) (4:6; see also Zeph 3:19) are feminine. Images of the powerful are masculine: YHWH appears like a warrior (1:3), and the ruler to come is male.

Feminist scholars have assessed differently the net effect of this imag-ery. Judy Fentress-Williams finds Micah's language sufficiently sexist to warrant resistance from feminist readers.[37] Sophia Bietenhard, on the other hand, finds Micah refreshingly absent of the troubling patriarchal imagery of the nation as YHWH's adulterous wife or a recalcitrant whore, and progressively female-affirming in assigning the feminine role of mourner to the prophet.[38]

Erin Runions, however, challenges such essentialist notions of gender (in the text and in the reader), pointing instead to the instability of Micah's gendered imagery. Throughout the book, the gender of pronouns and imagery frequently shifts, and in Mic 4 Daughter Zion assumes masculine characteristics: "she is a strong tower, she has an iron horn, she tramples the nations."[39]

As I will explain in detail in the body of the commentary, I find Micah's use of gendered imagery far less "queer" than Runions does, seeing instead recalcitrant gender scripts. Especially disturbing for me is the imagery of Mic 4 in which Daughter Jerusalem is depicted as an animal trampling others. Micah's feminine imagery neither challenges stereo-types of females as defenseless victims nor provides insight into the real-life women of the author's world—or my own.

The high degree of ambiguity in the language and message of Micah often frustrates translators and historians, as well as readers who want to determine its precise meaning, and yet Micah's language provokes the imagination. On the one hand, women may find these images gen-erative of hope: the imagery of swords beaten to plowshares, folks sitting in peace under fig trees, and a ruler emerging from the village of Beth-

37. Judy Fentress-Williams, "Micah," in *Women's Bible Commentary*, ed. Carol Newsom, Sharon Ringe, and Jacqueline Lapsley, 3rd ed. (Louisville, KY: Westminster John Knox, 2012), 328.

38. Sophia Bietenhard, "Micah: Call for Justice—Hope for All," in *Feminist Biblical Interpretation: A Compendium of Critical Commentary on the Books of the Bible and Related Literature*, ed. Louise Schottroff, Marie-Theres Wacker, and Martin Rumscheidt (Grand Rapids, MI: Eerdmans, 2012), 421–32.

39. Runions, *Changing Subjects*, 158.

lehem appeals to many desires. Micah's simple articulation of the religious life seems to distill the truth into a mantra: "what does the LORD require of you but to do justice, and to love kindness, and to walk humbly with your God?" (6:8), and the high degree of emotive language allows us to imagine an earnest prophet challenging injustice, as the language of lament and woe punctuates the accusations. If Jeremiah can be called the weeping prophet, then Micah is surely the lamenting one. On the other hand, such imagery can constrain thought and action. For example, in an ancient context in which mourning was "women's work," casting the male prophet as a mourner can be seen either as appropriating or denying women's role as mourner.

All these features and others that I will explore help Micah resonate with readers in different times and places. Micah arrests our attention with well-turned phrases and compelling imagery. The lack of details allows us to fill in our own, allowing us to feel that the book speaks directly to us in our own situation: we feel we know what Micah says because the words ring so true to our experience. Micah's ambiguity grants its language staying power, allowing readers of different times and places to find themselves within its pages. At same time, its familiarity can numb us to its power to reinforce the very stereotypes we resist.

Engaging Micah

When read from a Persian-period perspective, the book of Micah claims that both Israel and Judah were destroyed as YHWH's punishment for the sins of its leaders and elite citizens; because they seized the land of others, the nations were destroyed. The book both prays for and envisions a future time in which Judah's punishment will end and the city of Jerusalem will be exalted in the eyes of the world.

The book defines human justice as respecting the land rights of others and faithfully exercising the duties of one's office. The text also defines divine justice as a direct correlation between sin and punishment: because rulers seized land, the nation lost its land; because Samaria received a prostitute's pay, she will receive the punishment due a prostitute (1:7). The very names of the cities in 1:10-16 indicate their fate: Beth-leaphrah (בית לעפרה, "house of dust") should roll itself in עפר ("dust"). Because "the punishment fits the crime," YHWH's actions against Israel and Judah are justified. But because YHWH also honors commitments, Yehud can hope that the promises YHWH made to the ancestors might form the basis for its own promising future.

Feminist theologians and postcolonialist theorists have drawn our attention to the way that seemingly-universal claims about God actually reflect the ideology of the humans who formulate them. "Universal" theologies too often assume that certain people and experiences are the norm for all people, even though they actually serve the interests of some people over others. Asking feminist questions of the book of Micah, then, calls us to consider how its theology participates in the power dynamics of gender. At the same time, feminist interpreters must avoid their own forms of privilege. As womanist scholars have shown, white feminists have too often assumed that their own perspectives are universal and have overlooked the interests and perspectives of African American women.[40] And so our questions must continue to ask who benefits from claims made in and about the book of Micah. Whose realities does Micah's language—and our own interpretation—ignore or obscure from our view?

Micah 4–5 desperately hopes for a time in which Judah and Jerusalem will be prominent on the world stage, for Daughter Zion to transform from a woman writhing in pain to a strong ox treading her enemies underfoot, and yet the exaltation of a metaphorical daughter does not necessarily translate to the exaltation of real-life daughters (and wives and mothers). In political struggles around the world, the perceived needs of a marginalized community as a whole often supersede those of the marginalized within the community itself. Minority women in the United States, women living under occupation in Palestine, and African women in communities without healthcare and water are often counseled and often therefore choose to prioritize the rights of the community over their own concerns. Would a world in which all people stream to Jerusalem have benefitted those who did not share power in Jerusalem—women and men living in small villages?

In the commentary that follows, I will return to these and other questions raised by the book of Micah. Working systematically through Micah's poetry, I endeavor to lift up both its power and the difficult issues it raises. Throughout my discussion, I hope to keep a focus on real people's lives, imagining what these words might have meant for people's gendered lives in Persian Yehud and considering what they mean for our own gendered lives today.

---

40. See Valerie Bridgeman, "Womanist Criticism," in O'Brien, *Oxford Encyclopedia of the Bible and Gender Studies*, 2:431–39.

Micah 1–3

Judgments against Female Cities and Male Leaders

Superscription: What Micah Saw about Samaria and Jerusalem (Mic 1:1)

Micah's superscription instructs readers on how to interpret this book. The details of the opening verse invite us to imagine a particular time and place and to accept the speeches to follow as a prophet's faithful delivery of divine words. Paying attention to the book's history and to the dynamics of gendered power, however, challenges us not to conflate so easily the testimony of this book with divine will.

The three kings named—Jotham, Ahaz, and Hezekiah—ruled Judah in the eighth century BCE. The superscriptions of Isaiah and Hosea also include these kings, adding Jotham's father Uzziah. The mention of both Samaria and Jerusalem in Mic 1:1 further situates the prophet's speech within the period of the Divided Kingdoms, when Samaria stood as capital of the northern kingdom Israel and Jerusalem as capital of the southern kingdom Judah. According to this superscription, the prophet Micah was active from 759/743 BCE to 727/687 BCE, implying that he spoke before the fall of Samaria, after the fall of Samaria, and perhaps during the Assyrian siege of Jerusalem.

1

Mic 1:1

¹The word of the Lᴏʀᴅ that came to Micah of Moresheth in the days of Kings Jotham, Ahaz, and Hezekiah of Judah, which he saw concerning Samaria and Jerusalem.

A primary source for our understanding of the Assyrian period is 2 Kgs 15–19, part of a larger collection known as the Deuteronomistic History. The books of Kings portray the eighth century as one of political and military conflicts between Philistia, Israel, Judah, and Syria—all driven by Assyrian control of the Levant. It recounts various Assyrian blows to the region: the capture of Samaria in 722/721 BCE and the siege of Jerusalem in 701 BCE. From a Deuteronomistic theological perspective, 1–2 Kgs evaluates rulers on how faithfully they promote exclusive worship of YHWH in Jerusalem: Jotham receives positive marks, even though people worshiped at "high places" (e.g., 1 Kgs 14:22-23); Ahaz is judged as idolatrous (2 Kgs 16); and Hezekiah is praised for destroying worship sites outside Jerusalem (2 Kgs 18:4-5).

The body of Micah resonates well with Kings' description of the late eighth century, and many interpreters accept this "fit" as evidence that Micah preserves accurate memories of the Assyrian assault on Judah in 701 BCE. The connection between Micah and Kings, however, may derive less from historical context as from literary activity; the verbal parallels are strong enough to suggest the common editing of the books or even that the author of Micah may have derived knowledge of the eighth century from reading a version of Kings. In 2 Kgs 18:19-35, an Assyrian official mocks Judah's confidence in language echoed in Mic 5:6 and promises that defectors will eat from their own vines and fig trees (see also Mic 4:4).[1] Second Kings 19:4 and 31 describe a "remnant" of Jerusalem in ways similar to Mic 4:7 and 5:7-8 (5:6-7 MT). The reader's sense that these two literary collections corroborate one another may not be an accident but instead the accomplishment of Micah's author.

"Micah," perhaps a shortened form of "who is like Yah (weh)?" is a name shared with several other figures in the Hebrew Bible; a longer spelling is used for a figure in 2 Kgs 22:12. The superscription (as well as a reference in Jer 26:18) designates him as from Moresheth. If this is

---

1. James Nogalski, *The Book of the Twelve: Hosea through Jonah* (Macon, GA: Smith and Helwys, 2011), 511.

the same town as Moresheth-Gath (Mic 1:14), then it was likely in the area known as the Shephelah, near Judah's border with Philistia. Such a geographical location makes this literary character an outsider to both Samaria and Jerusalem.

The character of Micah is not explicitly called a prophet, but the style and particular vocabulary of the superscription categorize the book as the genre of prophecy. "The word of the LORD" appears in the superscriptions of ten prophetic books, while others include close parallels. The verb "saw" and the related noun form "vision" are technical terms for prophetic activity.

The role of the prophets has been variously understood over time,[2] yet evidence strongly suggests that throughout the ancient Near East prophecy was understood as one form of divine communication with humans. "Prophets—like dreamers and unlike astrologers or haruspices [entrail readers]—do not employ methods based on systematic observations and their scholarly interpretations, but act as direct mouthpieces of gods whose messages they communicate."[3] In texts from ancient Mari and Assyria, prophetic voices claim divinely granted knowledge about the future, including the outcomes of battles. Similarly, in the final form of prophetic books, prophets often speak of events prior to their actualization. The superscription of Isaiah, for example, sets the prophet in the eighth century, but Isa 45:1 reflects knowledge of Cyrus the Persian in the fifth century BCE. Deuteronomy 18:22 makes accuracy of prediction one mark of true prophecy, a theme carried through the stories about prophets in 1 and 2 Kings.

Persian-period readers, then, might easily understand Micah as a figure from the past whose words apply to diverse times and places, including their own. The superscription, in turn, grants the book's orientation to the future an atemporal dimension: while many modern scholars find the book's prediction of the fall of Jerusalem (3:12) to reflect a different period than hopes for its restoration (4:1-13), and the promise that the Assyrians will be rebuffed (5:5-6; 5:4-5 MT) to reflect a time earlier than the promise of an end to the Babylonian exile (4:6-7), ancient readers might attribute such insights to the special knowledge imparted to the prophet. "The book claims that it provides the readers who are

---

2. See Julia M. O'Brien, *Challenging Prophetic Metaphor: Theology and Ideology in the Prophets* (Louisville, KY: Westminster John Knox, 2008), chap. 1.

3. Martti Nissinen, *Prophets and Prophecy in the Ancient Near East* (Atlanta, GA: SBL Press, 2003), 1.

competent to read it both knowledge originating in the divine (i.e., YH-WH's word) and valid knowledge about the divine (i.e., an authentic representation of YHWH's positions, actions, plans, and indirectly of YHWH's character)."[4]

Within such an understanding of prophecy, the superscription renders the personality of the human prophet irrelevant to the message: the prophet Micah becomes the medium, not the origin, of the words to follow. The fact that the book will address readers directly, as if they were hearing the words just as delivered, further encourages the reader to hear the words of this book as God's words unfiltered by a human agent.[5]

The nature of the superscription also blurs the boundaries between the prophet and those who transmit and interpret the prophetic words. As Ehud Ben Zvi notes, the prophet provides access to God's intentions, but the scribe provides access to the prophet's words.[6] The superscription draws no overt attention to the scribe; indeed, Micah's opening (along with all prophetic superscriptions) obscures its own origins. Cast as divine speech unfettered by time, place, and human agency, the book says nothing about who recorded these words, why, and under what conditions. For Steed Davidson, such silences invite postcolonialist suspicion: "Exposing the mechanics of the production of knowledge and therefore the channels of power in the text remains one of the functions of a postcolonial enquiry."[7] He also notes that "the people to whom the words of the prophet are addressed neither speak, act, nor are mentioned in the records of the books," an absence especially noticeable when gender is considered.[8]

The superscription of the book of Micah mentions a male prophet identified by his location, three male kings, and two cities about whom the words pertain. It tells us nothing about the prophet Micah, his family, his social class, or his interests; nothing about the interests of the writer recording the words; nothing about the world of either the eighth century of the literary setting or of the fifth century of its composition. The presence of women in the royal houses, among the prophets, or within Sa-

4. Ehud Ben Zvi, *Micah*, The Forms of the Old Testament Literature, vol. 21B (Grand Rapids, MI: Eerdmans, 2000), 5.
5. Michael Floyd, *Minor Prophets, Part 2* (Grand Rapids, MI: Eerdmans, 2000), 171.
6. Ben Zvi, *Micah*, 16.
7. Steed Davidson, "Prophets Postcolonially: Initial Insights for a Postcolonial Reading of Prophetic Literature," *The Bible and Critical Theory* 6 (2010): 24.6–24.7.
8. Ibid., 24.8.

maria and Jerusalem is not imagined, nor are the lives of average people living in Samaria, Jerusalem, or smaller villages.

Attentive readers do well, then, to approach the book of Micah with a healthy dose of suspicion. Rather than a verbatim transcript of God's speech to all times and places, this work is one production of an anonymous male scribe writing in Persian-occupied Jerusalem in the fifth century BCE. This scribe's testimony may indeed be "inspired," but it is also shaped by the interests of its human author—interests that must be examined and, when necessary, critiqued.

When "universal" truths are advanced without attentiveness to the particularities of human living and apart from women's experience, what other voices need to be heard? What other realities need to be imagined beyond those recorded in these records? Womanist theologian Jacquelyn Grant recounts the words of Sojourner Truth, the former slave and women's rights activist, who refused to limit her preaching to the written word: "No honey, can't preach from de Bible—can't read a letter. When I preaches, I has jest one text to preach from, an' I always preaches from this one. My text is 'When I found Jesus!'"[9] Grant insists that contemporary persons without access to power must also interpret the Bible within the context of their own experience of God and listen to the ways in which the divine word is expressed from the margins of society.

While my exploration of the book of Micah endeavors to hear the "word of YHWH" within its pages, it also seeks to hear divine truth in other voices as well—in Micah's interpreters and in the world beyond Micah. Clearly, although the superscription of Micah suggests that its words extend *beyond* a particular time and place, the superscription also attests that its testimony emerges *from a* particular time and place—and therefore the testimony is a contextual truth that needs to be considered alongside other testimonies to truth. For that reason, the Contributing Voices in this volume bring in the concerns of Africa, of Israel and Palestine, of persons of varying sexual orientations and gender identities, and of artists.

In addition, I offer various excurses on the history of Micah's interpretation—in Christian interpretation and art—and contemporary reflections on themes of Micah, such as its hopes for the future and its

9. Jacquelyn Grant, "A Womanist Christology," in *Walk Together Children: Black and Womanist Theologies, Church, and Theological Education*, ed. Dwight N. Hopkins and Linda E. Thomas (Eugene, OR: Wipf and Stock, 2010), 171.

connection with remembered trauma. Throughout, questions of power (gendered and otherwise) remain as the focus of attention.

Judgment of Samaria and Jerusalem (Mic 1:2–3:12)

This first major block of Micah details the sins of Samaria and, in greater length, Jerusalem. When read from the viewpoint of the book's implied time period in the Assyrian period, this first block predicts the future fall of Samaria and Jerusalem. Read from the viewpoint of its Persian period authors and readers, the material explains why the northern and southern kingdoms were destroyed. Throughout this block, gender helps craft imagery that is powerful and problematic, stereotypical and yet occasionally unstable.

YHWH Appears and Addresses Humans and Earth for Judgment (Mic 1:2-5)

In language drawn from legal proceedings, the prophetic voice announces a suit against the whole earth and its inhabitants. YHWH will serve both as witness against the people and their judge. In a terrifying theophany (literally, "God showing up"), the Divine Warrior will charge from his[10] abode in the Jerusalem temple, destroying everything in his path. The earth as a whole will suffer because of the guilt of Samaria and Jerusalem. The image of YHWH as the avenging Warrior is ubiquitous in the prophetic books—opening the book of Nahum, ending the book of Habakkuk, and punctuating the books of Isaiah and Jeremiah. This imagery has strong ancient Near Eastern parallels: this description of YHWH parallels the descriptions of Baal in Canaanite myth and Marduk in Babylonian texts.

While in the Hebrew Bible[11] YHWH the warrior is described as male, elsewhere warrior language is not gender specific: Ancient Near Eastern

10. As explained in the introduction, I will utilize masculine language for Micah's description of YHWH. When describing my own understanding of God, I use non-gendered language.

11. Throughout the commentary, I will most often refer to the documents known to Christians as "Old Testament" and to Jews as "Bible" or "Tanakh" with the term "Hebrew Bible." This nomenclature is imperfect, since Roman Catholics recognize as canonical some "Old Testament" books that were originally written in Greek and since Christians are seldom willing to rethink the naming of the "New Testament." I am willing to follow the scholarly community in utilizing "Hebrew Bible," however,

Mic 1:2-5

²Hear, you peoples, all of you;
listen, O earth, and all that is
in it;
and let the Lord God be a witness
against you,
the Lord from his holy temple.
³For lo, the Lord is coming out of
his place,
and will come down and tread
upon the high places of
the earth.
⁴Then the mountains will melt
under him

and the valleys will burst open,
like wax near the fire,
like waters poured down a
steep place.
⁵All this is for the transgression of
Jacob
and for the sins of the house of
Israel.
What is the transgression of Jacob?
Is it not Samaria?
And what is the high place of
Judah?
Is it not Jerusalem?"

documents also describe warrior goddesses such as Ištar/Inana, Annunītum, Ulmašitum, Ninsi'anna, and Ninisin.[12] The raging anger of the offended YHWH also finds its parallel in descriptions of ancient Near Eastern deities of both genders. In various cuneiform texts, both masculine and feminine deities "are described as sullen, spoiled, impetuous, and disruptive when enraged. In order for a god to be calmed, be it Enlil when he chooses to destroy a city or land or Ereškigal when she flays Ištar, his/her heart must be cooled and his/her ego soothed."[13]

In the Hebrew Bible, YHWH's rage does not abate until vengeance is exacted. In her study of biblical depictions of anger, Ellen van Wolde notes that YHWH is "more than five hundred times represented as subjected to the explosive force of fury and aggression leading to violence."[14] Indeed, "the anger of the Lord will not turn back until he has executed and accomplished the intents of his mind" (Jer 23:20). In the prophetic books, YHWH's anger is always described as having been provoked by

---

in order to avoid the supersessionist implications of the term "Old Testament." Only when referring to specifically Christian understandings of the material will I retain the term "Old Testament."

12. Ilona Zsolnay, "Deity, Subentry Ancient Near East," in *The Oxford Encyclopedia of the Bible and Gender Studies*, ed. Julia M. O'Brien, 2 vols. (New York: Oxford University Press, 2014), 1:72.

13. Ibid.

14. Ellen van Wolde, "The Language of Sentiment," *SBL Forum*, n.p. (cited April 2007), http://sbl-site.org/Article.aspx?ArticleID=660.

8

acts of human injustice. Anger is not an eternal divine characteristic but an occasioned response to transgression.

The nature of Samaria's and Jerusalem's wrongdoing is ambiguously described in Mic 1:5. In parallel lines, Samaria itself is named as Israel/Jacob's transgression; Jerusalem is labeled as Judah's "high place," the language used in 1–2 Kings for idolatrous worship (e.g., 1 Kgs 3:4). These cities are condemned not for what they have *done* but for who they *are*.

Devadasan N. Premnath contends that the eighth-century prophet Micah condemns these urban centers because of their key role in an exploitative economy: "The cities, as the administrative centers of the state, functioned effectively in the process of penetrating and extracting the economic surplus from the rural areas. . . .The city stood as a symbol of the social stratification, which was based on a relationship of exploitation."[15]

Premnath's claim that Micah was antiurban is shared by many interpreters, and the prophet Micah is often seen as the rural counterpart to the Jerusalemite Isaiah. Such a conclusion, however, is problematic. The accusations against Samaria that follow are far too general for economic analysis, and the assumptions of a sharp divide between "urban" and "rural" are anachronistic—both for the eighth century in which Premnath locates the prophet Micah and in the Persian period in which I locate the book's production. As Lester L. Grabbe explains:

> Most recent study has emphasized that there was generally no sharp urban/rural distinction in antiquity. . . . The concept of an urban elite—in opposition to a rural elite—comes from the model of the medieval city, whereas the elite in antiquity was undifferentiated, dividing its time between the estates from which it obtained its wealth and the political activities that tended to be conducted in the city. . . . The concept of significant rural/urban alienation does not fit either what is known from other areas of the ancient Near East nor the primary data.[16]

In our own world, both urban *and* rural environments are difficult for women. The number of megacities (defined by the United Nations as metropolitan areas with a total population of more than 10 million people) continues to rise, increasing the number of urban poor in general

15. Devadasan N. Premnath, *Eighth Century Prophets: A Social Analysis* (St. Louis, MO: Chalice, 2003), 117.

16. Lester L. Grabbe, "Introduction and Overview," in *'Every City Shall Be Forsaken': Urbanism and Prophecy in Ancient Israel and the Near East*, ed. Lester L. Grabbe and Robert D. Haak, JSOTSup 330 (Sheffield: Sheffield Academic Press, 2001), 32.

and the female urban poor in particular: "In congested cities, women also face an increased risk of communicable diseases and infections. Women are more compromised than men under these urban conditions due to gender inequities and to a lack of awareness among urban developers and policymakers of their specific needs and concerns."[17]

Rural women, however, fare little better. "It is in the rural areas of the world where poverty is most severe in human terms, where the hunger, hopelessness, hardship, and despair commonly associated with entrenched poverty are most pronounced, where basic health services, sanitation, educational opportunities, and other common amenities are most lacking."[18] During the 2006–2008 global food crisis that raised international prices for staple foods, "poor rural women were particularly affected because they lag behind in access to resources like credit, land, technologies and infrastructure, which reduces their purchasing power. . . . As traditional food providers and carers for their households, they tend to act as 'shock absorbers,' giving their food to their children and their husbands to prevent them from going hungry, and spending more time caring for sick relatives as households cut back on health expenses."[19]

While Premnath and others pit rural versus urban in Micah, more attentive readers might ask how various genders and classes of people fare in each setting. In both the past and the present, access to basic goods is determined not just by social location but also by gender, class, race, and other human constructs. Although the opening oracle of Micah casts whole cities as transgressing, we can imagine that not all persons shared equally in the wealth—and in the blame—of Samaria and Jerusalem.

The inequities of power in the ancient world and in the present make me suspicious of Micah's totalizing language. Micah characterizes Samaria and Jerusalem as monolithically sinful entities deserving of punishment rather than locales inhabited by human agents whose choices affect themselves and others; Micah makes both everyone in general and

17. Afaf Ibrahim Meleis, Eugenie L. Birch, and Susan M. Wachter, *Women's Health and the World's Cities* (Philadelphia: University of Pennsylvania Press, 2011), 1–2.

18. Idriss Jazairy, Mohiuddin Alamgir, Theresa Panuccio, and International Fund for Agricultural Development, *The State of World Rural Poverty: An Inquiry into Its Causes and Consequences* (New York: NYU Press, 1993), summary.

19. Women-Watch, "Supporting Rural Women to Cope with High Food Prices," Women Watch: Rural Women and Development, October 2011, United Nations, http://www.un.org/womenwatch/feature/idrw/.

no one in particular accountable for the loss of life that the destruction of these cities would have entailed. While for a Persian-period scribe this generic language may have helped answer the theological problem of why Samaria and Jerusalem fell (we deserved it!), for me the language raises other theological problems. How can I believe in Micah's insistence that God is just when the realities of daily living are not factored into the theological equation? Abstract formulations may provide an explanation of reality, but they often do so by erasing the importance of individuals and the structures of power in which they live.

The Punishment of Samaria (Mic 1:6-7)

Having declared Samaria and Jerusalem guilty, YHWH immediately declares Samaria's verdict: the city will become a heap (the same threat will be applied to Jerusalem in Mic 3:12). The foundations of its buildings will be scattered. Most interpreters understand this threat as one of complete desolation, similar to the language of ancient Near Eastern treaty curses and as reflected in passages such as 1 Kgs 9:8 and Isa 17:1.[20] Daniel Smith-Christopher, however, argues that the second phrase in Mic 1:6 suggests that the writer envisions the conversion of urban space to agricultural land. Following the work of Premnath, he sets the passage within an eighth-century context and posits that Micah calls for "the redistribution of confiscated lands back into agriculturally productive land in the hands of the small farmers."[21] As noted above, however, the pitting of rural versus urban in the eighth century—as well as in the fifth century of the book's composition—is questionable.

Samaria is depicted as feminine. At first glance such gender assignment might be seen as merely stereotypical: throughout the Hebrew Bible and in other ancient Near Eastern documents, cities are personified as women. Micah 1:7, however, turns to specific feminine imagery: that of a prostitute who receives wages. The Hebrew term זונה literally refers to a professional prostitute: it is the same term used to describe the activities of Tamar (Gen 38) and Rahab (Josh 2), and its prohibition is paralleled with that of a male prostitute in Deut 23:18. By extension, however,

20. Delbert Hillers, *Micah: A Commentary on the Book of the Prophet Micah*, Hermeneia: A Critical and Historical Commentary on the Bible (Philadephia: Fortress Press, 1984).

21. Daniel L. Smith-Christopher, "On the Pleasures of Prophetic Judgment: Reading Micah 1:6 and 3:12 with Stokely Carmichael," in *Aesthetics of Violence in the Prophets*, ed. Julia M. O'Brien and Chris Franke (New York: T & T Clark, 2010), 85–86.

Mic 1:6-7

⁶Therefore I will make Samaria a heap in the open country, a place for planting vineyards. I will pour down her stones into the valley, and uncover her foundations. ⁷All her images shall be beaten to pieces, all her wages shall be burned with fire, and all her idols I will lay waste; for as the wages of a prostitute she gathered them, and as the wages of a prostitute they shall again be used.

זונה refers to any promiscuous woman. In Deut 22:21, for example, it describes a young woman found not to be a virgin, and Ezek 23:3 uses the term to accuse young women of promiscuous behavior. Like the modern term "slut," it is a slur for women who do not follow acceptable norms of sexual behavior, and the slur can be applied metaphorically to men. In the Hebrew Bible, idolatry is frequently compared to prostitution (זנה). First Chronicles 5:25-26, for example, claims that because Israel prostituted itself to other gods, YHWH stirred the Assyrians to destroy Samaria. Micah 1:7 draws on this typical association, linking prostitution to the worship of idols.

Many interpreters understand Mic 1:7 as explicitly labeling Samaria a harlot and thus in following the pervasive tendency of prophetic literature to denigrate Israel and Judah as "whores" deserving of brutal punishment.[22] From such a perspective, Judy Fentress-Williams points to the danger of the metaphor for women and calls modern readers to challenge it.[23] Sophia Bietenhard instead argues that Micah uses few of the offensive gendered metaphors found in other prophetic books, including the comparison of Israel to a whore and to Yahweh's wife.[24] In her extensive work on Micah, Erin Runions has argued that in Mic 1:7 Samaria is not actually accused of harlotry but rather of gathering a harlot's wages: Samaria is not a whore but a pimp. She claims that

---

22. For a fuller discussion, see O'Brien, *Challenging Prophetic Metaphor*, chaps. 2 and 4.

23. Judy Fentress-Williams, "Micah," in *Women's Bible Commentary*, ed. Carol Newsom, Sharon Ringe, and Jacqueline Lapsley, 3rd ed. (Louisville, KY: Westminster John Knox, 2012), 328.

24. Sophia Bietenhard, "Micah: Call for Justice--Hope for All," in *Feminist Biblical Interpretation: A Compendium of Critical Commentary on the Books of the Bible and Related Literature*, ed. Luise Schottroff, Marie-Theres Wacker, and Martin Rumscheidt (Grand Rapids, MI: Eerdmans, 2012).

interpreters have painted this passage with too broad a brush stroke and thereby overlooked its complicating, even "queer," potential.[25]

I recognize the way in which Micah's language differs from that of other prophets, but I find the language far more "typical" than "queer." Even if Micah's use of these sexually charged tropes is less extensive than Hos 1–2 or less scatological than Ezek 16 and 23, as Bietenhard suggests, this passage nonetheless perpetuates the association of women with illicit sex and illicit worship. I find Runions' reading to be an interpretive stretch. Samaria's identity as a prostitute may not be specified in Mic 1:7 but it is clearly implied. In Isa 23:17-18, Ezek 16:30-41, and Hos 9:1 the same Hebrew word for "wages" is linked with the (city personified as) prostitute herself. Moreover, if Runions is correct that Micah casts Samaria not as a prostitute but as a pimp then she simply becomes the exploiter of other nameless women. I find little comfort in imaging a female character as a manager of sex workers rather than a sex worker herself. A system that relies on the degradation of women is problematic, no matter who gets the cash.[26]

What might this passage have meant in Persian Yehud? The passage would have a clear retrospective function, joining other biblical material in blaming the previous fall of Samaria to the Assyrians on Israel's worship of other deities (Hos 4; 2 Kgs 18) rather than on YHWH's failure. At the same time, in the fifth century Samaria was also an active city to Jerusalem's north, perhaps even more prosperous than Jerusalem.[27] Deeming Samaria's worship as idolatry may have maintained the tension between Jerusalem's temple and the northern cult centers described in the books of Ezra and Nehemiah.

25. Erin Runions, *Changing Subjects: Gender, Nation, and Future in Micah* (London and New York: Sheffield Academic Press, 2001), 125. See eadem, "Zion Is Burning: 'Gender Fuck' in Micah," *Semeia* 82 (1998): 225–46. Also eadem, "Refusal to Mourn: U.S. National Melancholia and Its Prophetic Precursors," *Postscripts* 1 (2005): 9–45.

26. Queer theology might critique this statement, suggesting that my sexual mores reflect a heterosexist definition of "decent sex." See, for example, Marcella Althaus-Reid, *Indecent Theology: Theological Perversions in Sex, Gender, and Politics* (London and New York: Routledge, 2000). While some queer perspectives advocate for a variety of sexual expressions, including those engaged for economic gain, I continue to see the ancient and modern sex working industry as exploitative, far more often staffed by sex slaves than those freely choosing a career path.

27. Gary Knoppers, "Revisiting the Samarian Question in the Persian Period," in *Judah and the Judeans in the Persian Period*, ed. Oded Lipschits and Manfred Oeming (Winona Lake, IN: Eisenbrauns, 2006).

While not explicitly denigrating the religious lives of women, the passage does employ highly-polemical language not only about women's sexuality but also about their worship. As explained by Ann Jeffers, Hebrew Bible texts consistently challenge the legitimacy of women's religious practices, especially when they diverge from orthodox norms.[28] Ezekiel denounces women who weep for Tammuz, a Semitic deity (Ezek 8:14), and Jeremiah condemns women who worship "the queen of Heaven" (likely Ishtar, Jer 7:16-20; 44:15-25). The stories of Rachel (Gen 31:19-34) and Michal (1 Sam 19:13) associate both women with household idols, and the Woman of Endor (1 Sam 28) is portrayed as a necromancer. Erhard S. Gerstenberger suggests that many of these practices, and their denigration, continued into the Persian period: "On account of their religious traditions and functions in the postexilic community, women were especially suspected of embracing foreign cults and of representing a religious anger for orthodox men."[29] The book of Micah likely would not have created such suspicions anew, but it would have echoed other postexilic texts in portraying women as dangerous (Prov 5–8).

Working from a scholarly perspective, Jeffers attempts to read beyond the patriarchal bias of biblical accounts to discern the importance that lifecycle rites and worship of the ancestors would have had for ancient Israelite women. Working from a more popular perspective, Sue Monk Kidd's *The Dance of the Dissident Daughter* well explains why so many women are hungry for a more female-friendly deity and faith.[30] Novels such as Anita Diamant's *The Red Tent* have attempted to imagine a woman's perspective on biblical accounts of "idols," menstruation, and sex.[31]

I find Kidd's and Diamant's work entertaining but problematic. *The Red Tent* imposes contemporary notions about sex, marriage, gender, and mothering upon ancient women, not considering the differences between the past and present or the gender constructions that lead

28. Ann Jeffers, "Popular Religion and Magic, Subentry Hebrew Bible," in O'Brien, *The Oxford Encyclopedia of the Bible and Gender Studies*, 2:54–61.

29. Erhard S. Gerstenberger, *Israel in the Persian Period: The Fifth and Fourth Centuries B.C.E.*, Biblical Encyclopedia: An English Translation of Biblische Enzyklopädie (Atlanta, GA: SBL Press, 2011), 451.

30. Sue Monk Kidd, *The Dance of the Dissident Daughter: A Woman's Journey from Christian Tradition to the Sacred Feminine* (New York: HarperOne, 2006).

31. Anita Diamant, *The Red Tent* (New York: Picador USA, 1997).

modern readers to equate women with motherhood and romance. I am interested in naming and critiquing these constructions rather than simply giving them greater value.

The Punishment of Jerusalem (Mic 1:8–3:12)

While Samaria receives a quick verdict, the trial of Jerusalem is prolonged. She eventually receives the same sentencing as Samaria—both will be "made into a heap" (Mic 3:12, 1:6)—but not before the reader hears much more about the case against her.

FIRST LAMENT (MIC 1:8-16)

The shift of focus from Samaria to Jerusalem begins with an expression of emotion. A voice cries out in lamentation and then dramatically reveals the cause of its grief: the imminent destruction of Jerusalem. The voice then appeals to others to join in lamentation, to begin mourning already the city's fate. As I will explain, this strongly emotive language, paired with highly gendered imagery, emerges from and at times destabilizes the norms for men's and women's behavior in the ancient world.

The lament begins with standard ancient Near Eastern vocabulary for desolation. The speaker strips for the rites of mourning (see Isa 20) and compares the sound of his lament to the eerie, haunting cries of ostriches and hyenas (see also Jer 50:39 and Isa 13:21). In verses that follow, the rites of mourning continue as others are told to weep and roll themselves in dust. The Divine Warrior introduced in Mic 1:2-7 now marches against Zion: "disaster has come down from the LORD to the gate of Jerusalem" (1:12).

What disaster is being lamented in Mic 1? Even though many of the place names in 1:10-16 are otherwise unknown, Nadav Na'aman has argued that the list reflects Sennacherib's military campaign of 701 BCE. In the late eighth century, the Assyrian king advanced from Gaza through the Shephelah region on his way to Jerusalem. Numerous cities, including Lachish, were destroyed, and Jerusalem was placed under siege. According to 2 Kgs 18–19 and Isa 36–37, in response to the prayer of the Judean king Hezekiah the prophet Isaiah announced YHWH's granting of deliverance, and the Assyrian armies retreated. According to Na'aman, "It is clear that the most reasonable date for Micah's address is on the eve of Sennacherib's campaign of 701 B.C. . . . The results of the Assyrian campaign were disastrous for the kingdom as a whole, and in particular for Micah's place of birth, exactly as envisaged in his prophetic

Mic 1:8-16

⁸For this I will lament and wail;
 I will go barefoot and naked;
I will make lamentation like the
  jackals,
 and mourning like the ostriches.
⁹For her wound is incurable.
 It has come to Judah;
it has reached to the gate of my
  people,
 to Jerusalem.
¹⁰Tell it not in Gath,
 weep not at all;
in Beth-leaphrah
 roll yourselves in the dust.
¹¹Pass on your way,
 inhabitants of Shaphir,
 in nakedness and shame;
the inhabitants of Zaanan
 do not come forth;
Beth-ezel is wailing
 and shall remove its support
  from you.
¹²For the inhabitants of Maroth
 wait anxiously for good,
yet disaster has come down from
  the Lᴏʀᴅ

to the gate of Jerusalem.
¹³Harness the steeds to the chariots,
 inhabitants of Lachish;
it was the beginning of sin
 to daughter Zion,
for in you were found
 the transgressions of Israel.
¹⁴Therefore you shall give parting
  gifts
 to Moresheth-gath;
the houses of Achzib shall be a
  deception
 to the kings of Israel.
¹⁵I will again bring a conqueror
  upon you,
 inhabitants of Mareshah;
the glory of Israel
 shall come to Adullam.
¹⁶Make yourselves bald and cut
  off your hair
 for your pampered children;
make yourselves as bald as the
  eagle,
 for they have gone from you
  into exile.

words."[32] Many scholars, including Marvin Sweeney, concur with Na'aman's assessment: "From his location in Moreshet Gath, Micah would have witnessed each of these moves, and would easily have drawn the conclusion that Judah would suffer the same fate as Israel if it dared to challenge Assyria."[33]

Several factors, however, challenge such a precise historical grounding for Mic 1:10-16. Few of the towns have been otherwise identified and,

32. Nadav Na'aman, " 'The House-of-No-Shade Shall Take Away Its Tax from You' (Micah 1:11)," *VT* 45 (1995): 527. See also idem, "Sennacherib's Campaign to Judah and the Date of the *Lmlk* Stamps," *VT* 29 (1979): 61–86.
33. Marvin Sweeney, *The Twelve Prophets*, Berit Olam, vol. 2 (Collegeville, MN: Liturgical Press, 2000), 341.

as James Nogalski notes, the list does not follow a strict military campaign.[34] Moreover, the passage does not present all the towns in the same way. Some *do* face pending assault:

- Lachish (1:13) is called to prepare for its own punishment. Because Lachish led the way for Jerusalem's sin, it should prepare for invasion.
- Mareshah (1:15) will face a conqueror, as may Adullam.

Others, however, are described differently:

- Gath (1:10) is not itself addressed. The phrase, "tell it not in Gath," is used here as in 2 Sam 1:20 as a formulaic acknowledgment of the shame of mourning. The speaker tells others to hide from Gath their weeping for Jerusalem, lest it boast.
- The other five towns listed in 1:10-12 weep for Jerusalem (1:12). Their own fates are not indicated.
- The towns named in 1:14 are not addressed directly. Rather, this verse continues to address "you," last identified as Lachish, mentioning other locales that will benefit from or suffer from Lachish's downfall. Moresheth-Gath, for example, will receive a divorce settlement.[35]

The literary artfulness of this unit also raises questions about its historical precision. Many of the town names appear in stories of Israel's past and thus may function as allusions. Mareshah appears elsewhere only in Joshua and Chronicles, two books widely recognized as later reflections on Israel's history; in Samuel and Chronicles, Adullam is remembered as the site of the cave in which David took refuge. In addition, the unit also is rife with Hebrew puns not evident in the NRSV. Beth-leaphrah (בית לעפרה "house of dust") should roll itself in the dust (1:10); Achzib (אכזיב) is "deception" (אכזב) (1:14). Some translators assume that all place names were intended as puns and "restore" those apparently missing.[36] In Eugene Peterson's work, *The Message*, for example,

---

34. Nogalski, *The Book of the Twelve*, 531.

35. I see the passage as addressing Lachish, but Sweeney argues that Jerusalem is being addressed. Sweeney, *The Twelve Prophets*, 2:528.

36. Mays emends freely to restore the puns: "No plausible understanding of the MT, especially vvs. 10-15, is possible apart from reconstructions and emendations" (James Luther Mays, *Micah: A Commentary* [Philadelphia: Westminster, 1976], 51). Some translators attempt to render the puns in English: John Rogerson translates 1:10 as "In Dustville, roll yourselves in dust," and 1:11 as "Don't go out, citizens of Outtown." See John Rogerson, "Micah," in *Eerdmans Commentary on the Bible*, ed. J. D. G. Dunn and John Rogerson (Grand Rapids, MI: Eerdmans, 2003), 703–7.

every town name is treated as a pun, with Lachish becoming "Chariot-ville" and Adullam becoming "Glorytown."[37] Given the playful nature of Micah's language and the degree to which translators endeavor to emphasize its literary art, overconfidence about the historical situation reflected by 1:10-16 seems unwarranted.

For a Persian-period reader, the primary point of Mic 1:8-16 would have been to depict Jerusalem's fall as YHWH's intention. While some of the towns mentioned might have been remembered as affected by a long-past Assyrian campaign, their names would have evoked a general sense of "past." Jerusalem and Lachish, the only two cities directly addressed, would have had a "present" reality for Yehudites as well: a Jerusalem that had not yet regained its glory and a Lachish that was a Persian stronghold and district capital.[38]

Significantly, Jerusalem's fate in Micah is not simply *depicted* but extensively *lamented*, a task associated in the ancient Near East primarily with women. Although men in the Hebrew Bible do lament, women serve as professional mourners (2 Sam 1:24; Ezek 32:16; Jer 9:17-22). In other ancient and modern societies, public and communal lamentation is a female role.[39]

The *feminine* characterizations in Mic 1:6-16 follow ancient gender norms. Most of the towns in this unit are characterized as feminine. Beth-leaphrah, Shapir, Zaanan, Maroth, and Maresha are characterized as female mourners (the Hebrew word יושבת, translated in the NRSV as "inhabitants of" is literally "she who sits in"). The "you" figure who in 1:16 is told to shave in mourning because "your sons" went into exile is likely Jerusalem: she is called to join the towns in lamenting the fate of her inhabitants.

Masculine characterizations in this unit, however, diverge from these norms, calling males to lament. Weeping Beth-ezel (Mic 1:11) is addressed with a masculine imperative, and Lachish (1:13) is addressed with masculine as well as feminine imperatives. Most significantly, the "I" who declares his intention to lament and go barefoot and naked in 1:8 is masculine.

37. Eugene Peterson, *The Message: The Bible in Contemporary Language* (Colorado Springs, CO: NAV Press, 2002).

38. Alexander Fantalkin and Oren Tal, "Redating Lachish Level I: Identifying Achaemenid Imperial Policy at the Southern Frontier of the Fifth Satrapy," in Lipshits and Oeming, *Judah and the Judeans in the Persian Period*.

39. See L. Juliana M. Claassens, "Calling the Keeners: The Image of the Wailing Woman as Symbol of Survival in a Traumatized World," *JFSR* 26 (2010): 63–77.

Although interpreters disagree about the identity of this male voice, many agree that the attribution of a feminine role to a male speaker is subversive. Bietenhard identifies the speaker as the prophet who interrupts the divine accusation to mourn the fact that Samaria's fate now reaches Jerusalem and that her "wound" is incurable. Bietenhard argues that "incorporating the feminine in a patriarchal culture makes him [the speaker] a person at the boundary and a transgressor of boundaries."[40] Timothy Beal argues instead that the speaker of the lament is YHWH, and the same first-person voice that declared Samaria's destruction in Mic 1:6-7 now laments for Jerusalem. Beal suggests that this language casts the divine not only as feminized (as in Isa 42:14) but also as abject;[41] YHWH is less an impassive patriarch than one who is devastated with emotion. Runions claims that these grammatical shifts destabilize the implied gender of the nation and the implied gender of the reader.[42] In turn, they destabilize binary definitions of gender governed by heterosexist assumptions.[43] Male and female are not defined by nature but are fluid, socially constructed categories. In this way, Micah "queers" the prophet and/or YHWH.

I find the gender slippages in Mic 1:8-16 far less radical than do these interpreters. The lack of distinction between the prophet and YHWH, I argue, is not accidental but characteristic of this and other prophetic books in which prophetic speech *is* divine speech. Moreover, while masculine pronouns may slide into the discourse, feminine imagery governs the unit as the return to feminine address in 1:16 underscores. While I share with Runions the desire to see liberative potential in the fluidity of gender in Mic 1, I mostly am disheartened by the durative nature of the gender scripts on which it relies. Why, if gender is so fluid, do the scripts for gender so stubbornly persist? Why must emotion be evoked by feminine figures? Can YHWH be seen as compassionate only when he acts like a woman? Dressing the divine in feminine garb does little to challenge gender stereotypes. In addition, in this unit of Micah gender norms serve a rhetorical function that outweighs other considerations. The towns are not important in their own right but only for how the

40. Bietenhard, "Micah," 427.

41. Timothy K. Beal, "Opening: Cracking the Binding," in *Reading Bibles, Writing Bodies: Identity and the Book*, ed. Timothy K. Beal and David M. Gunn (London: Routledge, 1997).

42. Runions, *Changing Subjects*, 133.

43. Ibid., 27.

sound of their names relates to Zion's doom.[44] The loss of life that the destruction of Judah would have entailed—for women as well as for men—is left unnamed. Gendered imagery (even when it is fluid) obscures actual female and male lives.

Rather than focus on gendered pronouns alone, feminist and other readers may find hope instead in the insistence on lament in this passage. By moving "just punishment" from an abstract concept to the cause of pain, lament opens a space for readers to imagine the experiences of others. The expressions of lament that punctuate the book of Micah might help readers remain attentive to the existential reality that this book may reflect. In the conclusion to this commentary, I reflect further on lament, the legacy of complex trauma on the nation of Judah, and the role of gender in grief and mourning.

Second Lament (Mic 2:1-13)

In Mic 2, lament extends to those responsible for Judah's downfall. An interjection of distress often used in lamentations, "ah!" (הוי, 2:1; see 1 Kgs 13:30; Jer 22:18), is followed by accusations of land confiscation; despite their protest, the guilty receive punishment befitting their crimes.

The first subunit, Mic 2:1-5, offers the first concrete accusation of the book of Micah. An unspecified group is accused of using its power to confiscate the land and houses of others. As punishment, the accused will lose their own land. The direct correlation between cause and effect is underscored by vocabulary: because they devise wickedness and evil (2:1), YHWH will devise evil against them (2:3); because they seize fields (2:2), they will lose fields (2:4); because they rob a man's inheritance (2:2), they will lose their right to allocations of ancestral inheritance (2:5).

The precise meaning of Mic 2:4 is debated. In the MT, land will be given to "the one who returns"; the translational footnotes in the NRSV render this as "rebellious," in the sense of "one who turns away." The translation in the NRSV itself of "captors" derives from the translators' reconfiguration of the Hebrew consonants. In either translation, the land of the guilty will be granted to those they consider unworthy.

---

44. Contrary to Daniel Simundson in *Hosea, Joel, Amos, Obadiah, Jonah, Micah*, AOTC (Nashville, TN: Abingdon, 2005). While he sees the puns of Micah as conveying a sense of "poetic justice" (what people do literarily returns to them), in fact Micah enumerates no deeds that return to them in cosmic cause and effect. The poetry of Micah does not seek justice for the towns of the Shephelah but attempts to evoke pathos for Jerusalem's exiles.

¹Alas for those who devise wickedness
and evil deeds on their beds!
When the morning dawns, they perform it,
because it is in their power.
²They covet fields, and seize them;
houses, and take them away;
they oppress householder and house,
people and their inheritance.
³Therefore thus says the LORD:
Now, I am devising against this family an evil
from which you cannot remove your necks;
and you shall not walk haughtily,
for it will be an evil time.
⁴On that day they shall take up a taunt song against you,
and wail with bitter lamentation,
and say, "We are utterly ruined;
the LORD alters the inheritance of my people;
how he removes it from me!
Among our captors he parcels out our fields."
⁵Therefore you will have no one to cast the line by lot
in the assembly of the LORD.
⁶"Do not preach"—thus they preach—
"one should not preach of such things;
disgrace will not overtake us."
⁷ Should this be said, O house of Jacob?
Is the LORD's patience exhausted?
Are these his doings?
Do not my words do good

The second subunit, Mic 2:6-13, reiterates the accusations in response to the implied audience's protest. The people dismiss the speaker's negative preaching (2:6, 11), but the crimes of the house of Jacob warrant even further approbation. Because "those who devise wickedness" drive women and children from their houses, YHWH will raise up against them an enemy. Further accusation appears in 2:8; although the NRSV translation relies on several textual "corrections," most translations suggest that the guilty are accused of stealing from innocent victims.[45]

The imagery at the end of the subunit serves as an ironic announcement of further punishment. YHWH will first gather the survivors of Israel into a crowded sheepfold and then lead them out through its broken gate. Because the biblical image of YHWH as Shepherd is a com-

---

45. Various translations of this phrase include: "From the laborer you strip his cloak; you take the garments off the captives in war" (Hillers, *Micah*, 34) and "As robbers lie in wait for someone, so the priests are banded together; they murder on the road to Shechem, they commit a monstrous crime" (Nogalski, *The Book of the Twelve*, 34).

to one who walks uprightly?
⁸But you rise up against my
people as an enemy;
you strip the robe from the
peaceful,
from those who pass by trustingly
with no thought of war.
⁹The women of my people you
drive out
from their pleasant houses;
from their young children you take
away
my glory forever.
¹⁰Arise and go;
for this is no place to rest,
because of uncleanness that de-
stroys
with a grievous destruction.
¹¹If someone were to go about ut-
tering empty falsehoods,

saying, "I will preach to you of
wine and strong drink,"
such a one would be the
preacher for this people!
¹²I will surely gather all of you, O
Jacob,
I will gather the survivors of Israel;
I will set them together
like sheep in a fold,
like a flock in its pasture;
it will resound with people.
¹³ The one who breaks out will go
up before them;
they will break through and
pass the gate,
going out by it.
Their king will pass on before
them,
the Lord at their head.

mon image of protection, many interpreters read the image positively: YHWH will gather the remnant and lead it out in safety. For example, Ben Zvi argues that the language of "remnant" suggests salvation,[46] as it does in Isaiah's speech to Hezekiah: "for from Jerusalem a remnant shall go out, and from Mount Zion a band of survivors. The zeal of the Lord of hosts will do this" (2 Kgs 19:31). With Sweeney, however, I view this image as a continuation of the threat against the people. As in 2 Kings, the "remnant" is accorded punishment: "I will cast off the remnant of my heritage, and give them into the hand of their enemies; they shall become a prey and a spoil to all their enemies" (2 Kgs 21:14).[47] "Break-ing" (Mic 2:13) evokes images of warfare, as in Amos 4:3 in which captives depart for exile through breached city walls. The guilty cannot rest because they have rendered the land unclean through their crimes (Mic 2:10); even though they feel secure as sheep in a sheepfold, they should prepare for exile.

46. Ben Zvi, *Micah*, 67. So too, Nogalski, *The Book of the Twelve*, 541.
47. Sweeney, *The Twelve Prophets*, 2:366.

The imagery of this unit helps create a picture of coldhearted luxury. The wealthy lie awake in bed, hatching plans that they execute as soon as the sun comes up. They strip off the clothes of the poor and leave women and children homeless. As punishment, evil will be placed on their necks like a yoke and they will be penned in by YHWH like sheep in a fold. As Carol Dempsey points out, key Hebrew words and verbal roots recur in Mic 2 repeatedly: "evil" (רע, 2:1, 3); "field" (שדה, 2:2, 4); "preach" (נטף, 2:6, 11); "house" (בית, 2:2, 9), etc. The author also uses wordplay: in Hebrew, "parcels" (יחלק) and "inheritance" (חלק) come from the same verbal root (חלק), and משל, "taunt song" (2:4) and משליך, "cast" sound very similar (2:5). This verbal play grants the author's speech an air of coherence and rectitude: "The wordplays show up the folly of wickedness—sinners will receive their 'just deserts.' . . . Readers of the book are prompted to visualize a causal relationship between negative social behavior, namely, sin and divine punishment. The present vignette (vv. 1-5) suggests a direct relationship between the harshness of the actions of those who deserve punishment and the harshness of their own coming punishment."[48]

Indeed, chapter 2 is the key text for interpreting Micah as the champion of the oppressed. As discussed in the introduction, many interpreters view the prophet as defending poor individuals against the unscrupulous wealthy. As Dilbert Hillers explains, "Micah speaks of the achieving of social and religious ideal from which the covetous and their descendants will be excluded. The future 'assembly of Yahweh' will consist of the oppressed."[49]

Slightly differently, Matthew Coomber and Premnath maintain that Micah (along with Amos and Isaiah) protests the eighth-century shift to the economic system of latifundialization—the transition from small tribal allotments of farmland to large landholding estates: "This oracle is a strong invective against the accumulation of landed property by the ruling elite to the deprivation of the peasantry."[50]

As many interpreters have noted, the accusations of Mic 2 are general enough to apply to a wide range of situations. The charge that "you" take "their" land well fits many times and places, including economic

---

48. Carol J. Dempsey, "Micah 2–3: Literary Artistry, Ethical Message, and Some Considerations About the Image of Yahweh and Micah," *JSOT* 85 (1999): 19, 21.

49. Hillers, *Micah*, 33.

50. Premnath, *Eighth Century Prophets*, 105.

changes in Tunisia[51] and the loss of family farms in the United States due to the growth of agro-business and foreclosures.[52] Ben Zvi interprets this generality as indicating that the social justice component of Mic 2 would not have been important to its Persian-period writer. As an elite scribe living in Jerusalem, he would have been little concerned with land ownership, concerned instead with maintaining his own role as a broker of divine knowledge. Invoking the motif of "fairness" common in ancient Near Eastern literature, the literati would have used this passage to explain the failures of an earlier generation rather than their own.[53]

As explained in the introduction, I am skeptical that the concerns expressed here were a "dead" motif, that they had no resonance in the Persian period. With little demarcation between rural and urban, no one in the ancient world would have been as isolated from the sources of food as most people in the modern world are. While the general language of the passage does not allow us to pinpoint the exact practices being condemned, the writer clearly cares about the loss of ancestral land holdings and the ways in which people in power dispossess others. In Persian Yehud, these charges would have strongly resonated with the scenario described in Neh 5, in which people unable to meet heavy taxation demands lose land and children to debtors.

Micah 2:9 is often lifted up as evidence that the writer was directly concerned about the plight of women and children; by explicitly naming the homelessness of women, according to such interpretations, the book shows itself as attentive to women's circumstances. Such an assumption, however, should be questioned. The casting of women and children in the role of victim does not necessarily entail advocacy but may instead, like the use of feminine forms in Mic 1, serve to evoke emotion. This verse uses the plight of evicted women and children to evoke the reader's anger at the accused. These weak victims function as "affective magnets,"[54] figures who can evoke pathos. As in contemporary movies, the mistreatment of women and children serves as a literary cipher for

51. Matthew Coomber, "Caught in the Crossfire? Economic Injustice and Prophetic Motivation in Eighth-Century Judah," *BibInt* 19 (2011): 396–432.

52. Wendell Berry has been a tireless advocate in defense of the family farm. A recent anthology of his writing is Wendell Berry, *Bringing It to the Table: Farming and Food* (Berkeley, CA: Counterpoint, 2009).

53. Ben Zvi, *Micah*, 51, 65.

54. For women as "affective magnets" in white supremacist groups, see Ann Burlein, *Lift High the Cross: Where White Supremacy and the Religious Right Converge* (Durham, NC: Duke University Press, 2002).

the deterioration of a society. Indeed, throughout this chapter the weak
are described with feminine forms (including the sheep in 2:12), and the
land rights under consideration are those of men: in Hebrew, 2:2 reads
"they oppress the strong man and his house; a man and his inheritance."
This language, though powerful, does not necessarily indicate the writer's great empathy for the real women and children of his community.

In fact, the appearance of a concern for the oppressed can often mask
the details of what causes oppression. Not discussed in this chapter of
Micah are the social conditions of women and children that make them
a ready symbol for "the weak," the land rights of women, or the effects
on women of the confiscation of family land. Comparison with other
Persian-period literature helps illumine these gaps. While, as noted in
the introduction, Christine Yoder has argued that elite women in Persian
Yehud may have owned land, Persian-period texts such as Nehemiah
and Chronicles recount men as property owners and leaders of the household. Nehemiah 5, which decries the Persian period's economic situation,
mentions "the people" separately from "their wives" (5:1), and Chronicles' extensive male genealogies erase the role of women in procreation.[55]
Nehemiah 5, however, does acknowledge that daughters experience debt
slavery differently from sons: while children of both sexes are sold into
slavery, in Neh 5:5 only the daughters are "ravished" (נכבשות), the same
Hebrew word used to describe rape. Micah 2, however, describes the
plight of displaced women and children generically: they are victims.

Further gaps in Micah's explication of the plight of women can be
discerned when we compare Micah with Persian-period documents
outside of the Bible. Fifth-century marriage contracts from Elephantine
and other locations painstakingly document women's dowries; since
these assets fell under the control of the husband upon marriage, women
bringing higher dowries were considered more desirable. Yoder suggests
that such realities are reflected in the description of the "good woman"
of Prov 31: "a man married to a woman of high value, particularly one
who 'treats him well . . . all the days of her life' (31:12), might well never
lack for 'loot.' "[56] Girls whose families were landless and hence without
dowries would have been highly vulnerable economically.

55. Christine Mitchell, "1–2 Chronicles," in Newsom, Ringe, and Lapsley, *Women's Bible Commentary*, 184–90.
56. Christine Yoder, "The Woman of Substance: A Socioeconomic Reading of Proverbs 31:10-31," *JBL* 122 (2003): 435–36.

Women and Land Seizure in Micah

It is at the beginning of Micah's chapter 2 that the audience is given an indication of what kindled their god's wrath: people using their positions of power to better themselves by exploiting others. In the first case, the oppression comes through the seizure of arable lands (2:1-2). This scenario is congruent with either an Assyrian or Persian backdrop, as land seizures commonly occur as empires rise and seek to extract greater tribute and goods from peripheral regions. In efforts to maximize production, systems of coercion and debt are employed to overturn traditional subsistence-farming methods—which focus on spreading risk and the long-term needs of farmers' immediate communities—to make room for revenue-driven agriculture, which focuses on the short-term goals of trade and supplying tribute to more powerful states. The archaeological record shows that just this sort of transformation occurred in late eighth-century Judah, the time to which Micah is attributed. As a consequence for these crimes against Judah's collective farming communities, unnamed perpetrators would suffer humiliation and captivity (2:3-4). But while readers may be quick to notice YHWH's anger and punishment, the deity's concern for the victimized should not be overlooked.

The authors convey the degree of oppression that was inflicted on these unspecified victims of land seizures—who suffered displacement or a loss of autonomy at the hands of those who now controlled their lands—through the Hebrew word עשק (Mic 2:2). While Hebrew has numerous verbs for "to oppress," עשק implies violence, robbery, and the creation of poverty. The authors' use of עשק conveys the utter devastation that the corruption in Mic 2:1-2 would have inflicted on the citizens of an agrarian society, where access to arable land is paramount to survival. YHWH is keenly aware of not only the transgression of the corrupt but of the suffering caused among God's people, displaying that YHWH's interests reach beyond receiving personal glory and sacrifice; this is a god that places significant emphasis on the welfare of its subjects, an attribute the Israelite and Judean kings would have done well, but failed, to match. YHWH's desire for people to emulate such integrity in their interactions with one another conveys important lessons for today.

Woefully, little in Micah is said about the effects of corruption on Judean women. In fact—rather than championing the cause of women—the anthropomorphic renderings of Jerusalem and Samaria as an unfaithful woman or as a prostitute (see Hosea), against whom great violence should be inflicted (1:12; 3:12) before she can be restored (e.g., 2:12-13; 4:2, 8), do much to undermine the status of women. Such female imagery is not only indicative of how the biblical authors perceived women but all too often instruct and justify the ill-treatment of women in Abrahamic religious traditions. At the same time, however, concern for the well-being of the women who suffered during the land grabs of 2:1-2 are found in YHWH's charges that the seizures caused women to be driven out of their "pleasant houses" (2:9).

Matthew Coomber

The real-life plight of landless women in patriarchal systems is not named in Micah, but we can see it in our own world, as in the case of modern West Bengal. According to Seattle's Landesa "Security for Girls through Land" project, which seeks to improve the economic and social status of girls, land rights and ownership are key factors in the security of Bengalese girls. When a family has few resources, it is unable to provide an adequate dowry for a girl to enter a "good marriage." "Girls in these communities are sometimes subject to neglect, gender-based violence, malnutrition and human trafficking, primarily due to poverty caused by landlessness. . . . Poor families often have a financial incentive to wed their daughters early to avoid dowry or offer them as maids so the girls can earn their dowry."[57]

These parallels suggest that the loss of land ownership would have had profound implications for women and girls in Persian Yehud, yet Micah does not directly address the poverty caused by loss of land. Women and children are objects of concern in Micah, but not visibly active participants in society. Micah employs standard gender scripts to make a theological statement about fairness and strength and weakness, but it obscures the ways in which those same gender scripts hurt real people by equating women with victimhood rather than challenging the structures of their oppression.

---

57. Erika Schultz, "Seattle's Landesa Aims to Help Rural Girls in India," *The Seattle Times*, March 16, 2013, http://seattletimes.com/html/picturethis/2020485595 _westbeng.html.

God, the "Breaker" of Injustice in Zimbabwe

"The one who breaks out will go up before them; they will break through and pass the gate, going out by it." (Mic 2:13)

Christianity came to Africa as a foreign religion coated with Western culture. This was no more the Christianity which was earlier brought to Egypt by the Apostle Mark and nurtured by the African church fathers. Working hand in hand with colonialists, a number of missionaries ushered in oppression and pain on the Africans.

The oppression of the African people started with the unilateral decision by European powers to carve up Africa for their convenience and benefit, a decision in which the missionary movement functioned as a support mechanism for white social control and domination of the African people. Within the educational system, instead of teaching African students to think independently and to develop fully as human beings, much of the curriculum, especially the religious elements, trained the Africans to be obedient to their white masters. The Africans were trained to be dependent people, mainly satisfied with pittance handouts. The Africans' initiative, resourcefulness, and self-help were discouraged.

The God of justice, the Breaker of oppressive systems, raised people in the likes of Bishops Joseph Crane Hartzell and Ralph Edward Dodge of the Methodist Episcopal Church (MEC) in Zimbabwe (then Rhodesia) and Bishop Abel Tendekayi Muzorewa, first black bishop of the Zimbabwe United Methodist Church. Together with other sympathetic missionaries and a number of Christians from different denominations and the society at large, they started to break through the glass ceiling which was between the blacks and whites. Like Micah, stirred by the injustice and oppression associated with the Rhodesian regime, these men and women envisaged a decisive deliverance for the people from decades of poverty, humiliation, exploitation, and imperialism.

The great turning point of the American Methodist Church was its participation in the fight against colonial domination and racial segregation. In 1956, the Church in Rhodesia welcomed Bishop Ralph Dodge as its new bishop. In his first address to the pastors he said:

> I would like to visit all of you, my brothers, in your circuits and get to know the people and the church well. But I am going to be radical. I will not carry any food when I visit you. I will come and stay with you in

your homes, wherever you are. I know that is the African custom and we will observe it.[58]

Such action was radical break from the usual pattern of the missionaries. Many missionaries had always stayed in missionary guest houses and carried their own bedding and food plus a cook. Bishop Dodge's radical ideas continued to be manifested in his sermons, teachings, conversations, and, above all, his actions. The old pattern of racial segregation within the church was breaking down and what also lay ahead for Bishop Dodge was to break down the customs of the missionary community and the white settlers in the society at large.

These church leaders and many Christians in Zimbabwe fought to give "a total gospel to a total person."[59] This meant that to love as God loved meant to be in total service to the total person, spiritually and politically.

As far as Bishop Muzorewa was concerned, participation in politics was not a secular activity only but also part of the Christian duty. Little did the colonialists know that, through the church, God was breaking down their oppressive systems. God, a mighty breaker, was able to break down all opposition and clear a road out of all captivity for the Zimbabwean people. Finally, through the leadership of Bishop Abel Tendekayi Muzorewa, a devoted and God-fearing church and political leader, the Zimbabwean people won their country back in 1979, and he became the first black prime minister in this country.[60]

Beauty Maenzanise

Micah's scathing critique of land confiscation provides neither a systematic analysis of nor a concrete program for modern land justice. Its rousing poetry, however, can spur readers to discern the dimensions of justice in their own settings. I am far less concerned than the writer of Micah with patriarchal household inheritance (2:2) and far more con-

58. Ralph E. Dodge, *The Revolutionary Bishop: Who Saw God at Work in Africa; An Autobiography* (Pasadena, CA: William Carey Library, 1986), 116.

59. Bishop Abel T. Muzorewa, *Rise Up and Walk: An Autobiography* (Nashville, TN: Abingdon, 1978), 68.

60. Most of this information was first published in the *Methodist History* 46 (January 2008). Permission to reuse this information was granted by Rev. Dr. Robert Williams, the general secretary of the General Commission on Archives and History of The United Methodist Church, PO Box 127, Madison, NJ 07940.

cerned with the ability of women and men to earn fair wages and participate equally in the benefits and responsibilities of society. For that reason, I join this writer in protesting those who perform evil simply "because it is in their power" (2:1).

DIRECT ADDRESS TO LEADERS (MIC 3:1-12)

Following two units shaped as laments, this unit returns to the language of the trial begun in Mic 1:2 and directly addresses community leaders. In 3:1 and 3:9, they are commanded to "listen/hear" (שמעו־נא); although the NRSV uses two different English words, the same Hebrew word appears in both verses, as well as in the address to the people in 1:2. By the end of the unit, the case against Jerusalem that began in 1:8 reaches a verdict: like Samaria before her (1:6), Jerusalem is sentenced to be made into a heap (3:12).

The unit is marked with ואמר, "and I said" (Mic 3:1). Throughout the unit, the "I" seems to be the character of the prophet as introduced in the superscription. The deity is described in the third person, and 3:8 contrasts the speaker with untrustworthy prophets. While the actual writer of the book of Micah is an anonymous scribe of the Persian period, the use of the first person helps the reader imagine the figure described in the superscription: an eighth-century Micah who announced YHWH's judgment in the face of opposition. From the vantage point of the Persian period and our own day, the prophet becomes a figure of the past who predicted Jerusalem's fall as punishment for the sins of its leaders.

The listing of the leaders' crimes and resulting punishment provides few clues to their identity. They "devour" people, skinning them and eating their flesh (Mic 3:2-3). Such accusations are clearly metaphorical and hyperbole, as are the English idioms such as "being skinned alive," "fleeced," or "chewed up and spit out." Leaders build the city with blood and injustice (3:10), which are damning yet non-specific accusations. In response, YHWH will refuse to answer their prayers, since they have done evil deeds. Concerns with "justice" run throughout the unit (3:1, 8, 9), though the details of what such justice entails are not specified. One hint may be offered in 3:11: if the heads "judge for a price," then they hold positions of power, in which they may be bribed to favor one party over another.

Prophets also are accused of selling their services for monetary gain. They predict positive outcomes for those who provide them with food, but dire fates to those who cannot pay. YHWH's resulting refusal to

Mic 3:1-12

¹And I said:
Listen, you heads of Jacob
    and rulers of the house of Israel!
Should you not know justice?—
    ²you who hate the good and
        love the evil,
who tear the skin off my people,
    and the flesh off their bones;
³who eat the flesh of my people,
    flay their skin off them,
break their bones in pieces,
    and chop them up like meat in
        a kettle,
    like flesh in a caldron.
⁴Then they will cry to the LORD,
    but he will not answer them;
he will hide his face from them at
        that time,
because they have acted wick-
        edly.
⁵Thus says the LORD concerning
        the prophets
    who lead my people astray,
who cry "Peace"
    when they have something to
        eat,
but declare war against those
    who put nothing into their
        mouths.
⁶Therefore it shall be night to you,
        without vision,
    and darkness to you, without
        revelation.
The sun shall go down upon the
        prophets,

speak to the prophets takes on an ironic tone: "seers" will be in the dark; those whose mouths relay YHWH's word for a living will cover their mouths in shame. Unlike the prophet Micah who "saw" (חזה, root *ḥzh*) the fates of Samaria and Jerusalem (Mic 1:1), these prophets-for-hire will be granted no vision (חזון, root *ḥzh*; Mic 3:6).

The verdict decreed in Mic 3:12 against Jerusalem not only settles her case but also closes the case brought against both Samaria and Jerusalem in 1:2. Samaria's verdict, declared in 1:6, is now matched by Jerusalem's in 3:12. In the Hebrew of 3:11-12, the pronouns and verbs associated with Jerusalem are feminine: she, like her fellow female Samaria, will become a heap of ruins.

According to Sweeney, Mic 3:12 records the eighth-century prophet's prediction that Jerusalem would fall to the Assyrians, a prediction that did not come true.[61] In Jer 26:18, the prophet Jeremiah defends his own dire words by invoking the earlier precedent of Micah's prediction: according to Jeremiah, Micah's words led to Hezekiah's repentance, which in turn led YHWH to repel the Assyrian armies encamped against Jeru-

---

61. Sweeney, *The Twelve Prophets*, 2:376.

and the day shall be black over
them;
⁷the seers shall be disgraced,
and the diviners put to shame;
they shall all cover their lips,
for there is no answer from God.
⁸But as for me, I am filled with
power,
with the spirit of the LORD,
and with justice and might,
to declare to Jacob his transgression
and to Israel his sin.
⁹Hear this, you rulers of the house
of Jacob
and chiefs of the house of Israel,
who abhor justice
and pervert all equity,

¹⁰who build Zion with blood
and Jerusalem with wrong!
¹¹Its rulers give judgment for a
bribe,
its priests teach for a price,
its prophets give oracles for
money;
yet they lean upon the LORD and
say,
"Surely the LORD is with us!
No harm shall come upon us."
¹²Therefore because of you
Zion shall be plowed as a field;
Jerusalem shall become a heap of
ruins,
and the mountain of the house
a wooded height.

salem. Interestingly, Jeremiah remembers Micah's words as a call to repentance that was heeded, while in Micah the words are presented as the announcement of an inevitable judgment.

This rare quotation of one prophet by another is often cited as evidence for the work of the historical Micah. Several aspects of the quotation, however, suggest that the correlations between the prophetic books are more complex. For example, Isa 37 and 2 Kgs 19 credit the prophet Isaiah (not Micah) with turning the heart of Hezekiah and diverting the Assyrian threat. As I will explore further in discussion of Mic 4, the books of Micah and Isaiah share much material, suggesting either that one book has drawn from the other or that common hands have shaped both.

James Nogalski, who argues that Hosea through Malachi were intentionally edited to be read as a single coherent Book of the Twelve, traces multiple connections between Micah and other books of the Minor Prophets. These connections take place on the level of individual parallels: for example, Mic 3:2 complains that the leaders "hate good and love evil," falling short of the command of Amos 5:15 to "hate evil and love good, and establish justice in the gate." Larger patterns also emerge, Nogalski argues: Micah's shift in focus from Samaria to Jerusalem reorients not only the book itself but "an early corpus (Hos-Amos-Mic-Zeph) which utilized the destruction of Samaria as a warning of what was to befall Jerusalem."[62] The introductory formula "hear" in Mic 3:1 and 3:9 is "reminiscent of major blocks of Hosea and Amos, suggesting they may have been adapted for the developing corpus during the exile when these books appear to have been transmitted and edited together."[63]

I am less inclined than Nogalski to read the Book of the Twelve as a unit; rather, I see connections across all of the prophetic books—not just the Twelve, but also Isaiah, Jeremiah, and Ezekiel. Micah 4, for example, is (in)famously similar to Isa 2, and the parallels will be explored in our discussion of that chapter. The reference to the "spirit of YHWH" in Mic 3:8 is closely related to the use of the phrase in Isa 11:2: "The spirit of the LORD shall rest on him, the spirit of wisdom and understanding, the spirit of counsel and might, the spirit of knowledge and the fear of the LORD." Micah 3:8 is also echoed in Isa 61:1: "The spirit of the LORD GOD is upon me, because the LORD has anointed me; he has sent me to bring good news to the oppressed, to bind up the brokenhearted, to proclaim liberty to the captives, and release to the prisoners."

These critical dimensions underscore, as I attempt to do throughout the commentary, that Micah (like the entire prophetic corpus) was intended to speak to a postexilic audience. From the vantage point of the Persian-period audience, Jerusalem did fall—not to the Assyrians in 701 but to the Babylonians in 587. Micah 1–3 serves to explain why Jerusalem fell.

This explanation for Jerusalem's destruction would have had political implications for the setting in which the book of Micah was composed. While the accusation that the greed of the nation's leaders was the cause of Judah/Jerusalem's downfall is primarily an explanation of the past, it would have secondarily provided a critique of the leadership of Yehud.

The identity of these Persian-period leaders is unclear. They are described with four labels: heads, chiefs, prophets, and priests. Because the NRSV does not consistently translate each term, the repetition is better seen in Hebrew:

3:1 heads (ראשי) and chiefs (קציני)
3:5 prophets (נביאים)
3:9 heads (ראשי) and chiefs (קציני)
3:11 heads (ראשי), priests (כהניה), prophets (נביאים)

---

62. James Nogalski, *Literary Precursors to the Book of the Twelve*, BZAW 217 (Berlin and New York: de Gruyter, 1993), 123.

63. Nogalski, *The Book of the Twelve*, 512.

Other Persian-period biblical texts use the label "heads" for a variety of positions: leaders of ancestral houses (Ezr 1:5; 4:2-3; 8:1; Neh 7:70; 8:13); leaders of the people (Neh 10:14); leaders of priests (Neh 12:7, 12); and leaders of singers (Neh 12:46). Noteworthy are the leaders of the province (Neh 11:3), synonymous with the "princes" (שרי, translated as "leaders" by NRSV) described in Neh 11:1 as living in Jerusalem along with one-tenth of the province's inhabitants and a long list of temple personnel. Apparently, while "heads" could be used for various roles, it referred to only the leading 10 percent of the community's population.[64] As discussed in the introduction, these local elites would have been subject to and implicated in the Persian occupation of Yehud. In critiquing these "heads," the author of Micah would have critiqued not only wealthy individuals but, by extension, the colonial system in which their wealth was acquired and maintained. Ezra 7:25 makes clear that the law of YHWH and "the law of the king" were inseparable in Yehud.

Would the prophets mentioned in Mic 3 have had any real-life referent in the Persian period? Given the heavily theologically retrospective dimension of the prophetic corpus that I have been suggesting, Micah's reference to prophets would clearly have had the function of interpreting the past: Jerusalem fell because of the widespread failure of all of those in leadership. Persian-period texts, however, do mention the presence of living prophets, though their authority is contested. Nehemiah 6, for example, describes contemporary prophets in oppositional terms, including a female prophet named Noadiah.

The gender of the leaders in Mic 3 is unclear, given the plural forms and generic language used. In Neh 11, to which we compared this chapter, "heads" are male. In the Hebrew Bible as a whole, named prophets are predominantly male, though Miriam, Deborah, and Huldah join Noadiah in being described as prophets.[65]

The gender of rulers, however, is not the only way in which to evaluate Micah's gender justice, since the gender of those in power does not directly correlate to those who benefit from their policies. Women's leadership does not necessarily translate into policies that benefit women, and

---

64. Smith claims that the "heads" had significant social authority in the postexilic period: Daniel L. Smith [Smith-Christopher], *The Religion of the Landless: The Social Context of the Babylonian Exile* (Bloomington, IN: Meyer-Stone Books, 1989), 98.

65. Wilda Gafney argues for a large number of women prophets in ancient Israel: Wilda Gafney, *Daughters of Miriam: Women Prophets in Ancient Israel* (Philadelphia: Fortress Press, 2008).

a woman's inclusion in a patriarchal system does not necessarily challenge the system itself. For example, former prime minister of Great Britain "Iron Lady" Margaret Thatcher may have been a powerful woman, but her policies led to increased poverty—for women and men.[66] Clearly, not all men benefit from male leadership either. As I have underscored, the book of Nehemiah indicates a high degree of social stratification in Persian-period Jerusalem. Readers might well be skeptical of the claims of Neh 10–11 that all the people willingly agreed to take on the heavy financial commitment of maintaining the temple and its personnel, of financing a local bureaucracy as well as the Persian administration.

The real-life consequences of the critique of Israel's leaders in Mic 3—in the past and in the present—can be variously assessed. Positively, Micah clearly holds leaders accountable for the treatment of the people under their charge and decries those who set ultimate value on economic gain. Micah's text does not shy away from criticizing religious leaders, calling out their hypocrisy. The rhetorical force is unmistakable: seers lose sight; cities are built with blood; peace and war are bought and sold. The critique arrests polite sensibilities: its description of injustice as cannibalism extends *ad nauseum*, as the human body is systematically butchered into skin, bones, meat, flesh. Such language allows Micah to transcend its own time and place and find resonance in other situations, including overcrowded living conditions in early twentieth-century London.[67]

In many quarters within the contemporary United States, the critique of government officials and religious leaders has become more of a trope than a rallying cry. Movies and popular music regularly mock politicians and preachers, ironically remaining silent on the wealth and power of the entertainment industry. For people without power, however, employing language like that of Mic 3 is incendiary, especially when the language is accompanied with action. In 1980, four US churchwomen were ambushed, beaten, raped, and murdered in El Salvador as retaliation for their persistent challenge to the violence and repression of the Salvadoran National Guard. Like Oscar Romero before them, Maryknoll Sisters Ita Ford and Maura Clarke, along with Ursuline Sister Dorothy Kazel and lay missioner Jean Donovan, died for championing the cause of the poor

<hr />

66. Malcolm Dean, "Margaret Thatcher's Policies Hit the Poor Hardest—and It's Happening Again," *The Guardian*, April 9, 2013, http://www.theguardian.com/society/2013/apr/09/margaret-thatcher-policies-poor-society.

67. W. MacKintosh MacKay, *The Goodly Fellowship of the Prophets: A Homiletic Study of the Prophetic Literatures of the Old Testament* (New York: Richard R. Smith, 1929), 46.

against those who "hate the good and love the evil, who tear the skin off my people and the flesh off their bones" (Mic 3:2).

For all of its evocative power, however, the powerful language of Mic 3 does not address structures of injustice. Micah 3 critiques corrupt leaders but not the systems of power that fuel them. The same observation holds true for this first unit of the book, which now draws to a close. As a Persian-period explanation for the fall of Samaria and Jerusalem, Mic 1–3 lays the blame for the nation's destruction at the feet of its leaders, viewing their sin as justifying YHWH's destruction. These verses do not mention the armies of Assyria or Babylon that carried out this destruction. The brutality of those regimes is well documented in ancient Near Eastern literature and art but left unnamed here. The policies of the Persian under whose occupation these explanations were formulated similarly remain invisible.

Micah's Intertext: Nehemiah and Power

As an African American female whose cultural context is slavery and oppression, I am very sensitive to marginalized voices and those who are systematically silenced in society. This perspective makes it is easy for me to identify the oppressor and oppressed in the text of Nehemiah. Although Nehemiah was a religious man, he failed to seek counsel with the priests as to his intentions and plans (Neh 2:12). He also failed to speak with those who were to do the work. He justified his actions by indicating that this is what God wanted him to do. One might argue that Nehemiah's intentions were good, but he failed to consider the needs of the people and used his power to silence voices that did not agree with or support his agenda.

It is not hard for me to draw a parallel between Nehemiah and a plantation owner. As in the case of plantation slave owners, Nehemiah's authority and position intimidated those in Jerusalem. He used his authority to gather a workforce of people to complete the menial task of rebuilding the wall. He did not ask them for assistance but rather told them what they were to do and accomplish. Their input and voice were not needed because Nehemiah held the position of power. He intimidated them by reminding them not just that he carried the authority of the king but also that he carried the authority of God. The people are marginalized because they have no power and no voice.

Rev. Tracey Cox

On the one hand, Micah's silence on empire offers an important theological—and political—testimony. By insisting that YHWH alone determines Jerusalem's fate, the book of Micah denies ultimate power to human agents. "In the book of Micah, the destruction of Jerusalem is domesticated by explaining it in terms of the incredible sins of the monarchic elites and by characterizing it as an action of temporal—and in the long run, fleeting—importance."[68] On the other hand, however, this theological explanation of history runs the risk of minimizing the role that human systems of power play in the fates of nations and individuals.

Although Mic 1–3 provides no window into how the sieges of Samaria and Jerusalem were experienced by women, children, and men, we as readers know that national tragedy always entails human tragedy. We, in turn, can bring other voices into conversation with Micah—the voices of those who suffer today and those who have suffered in the past.

The book of Lamentations offers one such window into the trauma of the Babylonian destruction of Jerusalem. As such, it offers a fitting epitaph—and perhaps a response to[69]— Mic 1–3:

> Cry aloud to the LORD!
>> O wall of daughter Zion!
> Let tears stream down like a torrent
>> day and night!
> Give yourself no rest,
>> your eyes no respite!
> Arise, cry out in the night,
>> at the beginning of the watches!
> Pour out your heart like water
>> before the presence of the Lord!
> Lift your hands to him
>> for the lives of your children,
> who faint for hunger
>> at the head of every street.
> Look, O LORD, and consider!
>> To whom have you done this?
> Should women eat their offspring,
>> the children they have borne?

---

68. Ben Zvi, *Micah*, 104.

69. For Lamentations as a response to the Prophets, see Carleen Mandolfo, *Daughter of Zion Talks Back to the Prophets: A Dialogic Theology of the Book of Lamentations*, SemeiaSt 58 (Atlanta, GA: SBL Press, 2007).

Should priest and prophet be killed
    in the sanctuary of the Lord?
The young and the old are lying
    on the ground in the streets;
my young women and my young men
    have fallen by the sword;
in the day of your anger you have killed them,
    slaughtering without mercy.
You invited my enemies from all around
    as if for a day of festival;
and on the day of the anger of the LORD
    no one escaped or survived;
those whom I bore and reared
    my enemy has destroyed. (Lam 2:18-22)

Micah 4–5

Exaltation of Daughter Jerusalem and Her King

Announcement of Jerusalem's Future Salvation (Mic 4–5)

After three chapters of judgment, Mic 4 abruptly turns to descriptions of Jerusalem's bright future. The phrase "mountain of the house" serves as the link between judgment and salvation: Mic 3:12 ends with the threat that the mountain will become a high place in the forest, and 4:1 opens with the promise that "in days to come" the mountain will become the highest of all. Promises for the exaltation of Jerusalem extend throughout Mic 4 and 5. Jerusalem will be lifted up, the honor of Daughter Zion will be restored, a new ruler will emerge from Bethlehem, and Judah's enemies will be destroyed.

Clearly the work of the book's Persian-period author, these chapters reveal the author's hopes for, and in turn what he perceives as the failures of, the present. As Ehud Ben Zvi notes, "Everything that is to obtain in the ideal future is precisely what is lacking in the present as experienced by the community of readers."[1] The writer longs for the world to be

---

1. Ehud Ben Zvi, *Micah*, The Forms of the Old Testament Literature, vol. 21B (Grand Rapids, MI: Eerdmans, 2000), 99.

different than it is and provides a powerful portrait of an alternative reality. In this and other ways, these chapters parallel Martin Luther King Jr.'s "I Have a Dream" speech; when King shared his dream of a day in which people will not be judged by the color of their skin, he attempted to motivate hearers to challenge the present reality of racial prejudice. "It is this distance between imagination and present reality that provides the reading with rhetorical power."[2]

The imagery of these chapters serves to create an attractive alternative reality. It shows rather than tells us that war can end, that people can be at peace, and that the world can turn to God. At the same time, like other visionaries, this Persian-period writer is constrained in his imagination by his own social location. His culturally based assumptions about gender and the relationship between nations are the language and the boundaries of his vision for the future, even as the images hint at additional possibilities for human living.

Jerusalem Exalted (Mic 4:1-7)

The powerful vision in Mic 4:1-7—of nations streaming to Jerusalem and of swords beaten to plowshares—is well known, primarily from its appearance in the book of Isaiah. Micah 4:1-5 and Isa 2:1-5 are mostly identical. Both promise that "in the days to come" people and nations will stream to the mountain on which the temple sits; there, all will learn Torah ("instruction") and God will settle all disputes, so that weapons of war can be repurposed into tools for agriculture and military training can cease. Both passages include an image of people walking with God.

A careful comparison, however, reveals important differences between Micah's and Isaiah's versions of this vision. The image of men sitting at peace under their own vines and fig trees (Mic 4:4) finds no parallel in Isa 2, though it does appear in Isa 36:16 in the speech of an Assyrian official offering besieged Jerusalemites a better future. Only Micah promises that people will no longer be afraid (Mic 4:4). The difference between Isa 2:5 and Mic 4:4 is especially noteworthy. Isaiah calls Israel to walk in the Lord's light, not mentioning the nations, while Micah distinguishes between Israel and the nations: "all the peoples" follow their own gods, but "we will walk in the name of the LORD our God forever and ever." In Micah the unit extends several more verses through 4:7, promising

2. Ibid., 95.

Mic 4:1-7

¹In days to come
　the mountain of the LORD's
　　house
shall be established as the high-
　　est of the mountains,
　and shall be raised up above
　　the hills.
Peoples shall stream to it,
　²and many nations shall come
　　and say:
"Come, let us go up to the moun-
　　tain of the LORD,
　to the house of the God of
　　Jacob;
that he may teach us his ways
　and that we may walk in his
　　paths."
For out of Zion shall go forth in-
　　struction,
　and the word of the LORD
　　from Jerusalem.
³He shall judge between many
　　peoples,
　and shall arbitrate between
　　strong nations far away;
they shall beat their swords into
　　plowshares,
　and their spears into pruning
　　hooks;

nation shall not lift up sword
　　against nation,
　neither shall they learn war
　　any more;
⁴but they shall all sit under their
　　own vines and under their
　　own fig trees,
　and no one shall make them
　　afraid;
　for the mouth of the LORD of
　　hosts has spoken.
⁵For all the peoples walk, each in
　　the name of its god,
　but we will walk in the name of
　　the LORD our God
　forever and ever.
⁶In that day, says the LORD,
　I will assemble the lame
and gather those who have been
　　driven away,
　and those whom I have af-
　　flicted.
⁷The lame I will make the remnant,
　and those who were cast off, a
　　strong nation;
and the LORD will reign over
　　them in Mount Zion
　now and forevermore.

that exiles will be returned to Jerusalem and become a mighty nation ruled by YHWH from Mount Zion.

From these comparisons, I concur with most scholars who conclude that Micah's vision is less universal than Isaiah's vision. In Micah, the nations serve to magnify Israel, whose fortunes are restored. In Micah, the vision of all people streaming to Jerusalem is less a vision of global inclusion than the exaltation of Jerusalem as the center of the world.

The source of these strong verbal similarities is unclear. Did one book borrow from another? If so, which version is original? Or was the passage added to both books by a third party? As discussed in my treatment of Mic 1:1 and of Mic 3 (as well as ahead in Mic 6), the book of Micah bears many parallels with Isaiah and other prophetic books—especially Zechariah, Amos, and Isa 36–37. These connections are best explained as literary in nature. The small circle of Persian-period scribes responsible for the prophetic books (and indeed much of the Hebrew Bible) not only shared materials but also sought to portray the prophets of a proposed time and place as consistent in their message. Certainly, the *effect* of the connections between Isaiah and Micah is our impression that God communicated a clear and unified message to preexilic Judah.

In the literary context of the book of Micah, the vision of 4:1-7 resonates with themes already developed in Mic 1–3. Jerusalem, brought to trial in Mic 1 and sentenced with destruction in Mic 3, now is promised restoration. Agrarian life, described as disrupted and perverted in Mic 2–3, now becomes an image of tranquility. A man's ancestral land, depicted as stolen in 2:2, now becomes a transgenerational place of repose: given that grape vines and olive trees require more than one generation to produce, enjoying them requires more than one season of peace.

The situational reality fueling these hopes, of course, is much darker. Inferring from this wish list what is lacking, behind Mic 4:1-7 we can imagine a community with members still scattered abroad, a society economically and emotionally drained by support for war, and a Jerusalem without international standing.[3] Such a scenario well fits the description of Persian-period Yehud outlined in the introduction. The financial burdens of supporting both Persian and native officials weighed heavily on the community, as did the perceived gap between Jerusalem's true destiny and its current reality.

The prominence of the temple in this vision also contrasts with its reality in the Persian period. Within the Persian Empire, local temples such as the one in Jerusalem did not function independently of imperial control: "The temples were important to the Persian imperial government for their use as mechanisms of social control and possibly as custodians of imperial financial interests in their local areas (district or

---

3. What Premnath (and Brueggemann whom he cites) claim about the eighth century is true for multiple time periods: "In agrarian societies, one of the conditions that contributes to the impoverishment of the peasantry is war. . . . It is not only the military operations that are detrimental but also a tax system that provides for and sustains such enterprises." Devadasan N. Premnath, *Eighth Century Prophets: A Social Analysis* (St. Louis, MO: Chalice, 2003), 130.

provincial)."[4] In Micah's vision, however, the temple is ruled by YHWH alone, and here, as in other postexilic Persian prophetic texts, "Jerusalem becomes the center of the world." [5] Micah envisions Jerusalem's function not as a financial and administrative center but as a key source of instruction.

The word translated in the NRSV as "instruction" in Hebrew is תורה, literally "Torah," and the word translated "teach" derives from the related verbal root (ירה), suggesting that the writer refers to specific written documents. Erhard Gerstenberger's impressive study of the Persian period explains the key role of Torah in the crafting of Jewish identity after the exile. He points to Neh 10 in which the community commits to organize itself according to written texts: "Torah is the decisive power; it is the point of reference."[6] He also explores the ways in which the Persian-period concept of Torah extends beyond the Pentateuch proper to include prophetic writings: "For the [Persian-period] community, prophetic words were just as much Torah, words sent by Yahweh, as were the speeches of Moses."[7] This understanding of prophecy, he argues, may have been projected back into Israel's past, such that prophetic texts in their Persian-period final form support the Torah in its Persian-period final form: "The prophets charge Israel or individuals with departure from faith in Yahweh, as well with social and cultic misconduct, perceived as 'sin' during the Persian period, and they bring the liberating message of the renewed care of Yahweh, after years of humiliation and foreign rule. Behind their charges, the definite rules of the Torah can be recognized in the Persian period."[8]

In its privileging of Torah, the vision of Mic 4 clearly reflects the interests of the scribal class. Those who preserve, copy, read, and interpret Torah mediate its power; their power depends on its power. In Neh 8, this role is played not only by Ezra, the scribe of the law, but also by a long list of men who interpret it: "they gave the sense, so that the people understood the reading" (Neh 8:8). As a member of this scribal class, the

4. Jeremiah Cataldo, *A Theocratic Yehud? Issues of Government in a Persian Province,* LHBOTS 498 (New York and London: T & T Clark, 2009), 184.
5. Steed Davidson, "Prophets Postcolonially: Initial Insights for a Postcolonial Reading of Prophetic Literature," *The Bible and Critical Theory* 6, no. 2 (2010): 24-1.13.
6. Erhard S. Gerstenberger, *Israel in the Persian Period: The Fifth and Fourth Centuries B.C.E.,* Biblical Encyclopedia: An English Translation of Biblische Enzyklopadie (Atlanta, GA: SBL Press, 2011), 22.
7. Ibid., 309.
8. Ibid.

writer of Micah would have clearly benefitted from a future in which all people recognize the importance of the texts in which he is an expert; like the prophet whom he describes, the scribe is one through whom the all-important Torah is known.

Gender assumptions clearly mold understandings of the present and the future in Mic 4. Feminine forms describe the current state of weakness, while masculine pronouns are reserved for future strength. In Hebrew, the words for the lame, outcast, and "one removed" in 4:6-7 are all feminine participles (see also the use of feminine participles in Zeph 3:19), while male pronouns refer to the exalted mountain (4:1), Yahweh (4:3, 7), and future recipients of salvation (4:7). Mic 4:4-5, translated literally, says, "they will sit, a man under his vine and under his fig tree"; "all the peoples walk, a man in the name of his god." In the present, Yehud is unmanned, as weak as a woman; in the future, its honor and glory will be restored, as it becomes a mighty nation under YHWH its king.[9]

Desire—sexual and otherwise—is socially constructed. Early in life, we learn from those around us what and who is valuable, worth wanting, and necessary for "the dream life." Feminist theorists have long argued the role that gender scripts play in the shaping of desire. Patriarchy has set the criteria for "beautiful" art in the West; nude women meet our gaze, aware that they are the object of desire, while nude men gaze elsewhere, apparently unaware of the viewer. Perhaps even more so, patriarchy shapes our very physical responses to images of ourselves and others. Importantly, however, viewers can always respond differently from how the artist intends. When, for example, a lesbian views a nude image of another woman, or a woman of color refuses to identify with the white woman objectified on a movie screen, the power dynamics in viewing become complicated: "Black female spectators, who refused to identify with white womanhood, who would not take on the phallocentric gaze of desire and possession, created a critical space where the binary opposition . . . of woman as image, man as bearer of the 'look' was continually deconstructed."[10]

9. See Julia M. O'Brien, "Once and Future Gender: Gender and the Future in the Twelve," in *Utopia and Dystopia in Prophetic Literature*, ed. Ehud Ben Zvi (Helskini: Finnish Exegetical Society, University of Helskini, 2006), 144–59.

10. bell hooks, "The Oppositional Gaze: Black Female Spectators," in *Feminist Film Theory: A Reader*, ed. Sue Thornham (New York: New York University Press, 1999), 313.

The Universality of Micah 4 and Modern Jerusalem

The prophet Micah, generally thought to have lived in Isaiah's time, includes, like many of his colleagues, a dialectic of doom and consolation, judgment and hope. In the third chapter of the book, verses 1-12, he attributes the fall of Jerusalem to failures of leadership. Then, in chapter 4, there is a prophecy of a utopian future. This is, at least in verses 1-3, the same as Isaiah's prophecy in 2:2-4. But I want to focus on v. 5: "All the nations may walk in the name of their gods; we will walk in the name of the LORD our God forever and ever" (NIV).

In Mic 4:5, it appears that in the time of redemption there will be a balance between the particular and the universal. Jerusalem will be the center, but each nation will walk there in the name of its god. There is no need for all to adopt one uniform faith.

To be sure, it is possible some biblical and rabbinic texts have a much less pluralist approach— for example, Zech 8:20-23—but even those texts do not necessarily imply that all people must become Jews; they have been interpreted as referring to an adoption of the Seven Noachide Laws.[11] Several authors have suggested that it is the specifically ethnic character of Jewish identity, the idea that Judaism is the religion of the Jewish people, that prevents it from making universal, exclusivist claims.[12]

The entire dilemma in our verse may be focused on a one-letter word in Hebrew: ו. It can certainly be translated as a contrast, as in: "For let all the peoples walk each one in the name of its god, but [ו] [or 'while' or 'though'] we will walk in the name of the LORD our God forever and ever." However, it could also, as in the NIV, mean simply "and." I want to focus briefly on that reading.

Micah's vision of a multicultural and multi-faith Jerusalem has to some extent been fulfilled in our own day. Walking around the city today we see a multitude of different people, from many backgrounds. When praying at the Western Wall, it isn't uncommon for a Jew to hear, at the same time, church bells and the muezzin. Without ignoring the conflicts and problems, we must recognize—and, I would add, celebrate—the great diversity that enriches and enhances life in Jerusalem today.

---

11. Aaron Lichtenstein, *The Seven Laws of Noah* (New York: Rabbi Jacob Joseph School Press, 1981).

12. Shlomo Fischer and Suzanne Last Stone, *Guidelines for Teachers: Tolerance and Principles of Religion* (Sarajevo: International Forum Bosnia, 2004), 85.

This diversity exists on many levels: religious, cultural, ethnic, linguistic, gastronomic, and sartorial, to name but a few. As the Mishnah teaches (*Sanhedrin* 4:5), "people stamp many coins with one seal and they are all like one another; but the King of Kings, the Holy One, blessed is He, has stamped every person with the seal of the first man, Adam, yet none of them is like his fellow." In human diversity, we see God's greatness.

Deborah Weissman

In viewing Micah's image, then, feminist interpreters can both recognize the limitations of its vision of the future and also choose to reframe that vision in light of their own commitments. My own hope for the future includes not only the absence of war but also the full sharing of property rights and agricultural goods. I long for instruction that will include not only written words but also the wisdom of diverse people. Like the author of Micah, I yearn for a world different from the current one, but my own hopes are not identical with his. And, fully aware that my own hopes are limited by my social location and privilege, I await the voices of those who will help me hope for even more.

Daughter Zion Restored to Honor and Strength (Mic 4:8-13)

Feminine imagery for Jerusalem proliferates in this subunit. Addressed directly, Jerusalem is characterized as a daughter, a woman crying out in childbirth, and a woman threatened with public rape. As in the previous subunit, feminine imagery depicts the community's current reality of pain/shame; and yet, the imagery remains abstract, detached from the reality to which it attests.

All three images—daughter, laboring woman, and female victim of public assault—are common in biblical descriptions of distress and have been widely explored by feminist interpreters.[13] The images often appear in combination, with Daughter Zion seeming to provide the governing

---

13. Christl Maier, *Daughter Zion, Mother Zion: Gender, Space, and the Sacred in Ancient Israel* (Philadelphia: Fortress Press, 2008); Katheryn Pfisterer Darr, *Isaiah's Vision and the Family of God* (Louisville, KY: Westminster John Knox, 1994); Carleen Mandolfo, *Daughter of Zion Talks Back to the Prophets: A Dialogic Theology of the Book of Lamentations*, SBL SemeiaSt 58 (Atlanta, GA: SBL Press, 2007); Mark J. Boda, Carol J. Dempsey, and LeAnn Snow Flesher, *Daughter Zion: Her Portrait, Her Response*, AIL 13 (Atlanta, GA: SBL Press, 2012).

Mic 4:8-13

⁸And you, O tower of the flock,
  hill of daughter Zion,
to you it shall come,
  the former dominion shall come,
  the sovereignty of daughter Je-
    rusalem.
⁹Now why do you cry aloud?
  Is there no king in you?
Has your counselor perished,
  that pangs have seized you
    like a woman in labor?
¹⁰Writhe and groan, O daughter
    Zion,
  like a woman in labor;
for now you shall go forth from the
    city
  and camp in the open country;
  you shall go to Babylon.
There you shall be rescued,
  there the LORD will redeem you
  from the hands of your enemies.

¹¹Now many nations
  are assembled against you,
saying, "Let her be profaned,
  and let our eyes gaze upon
    Zion."
¹²But they do not know
  the thoughts of the LORD;
they do not understand his plan,
  that he has gathered them as
    sheaves to the threshing
    floor.
¹³Arise and thresh,
  O daughter Zion,
for I will make your horn iron
  and your hoofs bronze;
you shall beat in pieces many
    peoples,
  and shall devote their gain to
    the LORD,
  their wealth to the Lord of the
    whole earth.

metaphor. While some scholars have argued that the Hebrew phrase should be translated "daughter *of* Zion" and understood to address the inhabitants of the city as its daughter, I contend that it is best understood as a metaphor for the city itself.[14]

Prophetic depictions of Jerusalem/Zion as Daughter almost always underscore the vulnerability of the city. This is especially true in announcements of punishment, where the language underscores just how helpless are those from whom YHWH withholds protection. In Isa 1:8, for example, "daughter" is paired with other metaphors of isolation and vulnerability: "And daughter Zion is left like a booth in a vineyard, like a shelter in a cucumber field, like a besieged city." Even when receiving promises of salvation, Daughter Zion remains vulnerable. Zephaniah 3:14-20, for example, encourages Daughter Jerusalem//Daughter Zion to sing and rejoice at the prospect of imminent rescue by YHWH, her

14. Julia M. O'Brien, *Challenging Prophetic Metaphor: Theology and Ideology in the Prophets* (Louisville, KY: Westminster John Knox, 2008), chap. 7.

champion: "The LORD, your God, is in your midst, a warrior who gives victory; he will rejoice over you with gladness, he will renew you in his love; he will exult over you with loud singing" (Zeph 3:17).

Such vulnerability reflects the social status of daughters in ancient Israel. While all Israelite women were dependent on the males who controlled their lives, biblical texts attest to the extreme dependency of daughters. Fathers transacted daughters' marriages (Gen 29; 1 Sam 18; 25), authorized their daughters' vows (Num 30), were allowed to sell them into slavery (Exod 21:7), and could submit them to violence (Gen 19:8; Judg 11; 19:24); the sexual purity of the daughter was a matter of family honor (Gen 34). Like actual Israelite daughters, Daughter Zion was vulnerable and in need of protection.

The pain of childbirth is mentioned frequently in the Hebrew Bible, especially in the Prophets. The book of Isaiah compares writhing in labor to the agony of Israel's enemy (13:8), the terror of one seeing visions of doom (21:3), and anger of YHWH himself (42:14); its image of Jerusalem's restoration is that of a woman who labors without pain (66:7). Jeremiah depicts YHWH's devastation as contorting Jerusalem in as much pain as a first-time mother in labor:

> For I heard a cry as of a woman in labor,
> > anguish as of one bringing forth her first child,
> the cry of daughter Zion gasping for breath,
> > stretching out her hands,
> "Woe is me! I am fainting before killers!" (Jer 4:31)

Numerous prophetic passages describe the fall of cities as the public shaming of a woman, which can include stripping and rape. In Isa 47:2-3, daughter Babylon is stripped and humiliated; in Hos 2:2-3, stripping is preliminary to the death of the woman; and in Jer 13:22, Judah is not only exposed but also violated. Nahum 3:5-7 offers a particularly graphic image of Woman Nineveh's punishment:

> I am against you,
> > says the LORD of hosts,
> > and will lift up your skirts over your face;
> and I will let nations look on your nakedness
> > and kingdoms on your shame.
> I will throw filth at you
> > and treat you with contempt,
> > and make you a spectacle.
> Then all who see you will shrink from you and say,

"Nineveh is devastated; who will bemoan her?"
Where shall I seek comforters for you?

The word translated as "profaned" in Mic 4:11 is from the Hebrew root *ḥnf*. Elsewhere, the NRSV also translates as "profaned" another Hebrew root strongly associated with sexual violence. As Harold Washington explains, "Thirteen times a transitive form of this verb, *ʿinnâ*, occurs with a woman as the object: Gen 16:6, 9; 31:50; 34:2; Deut 21:14; 22:24, 29; Judg 19:24, 25; and 2 Sam [13]:12, 14, 22, 32. Euphemistic translations such as 'to humble, dishonor,' etc., obscure the fact that *ʿinnâ* typically refers to sexual coercion or violence, and in at least one instance, resistance (Tamar, 2 Sam 23)."[15]

The meaning of the additional title with which Jerusalem is addressed in Mic 4:8 is less clear. The phrase translated in the NRSV as "tower of the flock" is in Hebrew מגדל־עדר; the same phrase in Gen 35:21 is translated in the NRSV as "tower of Eder," a location near Ephrath/Bethlehem where Rachel died in childbirth. Marvin Sweeney suggests that Mic 4:8 alludes to the Genesis story, extending the imagery of childbirth with a reminder of Rachel.[16] As explored in the excursus on Christian interpretation of Mic 4–5 that follows, this association between Mic 4 with Gen 35 has a long history. This passage also alludes back to Mic 2:12, where the same word עדר was used to describe the flock in the pasture.

According to the NRSV, Mic 4:8 promises the return of "the sovereignty of daughter Jerusalem," suggesting a situation in which Jerusalem will be self-governing. This translation interprets the Hebrew preposition prefixed to Jerusalem as one of possession, as do many interpreters. The preposition ל, however, can also indicate location, indicating that kingship will return *to* Jerusalem. Such an understanding is reflected in the NIV translation: "the former dominion will be restored to you; kingship will come to the Daughter of Jerusalem."

In this understanding, Jerusalem does not herself rule but is promised that she soon will be ruled again by a Davidic king. This latter translation is more consistent with Mic 5, which promises that a male ruler will deliver Jerusalem, and with the gender assignments of Mic 4–5. Read in this way, Mic 4:6-8 is consistent in using feminine forms to describe the weakness and vulnerability of the people and city: *now*, Daughter

---

15. Harold Washington, "Sexual Violence, Subentry Hebrew Bible," in *Oxford Encyclopedia of the Bible and Gender Studies*, ed. Julia M. O'Brien, 2 vols. (New York: Oxford University Press, 2014), 2:351.

16. Marvin Sweeney, *The Twelve Prophets*, vol. 2 (Collegeville, MN: Liturgical Press, 2000), 383.

Jerusalem cries in agony and faces public shaming, but she should trust that *in the future* YHWH will rule (4:7) and kingship will return (4:8).

In Mic 4:13, the newly empowered Daughter Zion is pictured with horns of iron and hooves of bronze, treading the nations underfoot as if they were grain on a threshing floor. While James Nogalski identifies this animal as a "raging bull,"[17] the "you" addressed is feminine in form.

A female animal is also described as threshing in Hos 10:11: "Ephraim was a trained heifer that loved to thresh, and I spared her fair neck." According to Oded Borowski, the use of animals was one of four methods of separating grain from the stalk in Iron Age Israel: threshing was also done with a stick, with a threshing sledge, and with a wheel-thresher.[18] A more likely parallel, however, comes from ancient Near Eastern art. Carole Fontaine has pointed to the ways in which cows and bulls appear in Egyptian battle scenes, particularly on the Narmer, Bull, and Battlefield palettes, trampling the enemy underfoot.[19]

The significance of the imagery used for Jerusalem in Mic 4:9-13 is variously assessed. Sophia Bietenhard argues that Micah's use of feminine imagery for the city is hopeful for women, indicating that women's experiences are appropriate grounds for theological reflection.[20] To the contrary, I find this language problematic for women—and men. Presented in Mic 4 are not the real-life experiences of real-life women but rather stereotypes employed about women for rhetorical purposes. The images of daughter, laboring woman, and victim of assault highlight not the strength and value of women but their vulnerability—especially their sexual vulnerability. Similarly, in her discussion of film, Linda Williams notes the ways in which female characters are often presented to evoke particular emotions from viewers: when the director wants us to weep, women weep; when we are supposed to scream, women scream.[21]

---

17. James Nogalski, *The Book of the Twelve: Hosea through Jonah* (Macon, GA: Smith and Helwys, 2011), 561.

18. Oded Borowski, *Agriculture in Iron Age Israel* (Winona Lake, IN: Eisenbrauns, 1987), 63.

19. Carole R. Fontaine, *With Eyes of Flesh: The Bible, Gender, and Human Rights*, ed. J. Cheryl Exum, The Bible in the Modern World 10 (Sheffield: Sheffield Phoenix, 2008), 50–52.

20. Sophia Bietenhard, "Micah: Call for Justice—Hope for All," in *Feminist Biblical Interpretation: A Compendium of Critical Commentary on the Books of the Bible and Related Literature*, ed. Luise Schottroff, Marie-Theres Wacker, and Martin Rumscheidt (Grand Rapids, MI: Eerdmans, 2012), 421–32.

21. Linda Williams, "Film Bodies: Gender, Gender and Excess," in Thornham, *Feminist Film Theory*.

In Mic 4 as throughout the book, feminine imagery is not truly about women. Missing from this description are women's own testimonies of sexual assault, pain in childbirth, and their experience of total dependency on a father. While this Persian-period scribe seeks to evoke sympathy for Jerusalem's current state by comparing the city to an abject woman, he fails to provide any insight into the lives of the real women of his community. Did those women long for the exaltation of their city? For the dissemination of Israel's emerging corpus of Torah? Was sexual assault prevalent in their own lives? What was their own experience of childbirth?

The significance of the animal imagery used for Jerusalem in Mic 4:13 also has been evaluated in very different ways. James Luther Mays argues that it empowers the female by looking "for the transformation of the daughter of Zion into the irresistible power by which the peoples are overwhelmed";[22] Erin Runions sees the image as gender-bending, "more surprisingly reminiscent of masculine figures in the Hebrew Bible."[23] To the contrary, I find it disturbing that when seeking a feminine metaphor for empowerment the writer of Micah must turn to the animal world, apparently finding no image of a human woman sufficiently powerful to make his point. Moreover, I note that while a threshing heifer may pulverize everything underfoot, it is a draft animal subordinate to the will of others. In this passage, Daughter Zion may trample, but only because YHWH has prepared the threshing floor. She does not enjoy the fruits of her work; instead, all gain is devoted to YHWH, who enjoys the wealth of the nations.[24] Unlike Runions, I do not find this image to be challenging gender ideologies but compounding them by comparing Zion to Yahweh's beast of burden: in Delbert Hillers's language, the writer of Micah envisions a time in which "God the harvester will use Zion as the beast."[25]

Micah 4:13 is not alone among biblical passages in abandoning female personification when describing Jerusalem's turn to strength. Zechariah 12:2-3 describes Jerusalem as feminine: "on that day [of vindication]" Jerusalem will become not only "a cup of reeling" but also "a heavy stone," hurting all those who attempt to lift *her*. Yet, in the following

---

22. James Luther Mays, *Micah: A Commentary* (Philadelphia: Westminster, 1976), 108.

23. Erin Runions, *Changing Subjects: Gender, Nation, and Future in Micah* (London and New York: Sheffield Academic Press, 2001), 158.

24. For a more developed argument, see O'Brien, "Once and Future Gender."

25. Delbert Hillers, *Micah: A Commentary on the Book of the Prophet Micah*, Hermeneia: A Critical and Historical Commentary on the Bible (Philadelphia: Fortress Press, 1984), 61.

verses YHWH promises to provide strength not to her but to her *people*: "The inhabitants of Jerusalem have strength through the LORD of hosts, their God" (Zech 12:5). While Zech 9:9-10 describes the weakness of Daughter Jerusalem/Zion with feminine forms, in Zech 10 *the flock of Judah* (עדר, 10:3; see Mic 4:8 and 2:12) is empowered, and the *people* become warriors (גברים, Zech 10:5): YHWH strengthens (גבר, 10:6) Ephraim and Joseph (male pronouns used for both), such that Ephraim becomes like a strong man himself (גבר, 10:7). Prophetic texts rarely apply feminine pronouns or descriptors to the nation being strengthened for battle. Christl Maier outlines this de-feminizing process in the book of Isaiah. While the oracle of judgment in Isa 3:16–4:1 describes the humiliation of Daughter Zion and her women, the oracle of salvation that follows in Isa 4:2-6 turns to the imagery of Zion as an ungendered mountain: "The result of that process is a space of glory but void of female embodiment."[26]

As suggested above, the cause of the weakness and shame that drives the feminine imagery of Mic 4 can be inferred from the desires expressed: the costs of war and the lack of political power and prestige. A further cause is named in 4:10: Daughter Zion's exile to Babylon. When read from the vantage point of the eighth-century setting of the superscription, this passage predicts Zion's destruction two hundred years later, but when read as the voice of the fifth-century Persian-period author it attributes to YHWH the city's past (and ongoing) desolation, as well as the end of exile. The community's honor is held in YHWH's hands: YHWH can shame and YHWH can restore honor. As is the case for all women in patriarchal systems, the honor of Daughter Jerusalem depends on the goodwill and the strength of her guardian. For the writer of Micah, these messages serve metaphorically to underscore Jerusalem's current vulnerable state.

For ancient and modern readers, these messages are powerful and tragic reminders of the realities of too many women's lives—perpetual dependency on males, pain (and often death) in childbirth, and public humiliation via stripping and rape. It reminds us too of the real-life implications of theologies that reinforce female dependency. In response, resistant readers can attest that dependency, childbirth, and sexual vulnerability are not the only or even most important characteristics of what it means to be a human female; and childbirth can be a source not only of pain but also of joy and empowerment.

26. Christl Maier, " 'Daughter Zion' as Gendered Space in the Book of Jeremiah" (paper presented at the SBL Annual Meeting, 2003), 13.

Daughter Zion the Thresher

In Mic 4:13, phallic imagery destabilizes gender boundaries as the Lord calls Daughter Zion to arise (stand erect) and thresh. She is no longer profaned, no longer gazed upon. This passage denigrates female bodies, celebrates only male power in the sex act, and creates a deeply disturbing image of the Lord. It is also an instance of the use of the "threshing floor" as a euphemism for females in general and female genitalia in particular.

The threshing floor euphemism is found throughout rabbinic and biblical texts. The Babylonian Talmud compares threshing floors to different categories of women in order to answer a question regarding inheritance (b. Yebam. 100a). Elsewhere, the rabbis seek to avoid any impropriety and use one euphemism for genitalia to define another: "What is meant by threshing place?/The place where the attendant [euphemism for the male member] threshes" (b. Nid. 41b).

Prophetic texts frequently use the threshing floor euphemism to depict rape and violence against females, as well as illicit female sexual behavior. Portraying her defeat as a rape, Jer 51:33 calls Daughter Babylon a threshing floor at the time of being trodden. A textual discrepancy in Jer 2:25, along with the surrounding sexual imagery, offers the possibility of parallel euphemisms for male and female genitalia: "Withhold your feet from being bare and your threshing floor from being parched." "Floor" (גורנך) is based on the consonantal text of the MT (*kethib*, "what is written"), while the vowel pointing (*qere*, "what is read") suggests instead גרונך ("your neck/throat"). Descriptions of loin pain and a woman in labor precede the image of shattered idolatrous images lying fallen around female Babylon (Isa 21:3, 9). Isaiah 21:10 follows with the agonizing cry, "O my threshed one and the sons of my threshing floor" (מדשתי ובן־גרני). Defeated female cities lay shattered and threshed, as do her inhabitants.

Similar to Isa 21:10, threshing synonyms in Mic 4:12-13 emphasize a relationship between the female city's actions (ודושי) and the nations gathered to a threshing floor (גרנה). The doomed nations, female cities, and, inevitably, females in general become marred by violence and passivity as threshing/threshing floor vocabulary symbolizes sexualized violence that occurs on female genitalia.

In a shift that is supposed to appear triumphant, the Lord summons Daughter Zion in Mic 4:13 to enact metaphorical sexualized violence against other female bodies. She must become a female rapist, forcing herself upon the feminized enemy nations. More precisely, the she-city must execute not just masculinized force but animalized violence with her powerful horns and hooves. We witness the loss of her humanity. Perhaps even more troubling than this shifting gendered dimensions and sexualized animalistic violence is that the Lord initiates this brutality. The Lord makes the nations passive and feminized (gathered upon threshing floors), gives Daughter Zion her masculinized and animalistic tools, and orders her to perform sexual savagery. The image is more troubling than redemptive, more destructive than victorious. In a constant cycle of violence, the victim becomes perpetrator, and the Lord makes it so.

Jennifer J. Williams

EXCURSUS
United Nations Security Council Resolution 1820

Adopted 19 June 2008 (Excerpts)

[The Security Council]

Noting that civilians account for the vast majority of those adversely affected by armed conflict; that women and girls are particularly targeted by the use of sexual violence, including as a tactic of war to humiliate, dominate, instill fear in, disperse and/or forcibly relocate civilian members of a community or ethnic group; and that sexual violence perpetrated in this manner may in some instances persist after the cessation of hostilities. . . .

Reiterating deep concern that, despite its repeated condemnation of violence against women and children in situations of armed conflict, including sexual violence in situations of armed conflict, and despite its calls addressed to all parties to armed conflict for the cessation of such acts with immediate effect, such acts continue to occur, and in some situations have become systematic and widespread, reaching appalling levels of brutality. . . .

Demands the immediate and complete cessation by all parties to armed conflict of all acts of sexual violence against civilians with immediate effect; [and]

Demands that all parties to armed conflict immediately take appropriate measures to protect civilians, including women and girls, from all forms of sexual violence, which could include, inter alia, enforcing appropriate military disciplinary measures and upholding the principle of command responsibility, training troops on the categorical prohibition of all forms of sexual violence against civilians, debunking myths that fuel sexual violence, vetting armed and security forces to take into account past actions of rape and other forms of sexual violence.

United Nations Security Council Resolution 2122

Adopted 18 October 2013 (Excerpts)

[The Security Council]

Expressing concern at women's exacerbated vulnerability in armed conflict and post-conflict situations particularly in relation to forced displacement, as a result of unequal citizenship rights, gender-biased application of asylum laws, and obstacles to registering and accessing identity documents which occur in many situations. . . .

Expressing deep concern at the full range of threats and human rights violations and abuses experienced by women in armed conflict and post-conflict situations, recognizing that those women and girls who are particularly vulnerable or disadvantaged may be specifically targeted or at increased risk of violence, and recognizing in this regard that more must be done to ensure that transitional justice measures address the full range of violations and abuses of women's human rights, and the differentiated impacts on women and girls of these violations and abuses as well as forced displacement, enforced disappearances, and destruction of civilian infrastructure. . . .

Reiterating its strong condemnation of all violations of international law committed against and/or directly affecting civilians, including women and girls in armed conflict and post-conflict situations, including those involving rape and other forms of sexual and gender-based violence, killing and maiming, obstructions to humanitarian aid, and mass forced displacement. . . .

Requests United Nations peacekeeping mission leadership to assess the human rights violations and abuses of women in armed conflict and post-conflict situations, and requests peacekeeping missions, in keeping with their mandates, to address the security threats and protection challenges faced by women and girls in armed conflict and post-conflict settings.

The Promise of a New Ruler (Mic 5:1-6 [4:14–5:5 MT])

Jerusalem's future also depends on a strong ruler. In this subunit, the humiliation of the current "judge" is contrasted with the authority of a future ruler who will feed the flock in peace and defend the land from the attack of the "Assyrians." While these verses have a long history in Christian interpretation, the situation to which they originally referred is not easily pinpointed.

Mic 5:1-6

[1]Now you are walled around with
a wall;
siege is laid against us;
with a rod they strike the ruler of
Israel
upon the cheek.
[2]But you, O Bethlehem of Ephrathah,
who are one of the little clans
of Judah,
from you shall come forth for me
one who is to rule in Israel,
whose origin is from of old,
from ancient days.
[3]Therefore he shall give them up
until the time
when she who is in labor has
brought forth;
then the rest of his kindred shall
return
to the people of Israel.
[4]And he shall stand and feed his
flock in the strength of the
LORD,

in the majesty of the name of
the LORD his God.
And they shall live secure, for now
he shall be great
to the ends of the earth;
[5]and he shall be the one of
peace.

If the Assyrians come into our
land
and tread upon our soil,
we will raise against them seven
shepherds
and eight installed as rulers.
[6]They shall rule the land of Assyria with the sword,
and the land of Nimrod with
the drawn sword;
they shall rescue us from the Assyrians
if they come into our land
or tread within our border.

The identity of the leader under attack in Mic 5:1 (4:14 MT) is unclear. He is described as a judge (Hebrew, שפט) hit upon the cheek, an act of public shaming; in Lam 3:30, smiting on the cheek is poetically linked with receiving insults. Interpreters who focus on the eighth-century setting of Micah argue that it reflects the same Assyrian humiliation of Judah and its king described in Isa 10.[27] The language is generic enough, however, to refer to diverse situations, and I agree with Hillers that it is primarily metaphorical.[28] While Ben Zvi is right that Yahweh is often called "judge," his claim that God is the "judge" described here is unlikely.[29] Elsewhere in the Hebrew Bible, שפט describes the actions of judges (Isa 40:23), the Davidic king (Isa 16:5), and various leaders (2 Chr 1:2).

27. Sweeney, *The Twelve Prophets*, 2:387.
28. Hillers, *Micah*, 63.
29. Ben Zvi, *Micah*, 120.

TRANSLATION MATTERS:

Verse numbers in Mic 5 are not the same in all biblical translations. As indicated in most annotated Bibles, Mic 5:1 in the NRSV is numbered as Mic 4:14 in Hebrew texts, leading to a one-verse numbering difference throughout Mic 5. For example, the verses labeled as Mic 5:1-5 in the NRSV appear in the JPS Tanakh translation as Mic 4:14–5:4. This numbering difference derives not from ancient manuscripts but from later Christian and Jewish hands. In 1227, the archbishop of Canterbury Stephen Langton added chapter divisions to the Latin Vulgate, from which the English Wycliffe Bible and subsequent English translations were made; in 1551, the French printer Robert Estienne added verse numbers. Chapter and verse numbers were added to Hebrew Bibles around 1440 by Rabbi Isaac Nathan; while Nathan was strongly influenced by the Christian numbering system, his divisions attempted to honor notations in the Masoretic Text that indicate major and minor breaks in thought, leading to occasional differences in numeration. In this commentary, I follow the NRSV numbers while including the Hebrew numbering in parentheses.

Micah 5:1 (4:14 MT) addresses a feminine subject, likely still Jerusalem, but the description of her present distress varies widely among modern translations. According to the NRSV, she now is "walled around with a wall." The NIV, however, translates this verse as "Marshal your troops, O city of troops," and the Tanakh translation renders it, "Now you gash yourself in grief." This last translation stays closest to the Hebrew text, understanding the root גדד (*gdd*) from which both the verb and the noun derive to refer to the self-mutilation of mourning rites, as it does in Jer 41:5 and 48:37. The NIV draws from the secondary meaning of גדד as "(those who) attack" and understands the verb as instructing Jerusalem to prepare for battle. The NRSV translation is based on a proposed correction of גדד (*gdd*) to גדר (*gdr*) to match the Septuagint reading of "blocked."

None of these translations, however, reveal to the English reader that the verse includes yet another reference to "daughter."[30] My own literal translation of the Hebrew is "Now you cut yourself, daughter of cutting." This literal translation best fits the literary context of Mic 4–5. Like Mic 4, Mic 5 first depicts the now of Jerusalem's dire situation before revealing the then of the promised future. Now, Daughter Jerusalem cuts herself in mourning because the judge of Israel (NRSV: "ruler of Israel") is being shamed; soon, however, a powerful ruler will emerge from Bethlehem and reign in peace.

---

30. Jacobs translates, "Now gash yourself, daughter of the troops." Mignon R. Jacobs, *The Conceptual Coherence of the Book of Micah*, JSOTSup (Sheffield: Sheffield Academic Press, 2001), 243.

The new ruler described in Mic 5:2-5 (5:1-4 MT) is clearly linked with the figure of David by allusions to numerous "Davidic" texts. The ruler will come from Bethlehem, the ancestral home of David (1 Sam 16); he will "rule" as does Solomon (2 Chr 7:18); he will "come forth" (5:2 [5:1 MT]; the same Hebrew root used for "led out" and "brought in" in 2 Sam 5:2) and "shepherd" the people (Mic 5:4 [5:3 MT]; 2 Sam 5:2). The reference to a woman in childbirth in 5:3 (5:2 MT) refers back to Mic 4:10 and also may allude to the well-known Immanuel oracle in Isa 7:14, often understood as referring to a child in the line of David. The promise of victory over the Assyrians in 5:4 (5:3 MT) likely is an allusion to Isa 7:17, which also mentions the Assyrian threat; if so, Micah shifts the meaning of Isaiah's oracle. In Isaiah, God advises the Judeans not to fear the anti-Assyrian coalition besieging the city; the real threat they face is Assyria itself, whom God will use as the "rod of my anger" (Isa 10:5) to punish Judah's sins. In Micah, these words are those of promise: a postponed threat in Isaiah becomes a lasting promise in Micah.

The Persian-period writer of Micah apparently anticipated the rise of a human king in the line of David. As John Collins and Adela Yarbro Collins have well argued, biblical texts composed prior to the Hellenistic period make modest claims for desired future kings: they are understood to be fully human and, under the influence of Deuteronomic theology, as subject to the requirements of Torah.[31] Other Persian-period texts also hope for the return of the Davidic monarchy: Amos 9:11 claims that God will raise up the fallen booth of David, and Zech 3–4 envisions the future joint rule of king and priest in which people will invite each other to come and sit under their vine and fig tree (Zech 3:10; see also Mic 4:4).

The promise of protection against the Assyrians in Mic 5:5b-6 testifies to the book's *literary setting* in the eighth century rather than to the date of its *composition*. It alludes to 2 Kgs 19:32, in which God decrees that the Assyrians will not enter Jerusalem. Nogalski identifies the seven shepherds and eight princes mentioned in 5:5 (5:4 MT) as the eight kings who ruled from Hezekiah to Jerusalem's destruction,[32] suggesting that the writer of Micah is viewing the end of the monarchy in retrospect. From

---

31. John J. Collins and Adela Yarbro Collins, *King and Messiah as Son of God: Divine, Human, and Angelic Messianic Figures in Biblical and Related Literature* (Grand Rapids, MI: Eerdmans, 2008), 47.

32. Nogalski, *The Book of the Twelve*, 554. "These verses do not speak of a specific event but of an epoch that lasts from the eighth century through the duration of the seventh" (565).

his vantage point in the Persian period, the writer of Micah can reflect not only on the sixth-century Babylonian exile and its fifth-century end (4:10) but also on the eighth-century Assyrian threat to Jerusalem (5:5 [5:4 MT]). In recalling YHWH's decision to spare Jerusalem from the Assyrian armies in 701 BCE, this writer finds hope for Jerusalem's future deliverance from other enemies. In Micah as well as other texts from the Persian and Hellenistic eras, "Assyria" comes to stand for all of Israel's enemies: according to Erhard Gerstenberger, in this text, originating in the Persian period at the earliest, the designation " 'Assyrian' stands for any invader or tyrant."[33]

In the passage's focus on Bethlehem, many interpreters have seen an anti-Jerusalemite stance. John Rogerson, for example, claims that it is "a radical rejection of Jerusalem and the existing Davidic dynasty and a completely new start beginning from Bethlehem."[34] A. J. Petrotta claims that it challenges both Jerusalem and monarchical succession: "It is also an affirmation that God can once again work through humble means, as he did with David, and is not dependent on the royal city and household, which has so deteriorated."[35]

This proposed rejection of Jerusalem, which will be developed in later Christian interpretation (see "Excursus"), does not fit well with the book itself, given its strong Jerusalemite focus. Bethlehem more likely appears here not as the antithesis of Jerusalem but as the source of its salvation: just as David once was anointed to shepherd the people in peace, so too YHWH will appoint a new David who will complete the gathering of exiles (5:2 [5:1 MT]) and rule an independent Yehud.

In envisioning a utopian future, the writer of Micah holds to standard gender scripts. *Now* the city is a defenseless woman who gashes herself in grief. *Soon*, however, YHWH and his king will save her. The status of Jerusalem's ruler (or perhaps YHWH) will be exalted throughout the earth (5:4 [5:3 MT]), and she will remain under his protection. In keeping with traditional gender roles, Daughter Jerusalem is called not to act on her own behalf but to trust in the protection of others.

33. Gerstenberger, *Israel in the Persian Period*, 317. The pairing of Assyria and Nimrod appears elsewhere in the Hebrew Bible in Gen 10.

34. John Rogerson, "Micah," in *Eerdmans Commentary on the Bible*, ed. J. D. G. Dunn and John Rogerson (Grand Rapids, MI: Eerdmans, 2003), 5.

35. A. J. Petrotta, "A Closer Look at Matt 2:6 and Its Old Testament Sources," *JETS* 28 (1985): 50.

EXCURSUS
Early Christian Interpretation of Micah 4–5

By the first century CE, it is likely that many Jews believed that the Messiah would be born in Bethlehem. Targum Jonathan on Micah (TgJ Mi), a Jewish paraphrase whose date is placed anywhere from the second century BCE to the fifth century CE, reads "messiah" for "ruler" in Mic 5:2 (5:1 MT).[36] John 7:42 reflects this tradition, and, as we will explore, it features prominently in Matthew and Luke.

Matthew is the only gospel to explicitly quote a prophetic prediction for Jesus' connection with Bethlehem. According to Matt 2:5-6, when Herod asked the chief priests and scribes where the Messiah was to be born,

> They told him, "In Bethlehem of Judea; for so it has been written by the prophet: 'And you, Bethlehem, in the land of Judah, are by no means least among the rulers of Judah; for from you shall come a ruler who is to shepherd my people Israel.'"

The primary reference is to Mic 5:2 (5:1 MT):

> But you, O Bethlehem of Ephrathah,
> who are one of the little clans of Judah,
> from you shall come forth for me
> one who is to rule in Israel,
> whose origin is from of old, from ancient days.

But Matthew's prophetic quote also draws upon 2 Sam 5:2:

> The LORD said to [David]: It is you who shall be shepherd of my people Israel, you who shall be ruler over Israel.

The gospel writer is not simply quoting Micah but instead blends two passages from the Hebrew Bible into a single "prediction" of Jesus' birth.

To bolster his claims that Jesus is the long-awaited Messiah, the writer also makes other changes to the Micah text:

- Micah's "Bethlehem of Ephrata" becomes in Matthew "Bethlehem in the land of Judah," the tribe through which the lineage of David is traced.

- Micah's "clans of Judah" becomes in Matthew "rulers of Judah," high-

---

36. For additional Jewish sources, see Raymond E. Brown, *The Birth of the Messiah: A Commentary on the Infancy Narratives in Matthew and Luke*, 2nd ed., ABRL (Garden City, NY: Doubleday, 1993), 513.

lighting the royal dimensions of Bethlehem.

- Micah's "you who are one of the little clans" becomes in Matthew "you are by no means least," exalting Bethlehem's status as the birthplace of the Messiah.

Clearly, in his use of Mic 5:2 (5:1 MT), the writer of Matthew does not simply repeat an existing "prediction." Rather, the gospel writer reinterprets Micah in light of his own convictions about Jesus.

The differences between Matthew and Micah were recognized by the fifth-century interpreter Jerome. In a letter to Pammachius regarding translation, Jerome notes the differences between the prophet's words and the evangelist's quote but casts them in a positive light:

> From all these passages it is clear that the apostles and evangelists in translating the Old Testament scriptures have sought to give the meaning rather than the words, and that they have not greatly cared to pre-serve forms or constructions, so long as they could make clear the subject to the understanding.[37]

In his magisterial study of the infancy narratives of Matthew and Luke, Raymond Brown argues that the connections between the gospels and Micah go far deeper than a simple prediction-fulfillment scheme and instead imbue both accounts of Jesus' birth with distinctive nuances. Brown argues that both Luke and Matthew allude to Migdal Eder, which appears in Mic 4:8 as an epithet for Jerusalem (NRSV, "tower of the flock") and which in Gen 35:19-21 is mentioned in the context of the burial of Rachel on the way to Ephrathah/Bethlehem.[38]

As Brown shows, connections between Micah, Genesis, and 1 and 2 Samuel allow the gospel writers to develop their infancy narratives in various ways:

- By linking Mic 5:2 and 2 Sam 5:2, Matthew underscores the shepherding function of the Davidic ruler and thereby casts Jesus' Davidic nature not

37. Philip Schaff, *The Principal Works of St. Jerome: Nicene and Post-Nicene Fathers, Series 2*, vol. 6, Christian Classics Ethereal Library (New York: Christian Literature Co., 1893), 299.

38. Brown, *The Birth of the Messiah*, 247. Similarly, Targum Pseudo-Jonathan on Gen 35:21 reads, "The tower of the flock, the place from which it will happen that the King Messiah will be revealed at the end of days" (quoted in ibid., 423).

as an absolute ruler but as a servant.[39]

- The reference to Rachel weeping for her children in Matt 2:18 is dependent not only on a quote from Jeremiah but also on the connections already developed in Matt 2 with Mic 4–5, in which a woman in travail appears.

- Luke's inclusion of shepherds as receiving news of Jesus' birth draws from the "flock" resonances of Midgal Eder in Micah and Genesis.

- The angels' speech to the shepherds exalts Bethlehem over Jerusalem: by calling Bethlehem rather than Jerusalem the "city of David" (Luke 2:4, 11), the evangelist reverses the geographical priorities of Micah: "while Micah focuses on the triumph of Jerusalem/Zion through the ruler from Bethlehem, Luke shifts the total attention to Bethlehem."[40]

These interpretative connections that Brown traces are reflected in accounts of one of the earliest documented female commentators of Scripture: St.

Paula. The writings of Jerome relate that after the death of her husband a wealthy woman named Paula joined a semi-monastic religious community. After meeting Jerome in Rome, she went on pilgrimage to the Holy Land, settled in Bethlehem, and assisted Jerome in translating the Bible from Hebrew and Greek into Latin (the Vulgate). According to Jerome, Paula was proficient in Hebrew and edited his work.

In a letter to Paula's daughter Eustochium, Jerome recounts Paula's arrival in Bethlehem. Upon seeing the city, claims Jerome, Paula quoted various Old Testament Scriptures and, by expounding on the meaning of Hebrew words, connected them with Jesus' birth. Paula related Bethlehem, "house of bread," to Jesus the Bread of Heaven. Ephrathah, the land of fruit, she claimed, bears the fruit of Jesus. Paula explicitly quoted Micah, though in a form closer to the reading of Matthew (adding "not" to 5:2), and implied that "she who gives forth" in Mic 5:3 is the Virgin Mary. In his narrative, Jerome relates that after Paula saw the birthplace of Jesus she advanced to "Edar" (Hebrew, עדר, *eder*, connected to Migdal Eder—see above), the area "of the flock"

39. Ibid., 184.
40. Ibid., 422–23.

where the angels announced Jesus' birth to the shepherds.[41]

These typological interpretations of Micah continue in later Christian literature and art. In medieval and Reformation-era depictions, the prophet Micah is regularly shown holding a scroll on which appears the Latin of Mic 5:2. He (rather than the more commonly depicted Isaiah) appears in numerous annunciation scenes, hovering with his scroll behind or above the Virgin. In Jan van Eyck's Ghent Altarpiece, for example, Micah gazes down at Mary as the Holy Spirit descends upon her; the words on his scroll apparently apply "you" not to Bethlehem but to the Virgin herself: "out of you will come one who is to rule Israel."

In Christian art, the prophet Micah is also commonly portrayed in connection with nativity scenes, often pointing to the city in which the manger is set. In Reformation-era woodcuts available from the Pitt Library at Emory University, scenes of Micah regularly include one or two cities.[42] In a scene reproduced in a Luther Bible, Micah addresses men at a city gate (presumably Jerusalem), while in the background angels speak to the shepherds, with a city behind them, and a star shines over Mary, Joseph, and the baby (1541/1550Bib). In a similar piece by Virgil Solis, Micah addresses men wearing the distinctive pointed headgear that designates Jews in art iconography; he stands poised between their city on the right and the manger in a stylized building on the left (1560Soli). An etching by Matthaeus Merian, printed in a Luther Bible, shows Micah gazing at the manger behind which the city of Bethlehem rises; another city appears to the right, connected by a bridge (1704BiblC).

This contrasting city motif is portrayed in a particularly interesting way on the façade of the Orvieto (Italy) cathedral. The second pillar includes a Jesse tree which offers various Old Testament scenes as prophecies of the Messiah. In the left roundel of the eighth panel, a figure floating at the top of the scene points to a city on the left, in front of which appears a woman holding her abdomen; an opposing city appears on the right. Although in 1932 Elizabeth Rose identified these cities as Jerusalem and Babylon,[43] modern

41. Schaff, *The Principal Works*, 6:488–90.

42. Images may be accessed at *Pitts Theology Library: Digital Archives*, Emory University http://pitts.emory.edu/dia/listform.cfm.

43. Elizabeth A. Rose, "The Meaning of the Reliefs on the Second Pier of the Orvieto Facade," *The Art Bulletin* 14 (1932): 258–76.

art historians have followed the interpretation of Antonia Nava, Enzo Carli, Arthur Watson, and Michael D. Taylor that the scene depicts Mic 5 and the deity choosing Bethlehem over Jerusalem: hence the scene is dubbed either "the Malediction of Jerusalem" or the "Blessing of Bethlehem."[44]

Although art historians rarely note the connection, the imagery of the woman in travail develops the themes of Mic 4, which, as noted above, had been typologically linked to the Virgin by interpreters such as St. Paula at least since the fourth century. This roundel on the pillar devoted to the Jesse tree corresponds to the scene of Jesus' triumphal entry into Jerusalem on the third pillar, which is devoted to the life of Jesus.[45]

Other artistic representations of the Jesse tree also include Micah. As Pippa Salonius records, in the sixteenth century the pilgrim Franciscus Quaresimus reported that seeing Micah in the Jesse tree in the basilica of the Church of the Nativity in Bethlehem, and the "Painter's Manual" of Dionysius of Fourna, composed in the 1730s in Greece, prescribes Mic 5:2 as one of seven prophecies to be depicted in connection with the Nativity.[46] Micah also appears in wall paintings in various monasteries in Romania.[47] Missing from his description, as well as from other art of which I am aware, is Woman in Travail that appears in the Orvieto relief.

As seen in this cursory overview, females have played

44. Antonia Nava, "L'albero Di Jesse Nella Cattedrale D'orvieto E La Pittura Bizantina," *Rivista dell'Istituto nazionale d'archeologia e storia dell'arte* 5 (1936); Arthur Watson, "The Imagery of the Tree of Jesse on the West Front of the Orvieto Cathedral," in *Fritz Saxl, 1890–1948: A Volume of Memorial Essays from His Friends in England*, ed. D. J. Gordon (London: Thomas Nelson and Sons, 1957); Enzo Carli, *Le Sculture Del Duomo Di Orvieto* (Bergano: Instituto Italiano d'Arti Grafiche, 1947). Michael D. Taylor, "The Prophetic Scenes in the Tree of Jesse at Orvieto," *The Art Bulletin* 54 (1972): 403–17. This interpretation is assumed, though not argued, in Anita Fiderer Moskowitz and David Finn, *The Facade Reliefs of Orvieto Cathedral* (London and Turnhout: Harvey Miller Publishers, 2009).

45. I am grateful to Pippa Salonius for pointing out this correspondence to me. It is also mentioned in Pippa Salonius, "Arbor Jesse—Lignum Vitae: The Tree of Jesse, the Tree of Life, and the Mendicants in Late Medieval Orvieto," in *The Tree: Symbol, Allegory, and Mnemonic Device in Medieval Art and Thought*, ed. Pippa Salonius and Andrea Worm (Turnhout: Brepols, 2014), 213–41.

46. Ibid., 225.

47. See discussion in Michael D. Taylor, "The Local Motives in Moldavian Trees of Jesse with an Excursus on the Liturgical Basis of the Exterior Mural Programs," *Revue des etudes Sud-Est Europèennes* 12 (1974): 267–75.

various roles in the history of Christian interpretation of Mic 4–5. The feminine imagery used in Mic 4–5 to describe the travail of Jerusalem is used in Matt 2 to provoke pathos for the Slaughter of the Innocents; and in Christian art Micah's promise of salvation to Daughter Jerusalem is applied to the iconography of the Virgin Mary. Jerome's description of St. Paula suggests that females were not only the objects of these interpretations but also active participants in generating and expounding them. While the description of St. Paula is clearly the work of Jerome, he provides an early testimony to a woman who is drawing connections between the book of Micah and her own experience. Women today continue to do the same.

Julia M. O'Brien

Reading Micah 5
in Modern Bethlehem

As a daughter of a Palestinian Christian Lutheran family, I know Mic 5:2 by heart. Every year around Christmas, I hear these words in our Christmas Lutheran Church in Bethlehem, though in the version of Matt 2:6. As a little girl, I was thrilled to know that my little town was so important that even the Bible mentions it, paying little attention to the rest of the reading. As I became an adult and studied theology, I began to hear this verse with different ears. This verse, which seems at first glance to be a promise and a hope for what is to come, is actually a mirror of memories, of things that once were.

I was born in Bethlehem in 1969, two years after the beginning of the Israeli occupation. Thus, I belong to a generation of Palestinians whose lives are shaped by the Israeli occupation. I speak as a Palestinian Christian woman, born and raised under occupation, and a theologian belonging to a contextual and feminist theological school of thought.

Micah links the name Bethlehem to Ephrathah, a connection already found in Gen 35:16 and 48:7, both connected to the death of Rachel. To Christians who are not native to the "Holy Land," these references may not be noteworthy, but for a Palestinian Christian from Bethlehem Micah's references to Ephrathah and to Rachel have strong contextual connotations. All places mentioned in the Bible are part of the country to which I belong and are connected with real images and memories.

Bethlehem is a Palestinian city; since 1995 it has been formally under Palestinian Authority rule, but in practical terms since 1967 it has remained under Israeli occupation. For Palestinians today the name "Ephrathah" is integrally linked to the Israeli settlement southwest of Bethlehem named "Ephrathah," which is built on confiscated Palestinian land and on which seven thousand Israeli settlers live.

The connection between Bethlehem and the tomb of Rachel also has changed dramatically in the last two decades. An old religious site at the entrance to Bethlehem is believed to be the tomb of Rachel; though various biblical scholars doubt that this is the case, for centuries followers of the three monotheistic religions (Jews, Christians, and Muslims) visited this site. Many of the visitors were women—some infertile praying for children and others pregnant praying for an easy birth. Since the late eighties, however, the tomb of Rachel has been increasingly transformed into an Israeli "colony" within Bethlehem. The isolation of Rachel's tomb from Bethlehem was achieved covertly. First, military checkpoints were set up around the entrance; later access was denied to Palestinians (both Christians and Muslims); and in recent years the separation wall around Bethlehem was built in such a way as to segregate the tomb from Bethlehem and annex it to Jerusalem—part of the plans of a greater Jerusalem. Rachel's tomb as a religious site has been misused by the Israeli occupation and the ruling Israeli government to strangle Bethlehem.

For Palestinian Christians today to understand the prophetic voice of Micah, it is essential for us to remember that Micah was not predicting the future but rather explaining the past. The people Micah was talking to had gone through hardships, expulsion, and exile. In his social criticism Micah takes a clear stand in naming the injustice and its perpetrators and gives a voice to the voiceless. Micah did not include "other" religious or ethnic groups in his social criticism, as he was speaking to his own community, yet critical reflection on the past is at the core of Micah. And there lies the hope for me as a Christian Palestinian woman today.

Over the last decades, the Oslo Process has made us Palestinians prisoners of our own political rhetoric. It has made us forget what we stand for, or once stood for, which society we were and are fighting for, and on which ethical grounding our national struggle has stood and should stand. We have thought that hope would come from Washington, Brussels, or Tel-Aviv. We have joined the international community in selling the Oslo Process as a Peace Process, despite the fact that it allowed the occupation to continue building settlements and separation walls, confiscate land, and deprive the

Palestinians from living a life in dignity. We have professionalized the soft skill of negotiation while losing the passion for justice. We have been more concerned with the "other" than with ourselves, thus becoming alienated from our past, present, and future.

What we need today are Palestinian prophetic voices in the tradition of Micah who will dare to develop an internal social-political criticism. We need people who also have the courage, vision, and wisdom to translate this criticism into a tool of social-political transformation.

In the last two and a half decades, while the politics of negotiation have made Bethlehem an open-air prison, a ministry for social and political transformation was founded in the midst of Bethlehem now known as Diyar. The Diyar Consortium is a group of Lutheran-based, ecumenically oriented institutions serving the Palestinian community. Its mission is clear: "That We Might Have Life and Have It Abundantly." This mission takes a clear stance: "In a context of too much politics, Diyar believes in caring for the polis/city. In a context of exclusive forms of religion, Diyar believes in investing in culture of inclusion. In a context of too much disempowering aid, Diyar believes in empowering the individual and the community. In a context of too much segregation, Diyar believes in building bridges and platforms for intercultural dialogue. In a context of despair, Diyar believes in creating room for hope."[48]

When Micah named Bethlehem and not Jerusalem as the place from which the Messiah would come, he was making a clear religious and political criticism over and against the religious and political establishment of his own people. When I name Palestine the place for hope to come, I do so in recognition, appreciation, and solidarity of what is being done on the long path for justice.

Viola Raheb

48. For more information about Diyar, visit Diyar, *Diyar: That We Might Have Life and Have It Abundantly*, Diyar Consortium, 2015, http://www.diyar.ps/.

Hopes for the Remnant 5:7-15 (5:6-14 MT)

As description of the future salvation of the people expands, feminine forms yield to masculine forms. Envisioned as thriving in 5:7-9 (5:6-8 MT) is no longer Daughter Jerusalem but a "remnant." In 5:10-15 (5:9-14 MT), a masculine "you" becomes the object of God's punishment. The language becomes combative as well, as YHWH turns in anger against the nations.

The imagery used for the flourishing of the "remnant of Jacob" builds intensity over the course of two verses whose repetitive beginnings highlight their progression of thought:

> Then the remnant of Jacob,
>> surrounded by many peoples,
>>> *shall be like dew from the* LORD, *like showers on the grass,*
>>> *which do not depend upon people or wait for any mortal.*
> And among the nations the remnant of Jacob,
>> surrounded by many peoples,
>>> *shall be like a lion among the animals of the forest,*
>>> *like a young lion among the flocks of sheep,*
>>> *which, when it goes through, treads down*
>>> *and tears in pieces, with no one to deliver.*

The remnant of Jacob, who is surrounded by others, first becomes like dew and showers, unfettered by human control, nourishing the earth; while Hos 14:5 compares YHWH's favor to dew, Micah grants this role to the remnant. The remnant changes, however, when placed among the nations: it becomes like a lion among sheep, unstoppable by human hands, devouring whom it pleases. The contrast between these images of dew and lion is underscored by their juxtaposition in Prov 19:12: "A king's anger is like the growling of a lion, but his favor is like dew on the grass." The remnant that was once gathered as sheep (2:12) and described in feminine terms as weak and lame (4:7) now is masculinized as the one who mangles sheep and lifts his hand in triumph over foes. Building on the second image, 5:9 (5:8 MT) directly addresses the remnant as a masculine "you" whose hand is strengthened to "cut off" enemies. The same root, כרת, "cut off," is repeated four times in 5:10-15 (5:9-14 MT), though its subject is no longer the remnant but YHWH. As in Mic 4, descriptions of power rely on scripts of masculinity.

The abrupt shift from promises of salvation to threats in Mic 5:10 (5:9 MT) has been explained in different ways. Some interpreters argue that

[7]Then the remnant of Jacob,
 surrounded by many peoples,
shall be like dew from the LORD,
 like showers on the grass,
which do not depend upon people
 or wait for any mortal.
[8]And among the nations the remnant of Jacob,
 surrounded by many peoples,
shall be like a lion among the animals of the forest,
 like a young lion among the
 flocks of sheep,
which, when it goes through,
 treads down
 and tears in pieces, with no
 one to deliver.
[9]Your hand shall be lifted up over
 your adversaries,
 and all your enemies shall be
 cut off.
[10]In that day, says the LORD,

I will cut off your horses from
 among you
 and will destroy your chariots;
[11]and I will cut off the cities of your
 land
 and throw down all your
 strongholds;
[12]and I will cut off sorceries from
 your hand,
 and you shall have no more
 soothsayers;
[13]and I will cut off your images
 and your pillars from among
 you,
and you shall bow down no more
 to the work of your hands;
[14]and I will uproot your sacred
 poles from among you
 and destroy your towns.
[15]And in anger and wrath I will
 execute vengeance
 on the nations that did not obey.

it marks a return to judgment against Judah, last heard in chapter 3.[49] Mignon R. Jacobs concurs that "you" is Israel, but that the imagery is not of punishment but of purification: Israel who now lives among the nations must be cleansed in preparation for its return to the land.[50] Others suggest that the referent of "you" has shifted. The unit's ending judgment against the nations is seen as the theme of the unit as a whole, so that "you" in these verses refers to the enemy of the remnant rather than the remnant itself.[51] Runions and Ben Zvi underscore the ambiguity of the unit, in terms of both referent and theology.[52]

I concur with those who understand the object of YHWH's wrath as the nations. The enemy "you" is described as equipped with horses,

49. Sweeney, *The Twelve Prophets*, 2:392.
50. Jacobs, *Conceptual Coherence of Micah*, 155–56.
51. Nogalski, *The Book of the Twelve*, 567–68.
52. Ben Zvi, *Micah*, 137–39; Runions, *Changing Subjects*, 164–65.

chariots, and fortified cities. The enemy is accused of sorcery; spirit conjuring; idolatry; worshiping standing stones, hand-crafted images, and symbols of other deities (NRSV: "sacred poles"). While Devadasan Premnath identifies horses, chariots, cities, and strongholds "instruments of the elite's political and military power" in eighth-century Judah,[53] other biblical texts regularly attribute these items and practices to other nations. Haggai 2:22 describes the destruction of the nations as the over-throw of horses and chariots. Numerous prophetic texts accuse foreign nations with witchcraft and sorcery (Isa 2:6; 47:9, 12; Nah 3:4; Dan 2:2), and Deuteronomy sharply separates true Yahwism from the foreign worship of Baal and Asherah (Deut 16:21). When Israelites conduct such activities, they are accused of falling under the influence of the Other (2 Kgs 9:22). The mantra-like insistence that God will "cut off" the nations clearly indicates the writer's animosity against foreigners—either those outside of his land or those occupying his land.

In this way, Micah joins other Persian-period texts in referring to those now in Jerusalem as "remnant" (Hag 1:12, 14; 2:2; Zech 8:6, 12) and cast-ing them in opposition to surrounding nations who are construed as their enemies (Zeph 2:9; Zech 14). Steed Davidson attributes these preoc-cupations with the postcolonial situation in which the books were pro-duced: "The preoccupation with the foreign, at least to the extent of creating new cartographies of power, may well be one of the hallmarks of prophetic literature. . . .The prophetic texts reconstruct either a pris-tine identity that was spoiled and needs to be recovered or the constitut-ing of a new identity after the disaster."[54] Davidson's description well fits Mic 4–5, which envisions a Jerusalem at the center of the world to which the nations are either subordinate (Mic 4) or destroyed (Mic 5).

While these negative images of the foreign likely reflect the desire for governance independent of imperial control, they may have had addi-tional consequences for average women and men in the Persian period. The books of Ezra and Nehemiah recount that foreign women and their children were banished from Yehud: in Ezra 10, the whole community agrees to send them away, and Neh 13 claims that the people "separated from Israel all those of foreign descent" (13:3) and that Nehemiah berated and assaulted those who had married foreign women (13:25). Admoni-tions against the Strange Woman in Prov 1–9 may arise from such a social

53. Premnath, *Eighth Century Prophets*, 121.
54. Davidson, "Prophets Postcolonially."

situation.[55] In condemning the "nations," Micah's author would have been condemning the "others" within Yehud as well.

Ezra, Nehemiah, and Micah do not discuss the emotional and economic hardships caused by such banishment of "others," leaving the details to our imaginations. In our own world, we know too well the ways in which attitudes toward other nations and ethnicities affect families and communities, the ways that the political becomes personal. In our own world, we also know that particular attitudes are rarely limited to one gender: women as well as men can hold views about "those women." In reading Micah (and Ezra, Nehemiah, and Proverbs), we should remember that we do not know how widely this writer's views were shared by others in his own community, even as we remember that ideas carry over into the realities of people's lives.

Other real lives in the present may critique my perspective on exclusion rather than simply affirm it. The Black Theology movement, as exemplified in the work of James Cone[56] and evaluated in the work of Raphael Warnock,[57] underscores that *particularity* is essential to the dignity of the marginalized. As a white liberal Protestant in the United States, I can espouse the values of inclusion and downplay difference in part because my society does not demean me for being white. African Americans face a vastly different reality, and in this context Black Theology has insisted "Jesus is black" in an attempt to restore dignity and agency to those of African descent.[58] Similarly, the Black Lives Matter movement created in response to the tragic police shootings of unarmed African American teenagers between 2012 and 2015 insists that alternative inclusive taglines such as "All Lives Matter" obscures the reality that some lives are already assumed to matter more than others.

55. Harold Washington, "The Strange Woman of Proverbs 1–9 and Post-Exilic Judean Society," in *Second Temple Studies 2: Temple and Community in the Persian Period*, ed. Tamara C. Eskenazi and Kent H. Richards (Sheffield: JSOT Press, 1994), 217–42.

56. James Cone, *The Cross and the Lynching Tree* (Maryknoll, NY: Orbis, 2011).

57. Raphael G. Warnock. *The Divided Mind of the Black Church: Theology, Piety, and Public Witness* (New York: New York University Press, 2014).

58. Ibid., 145–50.

Micah 6–7

YHWH's Lawsuit and Daughter Jerusalem's Response

After two chapters of promised salvation for Jerusalem, Mic 6 returns to judgment. Like Mic 1–3, Mic 6 employs courtroom imagery and makes accusations of social injustice. Micah 7 encompasses a wider range of topics and emotions: the speaker's lament, which implies further accusations; Jerusalem's expression of confidence that YHWH will vindicate her in the face of her enemy; and a moving appeal for YHWH to be gracious.

The material in these chapters lacks much of the specificity found in Mic 1–3. Absent are allusions to the Assyrian period and long lists of the elites' misdeeds. What the language lacks in specificity, however, it gains in rhetorical power. Here we encounter one of the Bible's most rousing and memorable calls to ethical action, as well as a pathos-filled appeal to divine mercy. These words allow us both to imagine the plight and faith of Yehudites in the Persian period and to reflect on our own understandings of God and our responsibility to one another.

YHWH's Suit against Israel (Mic 6:1-16)

In many ways, Mic 6 echoes the judgment oracles found in Mic 1–3. Most obvious is the tone and vocabulary of legal disputation. The admonition to "hear," which called people to court in 1:2, 3:1, and 3:9, functions similarly in 6:1, 6:2, and 6:9; as earlier, unjust business practices are assailed (2–3; 6:10-12) and sentencing is announced with "therefore" (1:6; 3:12; 6:13-16).

In other ways, however, this chapter differs from Mic 1–3. Micah 6 makes no mention of priests, prophets, rulers, or specific geographical locations (neither Jerusalem nor Assyria is mentioned by name). Addressed instead are "my people," "the city," and a masculine "you." Attention here focuses more on general ethical norms and generic descriptions of punishment than on the specific acts of injustice named in Mic 2–3.

Micah 6 begins in a genre known as the covenant lawsuit. This form is called the ריב ("contend") based on the frequency in which the Hebrew word appears. ריב appears here in 6:1 (NRSV, "plead") and in 6:2 (NRSV, "controversy"). As in other examples of the ריב genre, "hear" (6:1, 2, 9) summons not only witnesses but also defendants.

Most interpreters understand the lawsuit as limited to Mic 6:1-5, which is then followed by the people's response in 6:6-8 and an additional oracle of judgment in 6:9-16. I will argue somewhat differently, suggesting that the entirety of Mic 6 constitutes an imagined legal dispute. YHWH's case against the people proceeds in this way:

> 6:1-2: Summoning of witnesses
> 6:3-5: Recital of YHWH's acts of faithfulness
> 6:6-8: Reminder of Israel's covenantal obligations
> 6:9-12: Israel's failures to meet its obligations
> 6:15-16: Sentencing

This chapter is neither dialogical[1] nor disjointed in literary style[2] but a divine monologue in which God is both accuser and judge.

Summoning of Witnesses (Mic 6:1-2)

Vocabulary such as "hear," "contend," and "controversy" immediately marks the unit as a divine lawsuit. As in Mic 1:2 and other examples of

---

1. For example, Ehud Ben Zvi, *Micah*, The Forms of the Old Testament Literature, vol. 21B (Grand Rapids, MI: Eerdmans, 2000), 143, 46–47. Wolff sees it as an "(imaginary) dialogue"; Hans Walter Wolff, *Micah: A Commentary* (Philadelphia: Augsburg Fortress, 1990), 168.

2. Francis I. Anderson and David Noel Freedman, *Micah: A New Translation with Introduction and Commentary*, AB24E (New York: Doubleday, 2000), 510.

Mic 6:1-2

¹Hear what the Lord says:
Rise, plead your case before
the mountains,
and let the hills hear your voice.
²Hear, you mountains, the controversy of the Lord,

and you enduring foundations
of the earth;
for the Lord has a controversy
with his people,
and he will contend with Israel.

this genre, nature itself is called to witness to God's case (Jer 2:12; Isa 1:2; Ps 50:4).[3] The accused is named in two parallel lines as "his people" and as "Israel." Because the lawsuit form is used to prosecute breaches of contract, this style implies that YHWH and Israel are bound by an agreement—a covenant. The terms of that covenant can be inferred by the way in which the lawsuit progresses.

YHWH's Fulfillment of Obligations (Mic 6:3-5)

Starting with a confrontational rhetorical question, YHWH testifies to past beneficent deeds done on Israel's behalf. YHWH liberated the people from slavery in Egypt and sent them Moses, Aaron, and Miriam (Exod 1–15); thwarted the treacherous plans of the Moabite king Balak (Num 22); and led the people from Shittim on one bank of the Jordan River (Josh 3:1) to Gilgal on the other (Josh 4:19-24). YHWH has honored the covenantal promise to protect Israel as "my treasured possession out of all the peoples" (Exod 19:5). In the words of Ehud Ben Zvi, "God has been a good patron."[4]

The author of Micah may not be alluding to ancient and well-known texts. Rather, if Theodore Mullen is right, the literary accounts of Genesis through Kings may themselves be Persian-period compositions. They provided "a narrative foundation for the reformulation and maintenance of 'Israelite' ethnic and national identity in the Second Temple period. . . . While many of the traditions contained in the final form of the Tetrateuchal and Pentateuchal stories might be ancient, the written form in

---

3. Herbert Huffmon, "The Covenant Lawsuit in the Prophets," *JBL* 78 (1959): 285–95.

4. Ben Zvi, *Micah*, 145.

Mic 6:3-5

³"O my people, what have I done
to you?
In what have I wearied you?
Answer me!
⁴For I brought you up from the
land of Egypt,
and redeemed you from the
house of slavery;
and I sent before you Moses,
Aaron, and Miriam.

⁵O my people, remember now
what King Balak of Moab
devised,
what Balaam son of Beor answered him,
and what happened from Shittim
to Gilgal,
that you may know the saving
acts of the Lord."

which we have them is no earlier than the Persian period."[5] In such a scenario, the Persian-period author of Micah joins with other scribes of the era in creating an account of YHWH's past acts of deliverance.

While such a listing of God's salvific acts is not rare in the Bible (e.g., Pss 105, 106; Neh 9; Josh 24), the mention of Miriam is. Indeed, the Bible mentions Miriam infrequently, elsewhere only tracing her genealogy (Num 26:59; 1 Chr 4:17; 6:3); her title of prophetess (Exod 15:20); her act of singing (Exod 15); her being struck with leprosy for challenging Moses (Num 12; Deut 24:9); and her death (Num 20). The NRSV translation of Mic 6:4 suggests that she is also a leader, but the infinitive "to lead" has been added to the Hebrew, which only says that Moses, Aaron, and Miriam were "sent before you." Tantalized by the lack of information about this female figure, interpreters through the centuries (especially women) have filled in the gaps of Miriam's story in ways that satisfy their own curiosities and reflect their own values (see *Excursus: Miriam Matters*).

In the context of the book of Micah, the list is noteworthy for stopping with the wilderness narratives. It offers no mention of any of YHWH's gracious acts leading up to the eighth-century setting of the book (there is no mention of divine assistance in the conquest of the land of the election of David) or to the time of the author (there is no mention of the end of exile). Rather, these "old, old" stories are offered as indisputable evidence that YHWH has been faithful.

---

5. E. Theodore Mullen Jr., *Ethnic Myths and Pentateuchal Foundations: A New Approach to the Formation of the Pentateuch* (Atlanta, GA: Scholars Press, 1997), 327–28.

EXCURSUS
Miriam Matters

Despite her relatively low profile in the Hebrew Bible, twentieth- and twenty-first-century feminists have devoted much attention to the character of Miriam, debating whether her story preserves remnants of a suppressed tradition of women's leadership or instead dresses patriarchy in a feminine guise. Three scenes from Miriam's life have garnered the most attention:

- her role in saving the infant Moses from Pharaoh's decree of death (assuming she is the same sister mentioned in Exod 2)

- her song and dance during the exodus event, during which she is called a prophet (Exod 15:20-21)

- her challenge to Moses' leadership in the wilderness, when she joins her brother in asking, "Has the LORD indeed spoken only through Moses? Has he not spoken through us also?" (Num 12:2); as punishment for her words, Miriam is stricken with leprosy and banished from the community for seven days

All three stories, but especially the last two, raise questions about Miriam's leadership in ancient Israel.

The dominant stream of male-dominated Jewish and Christian interpretation has downplayed or outright denied that these acts constitute true leadership on Miriam's part. As traced by Devora Steinmetz, the Jewish Midrashic tradition casts Miriam in a role of support, not only to Moses, but also to traditional family structures. The Babylonian Talmud (B. Sotah 11b; 12b-13a) identifies Miriam as Puah, one of the two Hebrew midwives in Exod 1, and claims that, before Moses' birth, she prophesied that she would have a brother who would save Israel. Various rabbinic tales depict Miriam as attempting to reconcile couples for the sake of bearing children, including her own parents and Moses and Zipporah (identified with the Cushite wife of Num 12). Even though the Bible does not mention Miriam's own marriage, Sifre Numbers identifies her with Azubah in 1 Chr 2:18, making her the wife of Caleb and an ancestress of King David.[6]

The Midrash develops the connections between Miriam and water already present in the biblical text. Since the account of Miriam's death in Num 20:1 is immediately followed by the statement that "there was no water" (20:2), the rabbis concluded that the two were

6. Devora Steinmetz, "A Portrait of Miriam in Rabbinic Midrash," *Prooftexts* 8 (1988): 35–65.

related, giving birth to the legend that Miriam had carried a well through the wilderness wanderings:

> The Midrash lists the well among the three gifts that were given to Israel by merit of their leaders. The manna was given on account of Moses, the pillar of cloud, by merit of Aaron, and the well, by merit of Miriam. The well that then reappeared by merit of Moses is the one mentioned in the song of the well (Numbers 21). All three gifts—the well, the manna and the cloud—finally disappeared upon the death of Moses (*Mekhilta de-Rabbi Ishmael, Beshalah* 5; T *Sotah* 11:1; BT *Taanit* 9a; *Num. Rabbah* 1:2).[7]

In a mural in the third-century synagogue at Dura Europos, Miriam's well is depicted as flowing toward the twelve tribes of Israel.

On the one hand, the Midrash honors Miriam:

> Miriam, like her brothers, died at Mount Nebo (BT *Sotah* 13b), that is also known as "the heights of Abarim." The names of the place of their burial denote the fact that these three prophets (*nevi'im*) did not die because of sin (*averah*) (*Sifrei* on Deuteronomy, 338; BT *Sotah* 13b). In the Rabbinic portrayal, the Angel of Death had no power over Miriam and she died with a kiss by God, which is a death reserved for the righteous (*Cant. Rabbah* 1:2:5; BT *Bava Batra* 17a). Miriam was one of the seven over whom worms had no power (*Masekhet Derekh Erez* 1:17).[8]

Yet, according to Steinmetz, just as the waters that Miriam encounters bring both life and death, the Midrash treats Miriam as an ambiguous figure.[9]

> Miriam, it seems, is cast by the rabbis in the mold of the biblical matriarchs. Like them, and unlike the biblical Miriam who sings with the women and complains about Moses, the midrashic Miriam claims no share of leadership for herself, but strives to insure that there be a male heir to carry on leadership of the developing nation. . . . If the rabbis chose, for a consistent and

---

7. Tamar Meir, "Miriam: Midrash and Aggadah," *Jewish Women's Archive: Encyclopedia*, 20 March 2009, http://jwa.org/encyclopedia/article/miriam-midrash-and-aggadah.

8. Ibid.

9. Steinmetz, "A Portrait of Miriam," 55.

sympathetic portrayal of Miriam, a model different from that suggested by the biblical portrayal, that model, quite possibly, reflects the rabbis' own view of the proper place of women within society. And, if Miriam's behavior within that model is still viewed with ambivalence, that ambivalence may reflect a discomfort with any challenge to the system from the outside, even with a challenge that does not claim a share in the system.[10]

Early Christian interpretation went even further than the Jewish tradition in denying any independent role to Miriam. Miriam became the prototype of the Virgin Mary, whose name she shares, and in turn was linked with the church (in Latin, *ecclesia*). Zeno of Verona, for example, claimed that "the water of the Red Sea is the antetype of baptism and Miriam of Ecclesia."[11] According to Michael D. Taylor, Miriam is depicted with a tambourine at the parting of the Red Sea in the second pillar

of the Orvieto Cathedral;[12] this scene from the Old Testament is paired with the annunciation to Mary on the third pillar, devoted to scenes from the New Testament.

In his treatise "Concerning Virgins," Ambrose claims that those who remain virgins pass unscathed through the sea of bodily temptations, just as did Miriam/Mary:

> And Miriam taking the timbrel led the dances with maidenly modesty. But consider whom she was then representing. Was she not a type of the Church, who as a virgin with unstained spirit joins together the religious gatherings of the people to sing divine songs? For we read that there were virgins appointed also in the temple at Jerusalem. (3.3.12)[13]
>
> What a procession shall that be, what joy of applauding angels when she is found worthy of dwelling in heaven who lived on earth a heavenly life! Then too Mary, taking her timbrel, shall stir

10. Ibid., 58.

11. Michael D. Taylor, "The Prophetic Scenes in the Tree of Jesse at Orvieto," *The Art Bulletin* 54 (1972): 412.

12. Ibid., 405. This is the same pillar on which the prophecy from Mic 5 appears. See the excursus on Mic 5.

13. Philip Schaff, ed., *Selected Works and Letters of Ambrose: Nicene and Post-Nicene Fathers, Series* 2, vol. 10, Christian Classics Ethereal Library (New York: Christian Literature Co., 1893), 805.

up the choirs of virgins, singing to the Lord because they have passed through the sea of this world without suffering from the waves of this world. (3.2.17)[14]

In his discussion of Num 12 in "Epistle LXIII: To the Church at Vercellae," however, Ambrose condemns Miriam for her rebellion against Moses: "this murmuring refers to the type of the Synagogue" (57).[15]

Later Jewish and Christian art, such as at the Sistine Chapel and in the work of Marc Chagall, shows Miriam dancing and playing music, but not in leadership alongside Moses or Aaron.[16] This image also appears in a thirteenth-century French Bible illustration (MS. Bodl. 270b).

In response to such denigrations of Miriam and her role, many feminist interpreters have attempted to reclaim her as a leader in ancient Israel and as a model for modern women. In a 1989 article titled "Bringing Miriam Out of the Shadows," Phyllis Trible, one of the best known feminist biblical interpreters of the twentieth century, argued that the androcentric editors of the Bible had attempted to neutralize the power of Miriam. Although the full text of the Song of the Sea (Exod 15) most likely harks back to Miriam, in the final form of Exodus the composition is attributed to Moses, with Miriam relegated to the role of leading only the women in song. Even though Num 12 recognizes that the people refused to travel as long as Miriam was exiled from the camp, the story as now recorded is a full-frontal attack on her leadership: "If reasons for the attack are difficult to discern, the threat that she represented to the cultic establishment is abundantly evident. And that threat testifies to her prominence, power and prestige in early Israel. So important was this woman that detractors tabooed her to death, seeking to bury her forever in disgrace. But detractors do not have the final word. Miriam emerges through fragments embedded in the very Scripture that would condemn her."[17] For Trible, the very attempts of the biblical editors to discredit Miriam reveal her importance to ancient Israel.

---

14. Ibid., 830.

15. Ibid., 987.

16. For more, see Elaine James, "Miriam and Her Interpreters," in *Women's Bible Commentary*, 3rd ed., ed. Carol Newsom, et al. (Louisville, KY: Westminster John Knox, 2012), 67–69.

17. Phyllis Trible, "Bringing Miriam Out of the Shadows," in *Feminist Companion to Exodus to Deuteronomy*, ed. Athalya Brenner, FCB 6 (Sheffield: Sheffield Academic Press, 1994), 179. Reprinted from "Bringing Miriam out of the Shadows," *BRev* 5 (1989): 14–25.

Similarly, Judith Plaskow, one of the most respected Jewish feminists of the twentieth century, argues in her classic *Standing Again at Sinai* that even fragmentary accounts of women's leadership in the Bible are indicators of women's important roles in biblical history:

> The Torah leaves us with tantalizing hints concerning Miriam's importance and influence and the nature of her religious role, but she is by no means accorded the narrative attention the few texts concerning her suggest she deserves. . . . The disparagement of Miriam's authority and the brevity of narrative concerning Huldah suggest an androcentric selection process that saw traditions about women as either threatening or unimportant. This scarcity of information about women's leadership cannot be assumed accurately to reflect women's actual influence or importance in a particular period. On the contrary, the fact that centuries of androcentric sifting and editing left any traditions concerning

women suggests that these may represent only a fraction of what we have lost.[18]

In such discussions, the inclusion of Miriam in Mic 6:4 alongside Moses and Aaron becomes a key testimony to the tradition's inability to write Miriam out of Israelite history. According to Trible:

> Beyond the Exodus and wilderness accounts, fragments of a pro-Miriamic tradition surface still later in the Hebrew Scriptures. If the priesthood has repudiated Miriam forever, prophecy reclaims her. In fact, it states boldly what others worked hard to deny, that in early Israel Miriam belonged to a trinity of leadership. She was the equal of Moses and Aaron. Thus the prophetic deity speaks in Micah 6.4 (RSV). Here prophecy acknowledges the full legitimacy of Miriam, its own ancestor, who was designated "the prophet" even before Moses. The recognition undercuts a hierarchy of authority with a male at the top.[19]

18. Judith Plaskow, *Standing Again at Sinai: Judaism from a Feminist Perspective*, reprint ed. (San Francisco: HarperOne, 1991), 39–40.

19. Trible, "Bringing Miriam," 181. This sentiment is echoed by Sophia Bietenhard, "Micah: Call for Justice—Hope for All," in *Feminist Biblical Interpretation: A Compendium of Critical Commentary on the Books of the Bible and Related Literature*, ed. Luise Schottroff, Marie-Theres Wacker, and Martin Rumscheidt (Grand Rapids, MI: Eerdmans, 2012).

Trible and Plaskow are key representatives of the second wave of feminist biblical interpretation, in which much effort was devoted to the task of reclamation and retrieval— recovering women's history from the androcentric biblical texts which attempted to squelch it. In this vein, in 1987 Rita Burns published a monograph-length attempt to reclaim Miriam as a key figure in biblical history.[20]

Numerous feminists explain why this task of retrieval is so important to the modern feminist enterprise. Speaking from a Jewish perspective, Plaskow claims, "We cannot redefine Judaism in the present without redefining our past, because our present grows out of our history. . . . Knowing that women are active members of the Jewish community in the present, even though large sectors of the community continue to define themselves in male terms and to render women invisible, we know that we were always part of the community— not simply as objects of male purposes but as subjects and shapers of tradition."[21]

Similarly, from a Roman Catholic perspective, Irmtraud Fischer casts Miriam as a model for all women who seek to challenge ecclesial traditions that deny them full status: "When [women in patriarchally constituted religious communities] rise up in a discussion to make an intervention and assert that God speaks also to us, we may well be right, but still be punished, treated with contempt for a while and excluded from the community. . . . Numbers 12 offers us at least this one consolation: the people will refuse to move on, the seven days will pass and the issue settled as we proposed."[22]

This reclamation of biblical women as leaders has found its way into some contemporary liturgical traditions. As explained on the website "Miriam's Cup," Jewish feminists have incorporated the legend of Miriam and her well into new, women-friendly forms of the Passover seder.

New rituals include the addition of "Miriam's cup," filled with water to symbol-

20. Rita Burns, *Has the Lord Indeed Only Spoken through Moses? A Study of the Biblical Portrait of Miriam*, SBLDS 84 (Atlanta, GA: SBL Press, 1987).

21. Plaskow, *Standing Again at Sinai*, 31.

22. Irmtraud Fischer, "The Authority of Miriam: A Feminist Rereading of Numbers 12 Prompted by Jewish Interpretation," in *A Feminist Companion to Exodus to Deuteronomy*, ed. Athalya Brenner-Idan, FCB 6 (Sheffield: Sheffield Academic Press, 2000), 172–73.

ize Miriam's miraculous
well. . . . In addition, an
orange sometimes is placed
on the seder plate, as a
gesture of solidarity with
Jewish lesbians and gay
men, and others who are
marginalized within the
Jewish community.

The first feminist seder was
organized by Esther Broner,
Marcia Freedman, and
Nomi Nimrod in Haifa in
1975. Inspired by this experience, Ms. Broner and
Nimrod wrote The Women's
Haggadah, first used in
New York and Haifa in 1976.
The Women's Haggadah
follows the traditional Seder
order, but alters the elements to insert the lives of
biblical and rabbinic women
in the story, to speak of past
and current oppression of
women, and to enhance the
spiritual journey of self-
discovery. Subsequently,
women throughout the
United States organized
seders, often composing
their own text.[23]

Included on the site is "Miriam's
Song" by Debbie Friedman; an
alternative version of the
Passover song "mi chamocha,"
Friedman's composition focuses
on Miriam as the singer of the
Song of the Sea.

Not all feminists, however, are
quite so quick to embrace
Miriam as a positive image for
women. Claudia Camp disagrees
with Trible that the community's
refusal to travel while Miriam
remains sequestered for leprosy
in Num 12 is a reflection of her
importance. Rather, Camp
suggests that the author casts
this refusal as yet another
example of the people's rebellion
in the wilderness, and she finds
it no accident that the
community moves forward only
after Miriam's death. In
Numbers, Miriam symbolizes all
that challenges male priestly
authority: as a sister she cannot
carry forward lineage; as a
woman she bears impurity; as a
voice of protest she threatens
Mosaic (and by extension
Aaronic) authority. Like the
"strange woman" of Proverbs
and foreign women in Ezra,
Miriam destabilizes the security
of the community.[24]

Restoring women to biblical
history is of little avail, argues
Carol Fontaine, if feminists do
not also question the ideology of
the texts in which women
appear. Is simply attributing the
Song of the Sea to Miriam rather
than to Moses helpful to women
(and to men)?

Now, even if we were to be
able to prove that these
psalms of thanksgiving

23. "Miriam's Cup: History," http://www.miriamscup.com/HistoryFirst.htm.

24. Claudia V. Camp, *Wise, Strange and Holy: The Strange Woman and the Making of the Bible*, JSOTSup (Sheffield: Sheffield Academic, 2000).

were authored by the women to whom they are attributed . . . has very much been gained by being able to point proudly to these passages as if they were written by women? Miriam's exultation in her war-god [Exod 15] easily glosses over the fate of the Egyptians; Hannah's joy in her pregnancy [1 Sam 2] expresses itself in the gleeful observation of the wicked getting their "just desserts"; and this same theme dominates Mary's Magnificat [Luke 2]. . . . Are the sentiments expressed, however human and understandable, actually sentiments we want to flourish and grow? Is the answer to the violence visited on women and children to mete out the same treatment to little boys and men? . . . Only by ending the cycle of violence once and for all, and not by perpetuating it through role reversal, can we have hope of bringing to a halt the reign of terror under which so many lives are lived.[25]

These various interpretations of Miriam, along with interpretations of other female biblical characters such as Sarah and Mary Magdalene, raise important questions about the definition and nature of feminism. Is feminism to be understood as including (or restoring) women to human history, telling their stories along with those of the men whose accounts have too long been the only history available to us? And/or does feminism call for challenging the power structures crafted under patriarchy— violence, war, competition, and hierarchy?

Perhaps Micah's greatest gift is that the writer does not tell us what to make of Miriam except that she, along with her brothers, was sent by God.

Julia M. O'Brien

25. Carole R. Fontaine, "The Abusive Bible: On the Use of Feminist Method in Pastoral Contexts," in *Feminist Companion to Reading the Bible* (Sheffield: Sheffield Academic Press, 1997), 96–97.

Miriam and Women's Leadership

In Mic 6:4, a strong point is made about both female and male leadership: Moses, Aaron, and Miriam are mentioned together. Because her death is immediately followed by a scarcity of water (Num 20:1-3), the Talmud (Ta'anit 9a) attributes the well from which the children of Israel drew water in the desert to the merit of Miriam. Some scholars have suggested that a well is a feminine image. Others have developed the connection between water and Torah, as "living waters." In this way, Miriam can be seen as a source of Torah—a particularly feminine, nurturing kind of Torah.

Perhaps the utopian prophecy of diversity we saw in Mic 4:4 connects with this vision of female leadership—a pluralistic vision of parallel paths without the need for competition or dominance. Female leadership often seems different from male leadership—less competitive, more cooperative, and more collaborative. We don't know if these attributes are innate or the result of millennia of conditioning. Only in recent history have women found prominence in politics, business, and other spheres of leadership. In a generation or two, if more women enter these fields, we will have enough examples of women leaders to draw conclusions about gender-related differences.

Perhaps these qualities of leadership associated with women are accessible to men, as well. The most primordial kind of pluralism in society is that of gender. Once you realize that males and females can be equal, though different, you have opened up possibilities for more such alternatives.

Deborah Weissman

"Miriam the Speechwriter"[26]

Moses, awkward, chose to be
mute
Aaron delivered
but it was Miriam who put
words in the mouth
words that flowed like honey
of bees that sting
sweet enough to make the
message palatable
thick enough to spread through
the crowd
sufficiently golden to reflect
     and remind of the calf.

Miriam the speechwriter is
remembered most for dancing
but she was the one who gave
voice
who swallowed the clouds and
spit them out in letters
who translated God to People
and moved them to reconsider
     and tears.
A woman's words, once again,
ghostly and potent
A woman's voice, once again,
silent and still.

        Janet Ruth Falon

"We All Stood Together"[27]

My brother and I were at
    Sinai.
He kept a journal
of what he saw
of what he heard
of what it all meant to him.

I wish I had such a record
of what happened to me there.

It seems like every time I want
    to write
I can't—
I'm always holding a baby,
one of my own,
or one for a friend,
always holding a baby,
so my hands are never free
to write things down.

And then
as time passes,
the particulars,
the hard data,
the who what when where why,
slip away from me,
and all I'm left with is
the feeling.

But feelings are just sounds
the vowel barking of a mute.

My brother is so sure of what
    he heard—
after all he's got a record of it—
consonant after consonant after
    consonant.
If we remembered it together
we could recreate holy time
sparks flying.

        Merle Feld

26. Reprinted by permission of Janet Ruth Falon. For more of Janet's poetry, visit her website: http://www.janetfalon.com.

27. Reprinted by permission from Merle Feld, *A Spiritual Life: Exploring the Heart and Jewish Tradition* (Albany: SUNY Press, 2007).

The People's Obligations (Mic 6:6-8)

The speaking voice of Mic 6:6-8 is unidentified. Many interpreters identify 6:6-7 as the people's response to YHWH's charges (what shall I do?), which is in turn answered by the prophet in 6:8 (here is what to do). In this understanding, the exaggerated nature of the people's questions (of course YHWH does not expect child sacrifice) depicts them as sorely misunderstanding divine expectations.[28] They had already been given clear and reasonable rules, expressed (as James Nogalski notes) earlier in the Book of the Twelve: "But as for you, return to your God, hold fast to love and justice, and wait continually for your God" (Hos 12:6).[29]

Other interpreters attribute all three verses to the voice of the prophet, who first asks rhetorical questions about YHWH's demands and then answers his own question. In this latter understanding, the prophet's speech echoes a particular cultic form, the temple entrance liturgy. Psalm 15 and 24 suggest that worshipers entering the temple may have voiced scripted rhetorical questions which were answered by temple personnel; the prophet's use of the form would have alluded to such rites and given it pedagogical power.[30]

My own understanding of Mic 6 differs, suggesting that the chapter implies one consistent speaking voice: that of YHWH. In 6:6-8, YHWH (not the prophet) recites a known temple entrance liturgy as a reminder that the people know what is required of them. While it may seem odd for YHWH to quote a liturgy and speak of the divine self in the third person, such a literary style is not uncommon in the Hebrew Bible. In Exod 34:6-7, YHWH speaks in the third person, articulating a profession widely believed to have been an ancient cultic credo (quoted in Neh 9:31; Pss 86:15; 103:8; 111:4; 112:4; 116:6; 145:8; Joel 2:13; Jonah 4:2).

> The LORD passed before him, and proclaimed,
>> "The LORD, the LORD,
>> a God merciful and gracious,
>> slow to anger,
>> and abounding in steadfast love and faithfulness,
>> keeping steadfast love for the thousandth generation,
>> forgiving iniquity and transgression and sin,

---

28. Ben Zvi, *Micah*, 148–49.

29. James Nogalski, *The Book of the Twelve: Hosea through Jonah* (Macon, GA: Smith and Helwys, 2011), 574.

30. Anderson and Freedman, *Micah*, 501. Marvin Sweeney, *The Twelve Prophets*, vol. 2 (Collegeville, MN: Liturgical Press, 2000), 398.

Mic 6:6-8

⁶"With what shall I come before
the LORD,
and bow myself before God on
high?
Shall I come before him with burnt
offerings,
with calves a year old?
⁷Will the LORD be pleased with
thousands of rams,
with ten thousands of rivers of
oil?
Shall I give my firstborn for my
transgression,
the fruit of my body for the sin
of my soul?"
⁸He has told you, O mortal, what
is good;
and what does the LORD require of you
but to do justice, and to love kindness,
and to walk humbly with your
God?

---

yet by no means clearing the guilty,
but visiting the iniquity of the parents
upon the children
and the children's children,
to the third and the fourth generation."

In Mic 6:6-8, YHWH mirrors back to the people what they regularly profess in a cultic form: they know that the deity calls not for child sacrifice and rivers of oil but for people to act justly.

The specific instructions are threefold, translated in the NRSV "do justice, love kindness, and walk humbly with your God." The first two nouns are mentioned frequently in the Hebrew Bible, yet in diverse contexts. The first, משפט ("justice"), is related to the verb for "judge or govern" (שפט) and thus implies a sense of "what is right" in ethical and legal terms; for this reason, the NRSV translates the same noun as "judgment" in 2 Chr 19:6; as "ordinance" in Num 27:11; as "just decisions" in Deut 16:18; and as "law" in Lev 24:22. The second, חסד ("kindness"), can be used in many ways but primarily refers to loyalty to one's commitments; the term frequently appears in biblical accounts of covenant making (Gen 24:27; 1 Sam 20:8). The third verb, צנע ("walk humbly"), appears only here in the whole Hebrew Bible; its translation is based on its similarity to a word meaning "be reserved" in later Hebrew texts and one word meaning "modest" in Prov 11:2. Rather than prescribing or proscribing particular behaviors, these statements set forth general virtues: Do what is right. Keep your promises. Do not think too highly of yourself.

Many interpretations, such as that of Rev. Kharma Amos (see p. 90), treat Mic 6:8 as the "punch line" of this chapter and of Micah as a whole, seeing this verse as a new and distinctive teaching of the prophet. And yet nothing expressed in Mic 6:6-8 would have been a new teaching in the ancient world. The Hebrew Bible resounds with calls to justice, righteousness, and faithfulness, and myriad Hebrew Bible and ancient Near Eastern texts insist that the proper treatment of other human beings takes priority over cult requirements, including Isa 1; Amos 5; Pss 40, 51; Prov 15, 21, 27; and the Egyptian "Tale of the Shipwrecked Sailor."[31] This passage is not a radical challenge to the sacrificial system as many have claimed, since even cultures and religious systems that value the sacrificial system stress the values of justice and righteousness. This "both-and" attitude toward sacrifices and ethics is evident in the common invocation of "justice" in the Psalms, which likely originated in temple worship; Ps 33 convenes temple musicians to celebrate that YHWH "loves righteousness and justice" (33:5). The covenantal requirements set forth in the Torah make no distinction between ethics and ritual, presenting all norms for Israel's behavior as commandments from YHWH.

As a reiteration of common knowledge that "doing the right thing" is the prerequisite for the upright life, Mic 6:6-8 is neither a "new teaching" nor the climax of the chapter. Rather, in the literary context of the chapter it serves to establish the grounds for YHWH's charges to follow. Because the people know they should "do justice, love kindness, and walk humbly with your God," their failure to do so is especially egregious.[32]

While social justice movements have often treated Mic 6:6-8 as the "message" of Micah, within the literary context of the book itself the real significance of the words comes from the context in which they are repeated. Similar cases in which authoritative ancient words are invoked as the "answer" to a situation appear throughout the Gospel of Luke. In Luke 10, Jesus does not author a new Golden Rule but instead quotes Lev 19:18 and Deut 6:5 in a context that expands its meaning: everyone may have known that faithful people were to love God and love neighbor, but few would have understood that moral dictum to apply to a Samaritan. In Luke 6:9, Jesus' declaration that human need takes precedence over the Sabbath is actually a well-known Jewish teaching, recorded in the Mishnah; Jesus scandalizes his audience not by quoting a well-known truth but by invoking it as justification for healing on the Sabbath.

---

31. Ben Zvi, *Micah*, 149.
32. Another perspective is offered in the Matthew Coomber's contribution.

Justice and Power

In Mic 6, YHWH claims the use of power to liberate subjects and win their trust (6:4-5). Missing this message, the people seek atonement by offering increasingly valuable gifts. Perhaps this last-ditch effort to save themselves reveals the priests' and judges' own expectations of receiving gifts in return for favorable prophecies and rulings (see 3:5). The prophet then issues the famous verse of 6:8, in which YHWH seeks only for people to be just and kind toward one another and to walk humbly with God.

The condemnations against corruption in Micah, and the book's prescription for right engagement with collective and individual power, speak to a variety of contemporary justice issues. Whether our power comes from an elected office or positions of societal privilege—gender, race, economic class, sexual orientation, health, or a combination—how we engage with power is a part of daily decision making. Will we use positions of power to better just ourselves or our communities? Will we engage in—or silently tolerate—racist, sexist, disability, or homophobic jokes? Will we speak out against the injustices or turn away? Some forms of corruption are so systemic that they are almost unavoidable due to our economic location: can I afford fair-trade products instead of those that are cultivated or manufactured under exploitative conditions? The condemnations against corruption in Micah, as well as in the greater prophetic corpus, encourage us to wrestle with the tough questions that surround our relationships to power and how we engage those who abuse theirs.

Matthew Coomber

Justice and Structural Change

Micah 6:8 is much beloved in Metropolitan Community Churches. It is painted on church walls, included in congregational mission statements, and recited with passion in contexts ranging from the personal to the legislative. In the midst of a too complicated world, this clarion call to return to the basics and do the right thing is refreshing. It strips away the pretense of religiosity and grounds us again in the simple (though not easy) charge to align ourselves with the heart of divine justice. But, justice itself is complicated, and what it looks like varies widely based on the perspective of the one(s) imagining it.

Along with other prophets, Micah has a heart for the disenfranchised and envisions a reversal of the status quo. Those who have no land will have it, those without voice will speak, and those who have enjoyed the privilege of power and wealth will be held accountable for their excess. This is certainly good news, but is it justice?

One of the most prioritized and publicized current "justice issues" in the queer community is that of "marriage equality." Much progress has been made, with same-sex marriage now legal throughout the United States and multiple other countries. For my part, I both celebrate and lament these advances. It is wonderful to know that "rights" previously granted to those whose sexually intimate relationships are deemed legitimate because they are heterosexual are now open (within limits) to same-gender loving couples who choose to marry. This still seems to me, however, a "tweaking" of an unjust system. The larger questions about whether or not any system should privilege people who conform to a particular structure/form of relationship remain unanswered. Redistribution of privilege does not do enough to deconstruct the system that affords that privilege in the first place.

In the case of Micah, to include more people in the ownership of land or people does not deconstruct "ownership" of land or people, neither of which should be "owned." In the case of marriage equality, to include more people in a system that promotes binary pair bonding as the only legitimate form of relationship does nothing to deconstruct the fear of scarcity of love, a renewable resource that is neither scarce nor limited. We would do better to talk about the qualities of justice, mercy, and kindness instead of focusing on what superficial shape they may take.

My denomination has spent much energy seeking to gain legitimacy in the eyes of the mainstream church and national legislative bodies. This has been a worthwhile effort. And, it has also distracted us from being who we are rather than who the world wants us to be. My hope, my prayer, is that we will heed Micah's call in a different, simpler way. I hope that we might let the familiar words—do justice, love kindness, walk humbly with God—strip away our pretense of religiosity and our desire for external validation and simply be at one with the heart of divine justice.

Kharma Amos

Justice in Biblical Perspective

Western philosophy generally summarizes the demands of justice as "give to each what is due" or "treat similar cases similarly." Injustice occurs when either of these formal requirements is violated, as when women doing work equivalent to that of men are not paid similarly. Determining what is "due," however, has proven contentious; are benefits due based on merit, need, effort, contribution, or some other quality? In the face of these difficulties, some contemporary philosophers and feminists believe that we can no longer find any universal standards for what is due to people. Justice seems to have lost its grounding even as cries for justice increase. Some feminists have also challenged the adequacy of justice as a framework, arguing that "care" requires us to be particular and contextual, whereas "justice" appears too abstract and formal to meet people's genuine needs.

In contrast in philosophical notions, biblical justice is grounded in remembrance of the saving activity of Yahweh and the covenant between Yahweh and the people. It entails bringing the world in line with God's intentions. Those intentions include: (1) shalom, a complete harmony and wholeness of being; (2) an "option for the poor," such that justice is never done when the poor are left powerless, hungry,

and suffering; and (3) a clear linking between justice and "mercy," as is evident in Micah. Further, (4) justice becomes an internal characteristic—a virtue, rather than simply an action to be taken, as in Micah's linking of justice with "humility." At the same time, (5) justice has primarily to do with structures and how they operate in the world to keep all people trapped in oppressive systems. Justice requires not simply *mishpat*, or the completion of specified duties, but also *sedaqah*, the fulfillment of righteousness in which ultimately everything is in "right relation."

A biblical perspective on justice further affirms that we live in the midst of injustice. In Micah, people have lost their ancestral lands and been thrust into poverty; the gap has grown between the rich elite and the poor peasants. Biblical justice means reversing this situation. This is reflected in the way that Mic 6 takes on the character of a courtroom drama in which Yahweh will bring accusations against the people and judge them for their failure to do what they have covenanted to do: justice, mercy, and humility.

If we live in the midst of injustice, then justice takes on the primary characteristic of being corrective or reparative. Philosophers tend to ignore the need for restorative justice, offering either a vision of an ideal approach to justice that is simply grounded in human reason under "fair" conditions (e.g., John Rawls), or a vision of justice as fairness in exchange (e.g., Robert Nozick). Although Rawls is greatly concerned that "starting points" in society disadvantage some people, he does not build a theory of justice designed to overcome concrete, historical injustices. Micah's vision and call does precisely this.

Since we live in the midst of injustice, oppression—and, hence, power and its use and abuse—becomes a central theme to any consideration of what it means to "do justice." Wealth and power tend to go together. Empowerment of the poor thus becomes a litmus test for justice.

In the midst of oppression, systems and structures ("powers and principalities") become primary subjects of justice. Justice can mean "doing the right thing" (*mishpat*), but it can also mean "letting justice roll down like waters and righteousness like an ever flowing stream" (Amos 5:24). I once lived in a small town in which a tiny stream ran right behind my house. During an El Niño year, the stream became a raging river. Rocks tumbled down from the sides of the embankment, entire trees were uprooted and floated down the torrents, and the road into town became blocked as the river rose over the bridge. I held my breath and prayed that the waters would not come all the way up to my house and wash it away too. The landscape was never the same again. This image of a justice that demolishes and leaves a different landscape behind is quite different from the injunction to "give to each what is due" that generally is taken to be the requirement of justice in philosophical circles. Biblical justice has this character, all-encompassing and requiring entirely new systems and structures and not just single acts of giving to each what is due. Justice is not simply a principle or standard but rather a command that is powerful, pervasive, and majestic.

Karen Lebacqz

Accusations of Breach of Covenant (Mic 6:9-12)

Prior to Mic 6:9, the chapter has established that (1) by protecting the people from harm, YHWH has honored his own covenantal obligations; and (2) Israel is bound by covenant to fulfill the obligations YHWH had set forth. Having laid this groundwork, the chapter now moves to the specification of the charges against the people and their sentencing. The courtroom setting is again invoked by the appeal to "hear!" (1:2; 3:9; 6:2).

Moving from the grounds for accusation to the accusation proper, YHWH now calls the people to admit their guilt. Specifically, YHWH

Mic 6:9-12

[9]The voice of the LORD cries to the city
(it is sound wisdom to fear your name):
Hear, O tribe and assembly of the city!
[10]Can I forget the treasures of wickedness in the house of the wicked,
and the scant measure that is accursed?
[11]Can I tolerate wicked scales and a bag of dishonest weights?
[12]Your wealthy are full of violence; your inhabitants speak lies, with tongues of deceit in their mouths.

calls to "the city," unspecified but likely Jerusalem. The meaning of the rest of 6:9 is unclear. The NRSV translation is based on the Septuagint: "it is sound wisdom to fear your name: Hear, O tribe and assembly of the city!" The MT more literally reads, "wisdom he fears your name; Hear, O tribe [or scepter]; For who will appoint her?" Most translations follow the Septuagint, although the New Jerusalem Bible leaves out the phrase altogether such that 6:9 reads, "Yahweh's voice! He thunders to the city, 'Listen, tribe of assembled citizens!'"

The charges that follow focus on the greed and dishonesty of the wealthy. The rich have filled their storehouses with wicked proceeds and been duplicitous in business—shortchanging customers in measures of grain (an *ephah* basket holds about forty liters) and trading with inaccurate scales and fraudulent measuring weights.

According to the book of Amos, such trade transgressions were both common in ancient Israel and abominable in YHWH's sight. Amos 8:4-6 announces judgment against those who

trample on the needy,
    and bring to ruin the poor of the land,
saying, "When will the new moon be over
    so that we may sell grain;
and the sabbath,
    so that we may offer wheat for sale?
We will make the ephah small and the shekel great,
    and practice deceit with false balances,
buying the poor for silver
    and the needy for a pair of sandals,
    and selling the sweepings of the wheat."

Leviticus 19:36 further clarifies that such practices were also breaches of Israel's covenantal obligations to God:

You shall have honest balances, honest weights, an honest ephah, and an honest hin [a liquid measure of about one gallon]: I am the LORD your God, who brought you out of the land of Egypt.

As in Mic 3:9-11, elites within the society are accused of perverting justice for their own financial gain. In 6:11-12, however, more direct focus is placed on the wealthy and on trade practices.

Marvin Sweeney suggests that the accusations may extend to the temple, since the word אצרות, translated as "treasures [of the wicked]" in the NRSV, is the same word used elsewhere for the storehouses of the temple (2 Kgs 12:19; 16:8; 1 Chr 26).[33] Similarly, Nogalski claims, "Micah 6:10 levies this accusation against the Jerusalem temple because it functions as a center of sinfulness."[34]

In extending its critique to the temple, the Persian-period author of Micah would have been accusing not only religious leaders but also the administrative leadership of the community. As discussed in the introduction of this commentary, Jerusalem's temple functioned within the context of the Persian imperial system, and its leaders played key roles within the larger imperial economy. Nehemiah 13:13 lists those put in charge of the temple treasuries: a priest, a scribe, a Levite, and "alongside them" a particular Hanan who also appears in Neh 8:7 as helping teach the people the law. Nehemiah 10 lists two persons with the name Hanan: one who is one of the "associates" of the Levites (10:10) and another who is one of the "heads" (ראש) of the people (10:26).[35] I find the resonances between Mic 6 and Neh 13 intriguing: Nehemiah mentions men who are put in charge of the treasures because they are trusted to be honest in "distributing" to the people, while Mic 6:10 blasts unjust treasuries. Claiming that the author of Micah was explicitly addressing the individuals named in Neh 13 is overly-speculative, but such a possibility reminds us that seemingly generic accusations are "personal" in particular times and places.

Sentencing (Mic 6:13-16)

As punishment for breaches of covenant obligations, "you" will be stripped of all gain. Judah's sentencing takes the classic form of futility curses included in the enforcement provisions of ancient Near Eastern

33. Sweeney, *The Twelve Prophets*, 2:40.
34. Nogalski, *The Book of the Twelve*, 575.
35. See the discussion of Mic 2 in this volume.

Mic 6:13-16

13Therefore I have begun to strike you down,
making you desolate because of your sins.
14You shall eat, but not be satisfied,
and there shall be a gnawing hunger within you;
you shall put away, but not save,
and what you save, I will hand over to the sword.
15You shall sow, but not reap;
you shall tread olives, but not anoint yourselves with oil;
you shall tread grapes, but not drink wine.
16For you have kept the statutes of Omri
and all the works of the house of Ahab,
and you have followed their counsels.
Therefore I will make you a desolation, and your inhabitants an object of hissing;
so you shall bear the scorn of my people.

treaties and the biblical texts modeled on them. Deuteronomy 28, for example, threatens that if the people do not obey YHWH's commandments (28:15), then

> you shall carry much seed into the field but shall gather little in, for the locust shall consume it. You shall plant vineyards and dress them, but you shall neither drink the wine nor gather the grapes, for the worm shall eat them. You shall have olive trees throughout all your territory, but you shall not anoint yourself with the oil, for your olives shall drop off. (28:38-40)

Prophetic texts such as Zeph 1:13 threaten the same:

> Their wealth shall be plundered,
>   and their houses laid waste.
> Though they build houses,
>   they shall not inhabit them;
> though they plant vineyards,
>   they shall not drink wine from them.

In Mic 6, YHWH reverses the image of prosperity captured in Mic 4. According to Nogalski, "The peace and fertility of the land anticipated in 4:3-4 will not happen before YHWH's punishment, which will then bring the opposite."[36]

36. Ibid., 576.

In the course of sentencing, another accusation is added to Israel's list: rather than following the statutes of YHWH, Israel has followed the statutes of Omri and Ahab. These two kings of Israel are excoriated in 1 Kings, with Omri deemed more evil than any king before him (1 Kgs 16:25) and Ahab described as yet more evil than his father (1 Kgs 16:30). The writer of Micah may allude to these kings because of their general evil reputation, or perhaps because of the resonances between one particular Ahab story and the charges made here. First Kings 21 recounts the tale of a landowner named Naboth whose ancestral fields are confiscated by Ahab and his wife Jezebel through trumped up legal charges. Both Ahab's and Micah's audiences are accused of sin (1 Kgs 21:22; Mic 6:13); Ahab "sold himself" to do evil (1 Kgs 21:20), just as the people are accused of doing; and both guilty parties are threatened with extinction (1 Kgs 21:21-24).

Assessing Micah 6

How might Mic 6 have resonated within the context of the Persian period? On a theological level, these accusations (like those in Mic 1–3) would have served to explain the reasons for the Babylonian destruction of Jerusalem; when read in the Persian period as the prediction of an eighth-century prophet of YHWH's just punishment for corruption, it would have underscored Judah's own responsibility for its fate. This second round of accusation might take on greater weight than the first round in Mic 1–3 since it follows two chapters of hopeful promises. In the literary context of the book, Mic 6 reiterates that while YHWH might in the future forgive Jerusalem, the sins of the wealthy justifiably outraged YHWH.

While the accusations against the wealthy and the futility curses leveled in 6:9-16 would have primarily characterized the sins of preexilic Judah, they may have resonated with a Persian-period audience as well. Olive oil and wine, items singled out for deprivation, were key elements of not only the Persian-period diet but also its economy. Zipporah Glass's study of Yehud's economy indicates that "the agricultural patterns in Yehud appear consistent with that known from the Iron Age, being an economic mix of agrarian production, primarily of grains, wine, oil, and animal husbandry. . . . Both domestic and industrial complexes, such as village-worked threshing floors, wine and olive oil-presses, played a part in maintaining the economy and supporting individual households."[37]

37. Zipporah Glass, "Land, Labor, and Law: Viewing Persian Yehud's Economy through Socio-Economic Modeling" (PhD diss., Vanderbilt University, 2010).

As foodstuffs, olive oil and wine were staples of the ancient Mediterranean diet. Nathan MacDonald has suggested that an Israelite may have received 11 percent of daily calorie intake from olive oil and consumed one liter of wine per day.[38] Both were also traded. As Christine Yoder notes, "Nehemiah describes the marketplace of Persian-period Jerusalem as bustling with merchants plying their goods, people treading wine-presses, and animals loaded with heaps of grain, grapes, and figs— even on the Sabbath (Neh 13:15-16; see also Neh 10:31)."[39] Olive oil was prized not only as food but also as lamp fuel and a rub for the body.

Such commodities, however, were not shared equally among all segments of the population. Glass argues that while food production in Yehud was adequate to feed the whole colony, the mechanisms of food distribution produced an inequality in access to food. As discussed more fully in my introduction, the burden of supporting both Persian imperial representatives and the Jerusalem temple personnel placed enormous burden on average Yehudites. Nehemiah 5 reflects a situation in which "the problem for the community was that the distribution of the increased average supplies was not towards those who were the most in need or food deprived but toward an elite group of consumers, so that the needy remained numerous."[40] Nathan MacDonald suggests that the same inequities arose when Judah operated under Assyrian imperial control in the eighth and seventh centuries: in preexilic Judah, it is likely that "olive oil consumption varied markedly with social class."[41]

In an economy in which the wealthy have greater control of and access to olive oil and wine, the futility curses of Mic 6 might be seen as a direct challenge to the province's elite. Their dishonest appropriation of food and trade stuffs gets them nowhere; the oil they produce cannot be used to anoint their bodies; the wine they produce cannot be drunk; and the savings they have hoarded will be lost. If the "house" in 6:10 refers to the storehouses of the temple (see above), then the wealthy being accused include temple personnel. The average Yehudite would have likely already experienced this futility, already having surrendered the fruits of their labors to the temple treasuries (Neh 13:12) and the "king's tax" (Neh 5:4).

---

38. Nathan MacDonald, *What Did the Ancient Israelites Eat? Diet in Biblical Times* (Grand Rapids, MI: Eerdmans, 2008).

39. Christine Yoder, "The Woman of Substance: A Socioeconomic Reading of Proverbs 31:10-31," *JBL* 122 (2003): 441.

40. Glass, "Land, Labor, and Law," 40–41.

41. MacDonald, *What Did the Ancient Israelites Eat?*, 24.

The "working poor" in contemporary societies share the experience of lower-class Yehudites. They know what it is to "eat but not be satisfied" with the food they can afford on minimal wages and never to be able to "anoint" themselves from what they earn. Micah's curses, it seems, threaten the wealthy with the realities of many people's daily lives.

In the past and in the present, economic privilege often follows gender lines. While in the contemporary era women's earnings and access to goods have increased globally, they still lag behind those of men. The fact that Mic 6 does not explicitly mention the dimensions of gender or class can be seen as both a shortcoming and a relief. As a shortcoming, it leaves unnamed the distinctive ways in which economic deprivation affects women—their increased likelihood of prostitution and sexual assault, as well as their additional burden of supporting children. As a relief, Micah avoids blaming wealthy women for the evils of their husbands, unlike Amos 5. As Judith Sanderson notes, "Amos specifically condemned wealthy women for oppressing the poor (4:1) but failed specifically to champion the women among the poor."[42] Although the masculine "you" condemned is not named, in Mic 6 a male figure shares the blame shouldered alone by Daughter Jerusalem in Mic 1–3.

The insistence of Mic 6:8 that the Divine One calls humans to "do the right thing" does not provide a program for addressing gender injustice. But for those of us who see the injustice inherent in our own society's rules for gender, the reminder to "do justice" can inspire and motivate us to continue our work.

Daughter Jerusalem's Response, in Conversation with YHWH (Mic 7:1-20)

Micah 7 returns to the lament form that is so prevalent in the first three chapters of the book, as the speaker decries the lack of justice in the community. The mood shifts in Mic 7:7, with an expression of confidence in YHWH that builds in intensity and concludes with a moving paean (and implied appeal) to divine mercy. The chapter (and book) end in trust that YHWH will be loyal to the present community just as YHWH was loyal to the ancestors.

42. Judith Sanderson, "Amos," in *The Women's Bible Commentary*, ed. Carol Newsom and Sharon H. Ringe (Louisville, KY: Westminster/John Knox Press, 1992), 206.

> **Institute for Women's Policy Research Fact Sheet, April 2014**
>
> Women's median earnings [in the United States] are lower than men's in nearly all occupations, whether they work in occupations predominantly done by women, occupations predominantly done by men, or occupations with a more even mix of men and women. Data for both women's and men's median weekly earnings for full-time work are available for 112 occupations: there are only three occupations in which women have higher median weekly earnings than men. In 101 of the 112 occupations, the gender earnings ratio of women's median weekly earnings to men's is 0.95 or lower (that is, a wage gap of at least 5 cents per dollar earned by men): in 17 of these occupations the gender earnings ratio is lower than 0.75 (that is, a wage gap of more than 25 cents per dollar earned by men). During 2013, median weekly earnings for female full-time workers were $706, compared with $860 per week for men, a gender wage ratio of 82.1 percent.[43]

Identifying the speaker(s) of the chapter is difficult. Especially when read in Hebrew, the person, number, and gender of speaker and addressee shift several times, usually without identification:

- in vv. 1-10, speaker is a first-person singular "I," with YHWH described in third person

- in v. 11, an unidentified speaker refers to "your" walls, using a feminine singular pronoun

- in v. 12, the "you" to whom peoples will come is masculine singular

- in v. 14, imperatives call a masculine singular "you" to shepherd "your" people, apparently addressing YHWH

- in v. 15, a masculine "you" is said to have come out of Egypt, while a first-person singular "I" promises to show wonders: while the NRSV reads "show us" as an imperative, the NRSV textual footnote acknowledges that the Hebrew reads, "I will show him"

43. Ariane Hegewisch and Stephanie Keller Hudiburg, "The Gender Wage Gap by Occupation and by Race and Ethnicity, 2013," IWPR #C414, Institute for Women's Policy Research, http://www.iwpr.org/publications/pubs/the-gender-wage-gap-by-occupation-and-by-race-and-ethnicity-2013.

- in vv. 16-20, YHWH is described as "our God" and called "you" and "he"[44]

Many scholars suggest that the changing voices in Mic 7 indicate that some or all of the chapter constitutes a temple liturgy with different speaking parts for communal reading. This possibility is strengthened by the stylistic similarities between Mic 7 and other liturgical compositions in the Hebrew Bible. For example, the chapter begins with complaint, turns to an expression of confidence, and ends with an assurance of salvation, the same pattern for most psalms of lament; it ends with praise of a YHWH who saves, as does Hab 3 (which is marked in the biblical text as a psalm); and its alternating voices may reflect that it was used responsively, as suggested in Ps 24. Based on these similarities, in 1903 Bernhard Stade designated Mic 7:7-20 as a psalm, and in 1928 Hermann Gunkel argued that it was a "prophetic liturgy"—a responsive reading for use in worship, based on the teaching of the prophet. Reading along similar lines, Marvin Sweeney recognizes two liturgical forms in the book: a lament in 7:1-6 and a (prophetic) psalm of confidence in 7:7-10.[45]

Rex Mason understands the entire chapter as one single prophetic liturgy which he outlines in this way: 7:1-6, the complaint of the prophet; 7:7-10, the prophet's expression of trust; 7:11-13, YHWH's promise of salvation; 7:14-17, the prophet's renewed prayer of trust; 7:18-20, affirmation of faith and trust in the future. He claims that the teaching of the eighth-century prophet Micah was recited in the temple in this liturgical form in the postexilic period: "Parallels to other such prophetic liturgies (e.g., Hos 14.1-7), to some of the Psalms, and to Lamentations show that here the theological statements of the book and general post-exilic prophetic themes have passed over into the language of worship. . . . The book of Micah, then, shows how the words of a pre-exilic prophet could become the text for a proclamation of the certainty of God's salvation for the people who had suffered, and in many ways were still suffering, the judgments of which the prophet had spoken."[46]

---

44. Erin Runions points out even additional shifts: *Changing Subjects: Gender, Nation, and Future in Micah* (London and New York: Sheffield Academic Press, 2001), 173–81.

45. Sweeney, *The Twelve Prophets*, 2:406.

46. Rex Mason, *Micah, Nahum, and Obadiah*, OTG (Sheffield: JSOT Press, 1991), 53. Similarly Nogalski: "Micah 7:8-20 . . . is a late composition that is intended to be read as a prophetic liturgy set in the time of Hezekiah at the end of the eighth century, but whose message anticipates the fate of Judah over the seventh century." Nogalski, *The Book of the Twelve*, 585.

Other scholars have raised the possibility of a female speaker within the chapter. With others, Judith Sanderson identifies the speaking voice of Mic 7:8-10 as Daughter Jerusalem.[47] James Nogalski recognizes that the speaker of 7:1-10 might be understood as either Daughter Jerusalem or the prophet, but he argues that the identification of the speaker as the prophet makes better rhetorical sense.[48]

My own claim is that a feminine voice runs throughout Micah: the chapter as a whole is an imagined dialogue between Daughter Jerusalem and YHWH.[49] In 7:1-10, the feminine city responds to the speech that was made against the city in the previous chapter. In 7:11-13, YHWH promises her deliverance. In 7:14-20, Daughter Jerusalem appeals to YHWH, with a brief interruption of YHWH's voice in 7:15.

While I recognize the influence of liturgical forms highlighted by other scholars, my own interpretation focuses primarily on the way in which the chapter returns to and completes the motifs and themes developed earlier in the book of Micah. Micah 7 completes the story of Daughter Jerusalem's judgment and salvation, returning to the themes of shepherding, exodus, and the ancestors. Like the book of Lamentations, in which Daughter Jerusalem laments her fate and appeals for divine mercy, the book of Micah imagines the community's current dire situation and its hopes for the future as that of the situation of a suffering woman. And yet, as elsewhere in the book, the writer of Micah leaves invisible the suffering women—and men—of his own community. His universalizing theological formulations affect people's real lives but do not necessarily reflect the experiences or nourish the imaginations of all humans.

Daughter Jerusalem's Lament and Expression of Confidence (Mic 7:1-10)

The opening interjection אללי (NRSV, "woe") reproduces the sound of wailing, as does the modern term "ululation," which also derives from this Semitic root. As noted above, most interpreters understand the voice as that of the prophet and/or the liturgical leader who speaks in the

---

47. Judith Sanderson, "Micah," in Newsom and Ringe, *Women's Bible Commentary* (1992), 216.

48. Nogalski, *The Book of the Twelve*, 578.

49. I recognize the legitimacy of identifying Mic 7:1-10 as the voice of the prophet. Such identification would link 7:7 with 3:8: in both, a speaker trusts in YHWH, in opposition to those who pervert justice. For reasons explained above, however, I believe that the speaker is better identified as Daughter Jerusalem.

prophet's name; some suggest a shift in speakers midway through the unit, with the prophet and/or implied author speaking in Mic 7:1-7 but Daughter Jerusalem appearing in 7:8-10.

My claim is that Daughter Jerusalem is the single implied voice of Mic 7:1-10. Having received her sentencing (6:1-16), she now takes on the role once played by others: the prophet and the cities of the Shephelah once lamented her fate (1:8-16; 2:1-5), but now she laments for herself. Her expression of pain, however, does not rule out her confidence in the divine promises already made. In Mic 4, YHWH promised to empower Jerusalem (4:12-13) over the enemies who clamored to gaze at her public defilement (4:9-11). In Mic 7, she acknowledges her situation (7:1-6) but remains convinced that YHWH will turn the tables so that she can be the one who gazes on the public shame of another (7:7-10).

Jerusalem's lament depicts her current situation with agricultural metaphors and with moving realistic depictions of community dissolution. The first such metaphor is that of fruit: even after the harvest, she finds no grapes or fig to eat. As Nathan MacDonald explains, both fruits were significant to the ancient Israelite economy and also "had emotional and symbolic resonances in the Old Testament."[50] Given that the ancient Israelite diet included few sweets, the first fruit of spring would have been especially desirable (Isa 28:4; Hos 9:10), when grape vines and figs give forth their sweet fragrance (Song 2:13). Like one without a taste of sweet fruit after a long winter, Jerusalem laments that nothing is pleasant.

The breakdown of social relationships is described in totalizing terms. Jerusalem complains that the world is completely devoid of pious and upright people and that a man hunts his brother with a net. This metaphor of entrapment also appears in Hab 1:15-17, and in Eccl 7:26 it describes a promiscuous woman, "whose heart is snares and nets." In her time of pain and crisis, Daughter Jerusalem sees everyone as corrupt.

Returning to themes developed earlier in the book, Mic 7:3-4 decries the corruption of officials controlled by bribes. In Mic 3, "heads" (root ראש) were blamed for "judging" (root שפט) for a price and were twice paralleled with "chiefs" (root קצנ).[51] In 7:3, a new term, "official" (root שר), is paired with "judge" (root שפט). All of these terms used in Micah for leaders appear in postexilic texts and are sometimes used interchangeably. For example, in 1 Chr 29:6, "official" (root שר) describes the

---

50. MacDonald, *What Did the Ancient Israelites Eat?*, 29.
51. See discussion of Mic 3 above.

Mic 7:1-10

¹Woe is me! For I have become like one who,
after the summer fruit has been gathered,
after the vintage has been gleaned,
finds no cluster to eat;
there is no first-ripe fig for which I hunger.
²The faithful have disappeared from the land,
and there is no one left who is upright;
they all lie in wait for blood,
and they hunt each other with nets.
³Their hands are skilled to do evil;
the official and the judge ask for a bribe,
and the powerful dictate what they desire;
thus they pervert justice.
⁴The best of them is like a brier,
the most upright of them a thorn hedge.
The day of their sentinels, of their punishment, has come;
now their confusion is at hand.
⁵Put no trust in a friend,
have no confidence in a loved one;
guard the doors of your mouth
from her who lies in your embrace;

head of a group called the "ancestral houses" (אבות) while in Ezra 1:5 the "ancestral houses" (אבות) are led by the "heads" (root ראש). In 2 Chr 19:8, Levites, priests, and the "heads" of the "ancestral houses" (אבות) take on the role of "judge" (root שפט). As noted in my discussion in this volume of Mic 3, Daniel Smith(-Christopher) argues that these labels reflect the organization of the postexilic community, in which large groups were bound together by fictions of kinship within the parameters of an imperial system.⁵² Since all leaders of the community—whether Yehudite or Persian—would have functioned within the framework of Persian imperial control, Micah's complaint has an implied political edge.

Micah 7:4 is difficult to translate, though the NRSV reading reflects its gist quite well: a day of recompense is coming. While now "everyone" inflicts pain like briers and thorns, lookouts ("sentinels") will soon announce that the time of "everyone's" punishment has arrived, throwing them all into confusion. Such vocabulary echoes descriptions of the Day of YHWH that appear throughout the prophetic books. The Day is a time in which God will bring justice, either reversing Israel's subordination

52. Daniel L. Smith, *The Religion of the Landless: The Social Context of the Babylonian Exile* (Bloomington, IN: Meyer-Stone Books, 1989), 98. (See also Daniel L. Smith-Christopher.)

⁶for the son treats the father with
contempt,
the daughter rises up against
her mother,
the daughter-in-law against her
mother-in-law;
your enemies are members of
your own household.
⁷But as for me, I will look to the
LORD,
I will wait for the God of my
salvation;
my God will hear me.
⁸Do not rejoice over me, O my
enemy;
when I fall, I shall rise;
when I sit in darkness,

the LORD will be a light to me.
⁹I must bear the indignation of the
LORD,
because I have sinned against
him,
until he takes my side
and executes judgment for me.
He will bring me out to the light;
I shall see his vindication.
¹⁰Then my enemy will see,
and shame will cover her who
said to me,
"Where is the LORD your
God?"
My eyes will see her downfall;
now she will be trodden down
like the mire of the streets.

to others (Obad 15) or, more commonly, punishing Israel for its sins (Amos 5; Isa 13). Sentinels, sometimes prophets, will announce its arrival (Isa 21:11; Ezek 3:17; 33:2-7; Hos 9:8), and confusion and destruction will ensue (Isa 22:5).

In Mic 7:5, Jerusalem's lament turns to advice: do not trust your family or friends. Underscoring the totality of the community's dissolution, her list of those not to trust grows progressively more intimate: you cannot trust a friend > your best friend > the one with whom you sleep. Micah 7:6 complains that "normal" household relationships are no longer safe: the generational hierarchy within the household is in disarray.

This description of the "bad" family indicates, of course, what the writer assumes about the "good" family: its patriarchal structure. Sons owe respect to their fathers (see Mal 1:6) and daughters should defer to mothers. Other subordinate women in the household are expected to remain within their subordinate roles. The term translated as "daughter-in-law" in the NRSV in Hebrew describes women in various states of dependency: in Isa 49:18 and 2 Sam 17:3 it is translated as "bride," suggesting that the woman here described is expected to submit to the control of her husband's family upon joining his household. The term for "mother-in-law" appears elsewhere in the Hebrew Bible only in the book of Ruth, where it describes Naomi.

In the Gospels of Matthew and Luke, this passage is invoked in the context of Jesus' description of the disruption to family loyalties to be experienced by those who follow him. In a passage likely deriving from the Q source, Matt 10:35 and Luke 12:53 insist that following Jesus is not a family-friendly enterprise. Rather than beat swords into plowshares, claims Matthew, Jesus comes to bring a sword.

In Mic 7:7, Jerusalem turns from complaint to trust. As in psalms of lament, the one who suffers expresses trust in YHWH to save. Emboldened with confidence, she can speak back to her enemy (7:8). Jerusalem anticipates a reversal in fortunes, described with pairs of opposites: though she now falls, she will soon rise; though she now dwells in darkness, light will soon come; though others once threatened to make Daughter Jerusalem into a public spectacle (4:11), she now threatens her feminine enemy with the same fate. Because she accepts her current dire straits as God's just punishment for her sins, she can trust when God's anger subsides she will be redeemed.

In this unit, numerous literary features function to underscore its pathos. As earlier in the book, the use of metaphor allows the complaints to resonate with a wide range of readers. Rather than list a series of wrongs, the writer poetically describes what devastation *feels* like. Betrayal feels like being trapped in a net, devastation feels like being in the dark, and in times of despair we feel that no one can be trusted. Most of us know that being betrayed by the ones we most trust leaves us feeling that we cannot trust anyone and that the whole world is corrupt. Describing the feeling of being alone in an unjust world, the writer of Micah names the pain that centuries of people have felt. We know what this feels like.

Gendered imagery intensifies this pathos. Daughter Jerusalem, whose plight was described in Mic 4 as a woman writhing in labor, threatened with public sexual violation, and cutting herself in anguish, here accepts responsibility for her fate and turns to YHWH for protection. Now contrite and recognizing her dependence, she rises from her humiliation to outshine her enemies. While in 4:11-13 the empowerment of Daughter Jerusalem entailed her masculinization, in 7:8-10 both Jerusalem and her enemy remain feminine. The feminization of her enemy activates gender scripts of the competition among women and of the desire for the good woman to triumph over the evil woman.

Numerous commentators have suggested that the feminine enemy is implied to be Nineveh, the capital of the Assyrian empire. Nogalski explores this identification at length, tracing the unit's allusions to the

> **Matthew 10:34-39**
>
> [34]"Do not think that I have come to bring peace to the earth; I have not come to bring peace, but a sword. [35]For I have come to set a man against his father, and a daughter against her mother, and a daughter-in-law against her mother-in-law; [36]and one's foes will be members of one's own household. [37]Whoever loves father or mother more than me is not worthy of me; and whoever loves son or daughter more than me is not worthy of me; [38]and whoever does not take up the cross and follow me is not worthy of me. [39]Those who find their life will lose it, and those who lose their life for my sake will find it.

anti-Assyrian polemic in Isa 9–10 and pointing to the larger literary framework of the book of Micah, which is set by the superscription in the eighth-century Assyrian context and which explicitly refers to Assyria in Mic 5.[53] He notes the verbal linkages between Mic 7:10 and the prediction of Woman Nineveh's humiliation in Nah 3:14 and suggests that these books are intentionally linked in the larger pattern of the Book of the Twelve: "In the canonical order [of the Twelve], one can even read the two verses as a prediction and (ironic) fulfillment. In Nahum 3:14, [Nineveh] is told to enter the mud and trample the clay, thus essentially doing to herself (in a futile effort to save herself) what Lady Zion anticipates will happen to her in Mic 7:10."[54]

Clearly, Mic 7 pits the feminine Judah/Jerusalem against feminine Nineveh in ways similar to the book of Nahum. In Nahum, Judah is depicted as a woman whom God once punished but will now save (Nah 1:12), while Nineveh is a woman on whom YHWH will exact punishment (Nah 3:4-7): called a whore, Nineveh is sexually humiliated/raped as punishment for her "countless debaucheries," as others are called to watch. One woman is pitted against another, and yet both the good woman and the bad woman are defined according to a single patriarchal gender script.[55] Judah is good because she remains dependent on and loyal to YHWH; Nineveh is bad because she does not. The same script

53. Nogalski, *The Book of the Twelve*, 586.
54. Sweeney, *The Twelve Prophets*, 2:587.
55. For a fuller analysis of gender scripts in Nahum, see Julia Myers O'Brien, *Nahum* (Sheffield: Sheffield Academic Press, 2002).

constructs Mic 7. As Judith Sanderson explains, in Mic 7, "God is a good and just and forgiving male, while the people is at worst an evil and corrupt female and at best a repentant female."[56]

Elsewhere, I have explored Nah 3's depiction of Nineveh's sexual violation in conversation with film studies. Film critic Laura Mulvey's claim that the gaze of the camera in movies such as Hitchcock's *Rear Window* forces us to see the story through a man's eyes finds its parallel in Nahum. In both cases, we see from the male point of view, and the object of our gaze is a female.[57] In contrast, what makes Mic 7 especially interesting is that it shows one woman taking pleasure in imagining the sexual humiliation of another woman. We might see this dynamic as the projection of men's heterosexual desire onto women, but it also could be interpreted as challenging the heterosexual assumption that only men find pleasure in viewing women.

What real-life situation is reflected in the dismal scene depicted in Mic 7:1-10? Sweeney, who interprets the book of Micah within the eighth-century setting of its superscription, suggests that these verses describe the Assyrian siege of Jerusalem in 701 BCE. While the city was closed up under siege, "a refugee such as Micah would likely find himself on the streets of the city scrounging for food."[58] In the Persian period in which I am interpreting Micah, I pinpoint no single event but instead understand the writer as poetically expressing his despair about social dissolution. The claim that people are out to get each other, that children do not show parents proper respect, and that there is no one righteous in the whole earth are perennial laments in human societies. This elasticity of language would allow the poem to be read in the Persian period as both about the past and about the writer's own era. The "family values" expressed in 7:1-10, however, are not universal. Throughout, they reflect the ideology of the patriarchal household, in which even adult children submit to their parents, a woman brought into a family submits to her husband's mother, and one woman's honor is restored when another woman is humiliated.

---

56. Judith Sanderson, "Micah," in *Women's Bible Commentary*, ed. Carol Newsom and Sharon H. Ringe. 2d ed. (Louisville, KY: Westminster John Knox, 1998), 216.

57. Julia M. O'Brien, "Violent Pictures, Violent Cultures? The 'Aesthetics of Violence' in Contemporary Film and in Ancient Prophetic Texts," in *Aesthetics of Violence in the Prophets*, ed. Julia M. O'Brien and Chris Franke (New York and London: T & T Clark, 2010), 112–30.

58. Sweeney, *The Twelve Prophets*, 2:407.

Not everyone considers disruptions to the traditional family as tragic, as the intertextual connections between Mic 7:5-6 and Jesus' description of the kingdom in Matt 10:35 and Luke 12:53 remind us. Other values are possible. Havor Moxnes's study of Jesus' sayings on the family underscores that the earliest traditions of Jesus cast him as challenging patriarchal family structures and perhaps even loyalty to the family itself:

> There are no images of a complete, patriarchal household in sayings about the followers of Jesus or about the kingdom household. . . . The kingdom was not a mirror image of the patriarchal household, it transgressed its boundaries, it had a different composition, and it lacked its hierarchy. Therefore we may say that the household in the kingdom has been "queered." The traditional order has been questioned and twisted. . . . By not fasting, but instead explicitly feasting with persons who were outside the social order, Jesus challenged its boundaries and the way they created divisions among people. Jesus was an ascetic who transgressed the boundaries of what it meant to be male in first-century Palestine. Moreover, he introduced that transgression as characteristic of the kingdom.[59]

The unbinding of traditional family values which is lamented by Daughter Jerusalem in Mic 7:6 is seen as the harbinger of God's kingdom in the gospels.

What were the intergenerational dynamics of the Persian period? Why did members of the younger generation refuse to submit to their parents? The author of Micah does not answer these questions, assuming that his readers will share his values and accept the transgression of family rules as an indicator of community chaos.

YHWH's Promises of Deliverance (Mic 7:11-13)

In Mic 7:11-13, YHWH rewards Daughter Jerusalem's profession of trust with an announcement that the day has come for the building of her walls and the ingathering of her people. While Mic 4 envisioned Jerusalem's exaltation as a future event, in 7:11-13 YHWH announces that the time for her exaltation—and expansion—has come.

The walls of ancient cities represented their security and strength. Primarily defensive structures, they guarded against invading armies

59. Halvor Moxnes, *Putting Jesus in His Place: A Radical Vision of Household and Kingdom* (Louisville, KY: Westminster John Knox Press, 2003), 105.

Mic 7:11-13

11A day for the building of your
        walls!
    In that day the boundary shall
        be far extended.
12In that day they will come to you
    from Assyria to Egypt,

and from Egypt to the River,
    from sea to sea and from
        mountain to mountain.
13But the earth will be desolate
    because of its inhabitants,
    for the fruit of their doings.

and signaled the city's ability to protect its people. The archaeological record of Jerusalem attests to the frequency with which its walls were broken in times of destruction and rebuilt in times of strength. The strategic and symbolic importance of city walls is also reflected throughout biblical literature: the fall of cities is described as the "breach" of their walls (2 Kgs 25:4; Amos 4:3); strong kings are said to have strengthened the city walls (2 Chr 32:5); nations both mock and plunder Jerusalem when it lacks walls (Ps 80:12); and secure city walls serve as a symbol of safety (Ps 144:14).

Postexilic texts underscore the importance of Jerusalem's walls to the community of Yehud. The books of Ezra and Nehemiah narrate the trials and tribulations of the returnees who sought to restore Jerusalem to the status of a walled city, in the face of opposition from neighboring peoples:

> For we are slaves; yet our God has not forsaken us in our slavery, but has extended to us his steadfast love before the kings of Persia, to give us new life to set up the house of our God, to repair its ruins, and to give us a wall in Judea and Jerusalem. (Ezra 9:9)

> Then I said to them, "You see the trouble we are in, how Jerusalem lies in ruins with its gates burned. Come, let us rebuild the wall of Jerusalem, so that we may no longer suffer disgrace." (Neh 2:17)

> Now when Sanballat heard that we were building the wall, he was angry and greatly enraged, and he mocked the Jews. (Neh 4:1)

Postexilic prophetic literature such as Third Isaiah similarly includes Jerusalem's walls in the hopes for the city's restoration.

> Foreigners shall build up your walls,
>   and their kings shall minister to you;
> for in my wrath I struck you down,
>   but in my favor I have had mercy on you.

Your gates shall always be open;
>   day and night they shall not be shut,
> so that nations shall bring you their wealth,
>   with their kings led in procession. (Isa 60:10-11)

The postexilic ending of Amos may envision not only the restoration of the Davidic monarchy but of Jerusalem as David's citadel:

> On that day I will raise up
>   the booth of David that is fallen,
> and repair its breaches,
>   and raise up its ruins,
>   and rebuild it as in the days of old. (Amos 9:11)

That Mic 7:11 envisions the building of Jerusalem's walls as imminent but not yet accomplished could indicate that it was composed prior to 445, the date of the completion of the walls based on the chronology presented in Nehemiah. Seen in this way, Mic 7 may call for and anticipate the building of Jerusalem's walls just as Zechariah calls for and anticipates the building of the second temple. The retrospective nature of the book of Micah, however, complicates such precise dating. Because the book is presented as the predictions of an eighth-century prophet, any time period after the eighth century may be reflected: either events between the eighth and fifth centuries (events known to the Persian-period writer of Micah) or events after the fifth century (hoped for by the Persian-period writer).

In this short unit, however, the building of Jerusalem's walls does not stand as a singular event. Rather, wall building will inaugurate the expansion of the land's borders (Mic 7:11), the ingathering of its dispersed from the far reaches of the earth (7:12), and the desolation of the nations who once troubled Judah (7:13). While related to the vision of Jerusalem's exaltation in Mic 4, the vision of 7:1-13 focuses on the fate of the return of exiles. In this way, it parallels hopes expressed in other postexilic prophetic literature:

> I will bring them home from the land of Egypt,
>   and gather them from Assyria;
> I will bring them to the land of Gilead and to Lebanon,
>   until there is no room for them. (Zech 10:10)

> On that day the LORD will extend his hand yet a second time to recover the remnant that is left of his people, from Assyria, from Egypt, from Pathros, from Ethiopia, from Elam, from Shinar, from Hamath, and from the coastlands of the sea. (Isa 11:11)

As Hans Walter Wolff explains, the promise of Mic 7:11-13 is "broad enough to include the last dispersed Israelites as well, wherever they might be scattered between the Mediterranean and the Persian Gulf, between Sinai and Lebanon. . . . With the consummation of YHWH's lawsuit with his people, the end is coming not only to the judgment upon Jerusalem and its (hitherto narrowly drawn) borders, but also to Israel's dispersion."[60]

While the book of Zechariah pins its future hopes on the rebuilding of the temple and the book of Micah focuses on the building of the walls, both long for Jerusalem's expansion, a swell in its population, and recompense against the nations.

> Proclaim this message: Thus says the LORD of hosts; I am very jealous for Jerusalem and for Zion. And I am extremely angry with the nations that are at ease; for while I was only a little angry, they made the disaster worse. Therefore, thus says the LORD, I have returned to Jerusalem with compassion; my house shall be built in it, says the LORD of hosts, and the measuring line shall be stretched out over Jerusalem. Proclaim further: Thus says the LORD of hosts: My cities shall again overflow with prosperity; the LORD will again comfort Zion and again choose Jerusalem. (Zech 1:14-17)

The hopes expressed in Mic 7 could reflect either the writer's hopes for the future construction of the wall or the writer's hopes that the recently completed construction of the wall portends other divine acts of salvation.

Daughter Jerusalem's Final Appeals (7:14-20)

In response to YHWH's promise to once again favor Jerusalem, the city issues a plaintive plea for a return to earlier days, in which YHWH served as the people's shepherd. Earlier in the book, Jerusalem's future king and its princes were described as shepherds (Mic 5:4-6; 5:3-5 MT); here, YHWH alone is shepherd. Images of lush pastureland are evoked by references to Carmel and Bashan. The Hebrew word translated as "garden land" is literally "Gilead," opening the possibility that a third agrarian location is imagined. In other postexilic prophetic texts that develop similar sheep/shepherd imagery, these locales characterize the peace of the people:

60. Wolff, *Micah*, 225.

EXCURSUS
The Irony of Walls

Walls serve many functions. They define places of refuge, but they also form prisons. They exclude. They define. They exalt (Mic 7:11), but they also hem in (Mic 5:1; 4:14 MT).

History attests to the complex dynamics of walls, how the same barriers that are touted as necessary for safety can become mechanisms of oppression for those who find themselves on the "wrong" side. The walls of the Jewish ghettos throughout Europe were claimed as necessary to protect Christians from Jews and Jews from Christian mobs, and yet they became boundaries of deprivation and massacre. The Berlin Wall was built to protect its people from fascists, though it became an oppressive "Iron Curtain" between East and West.

Though its builders claim that the Separation Barrier that separates the state of Israel from the Palestinian West Bank is necessary to protect Israel from terrorist attacks, the Israeli Committee Against House Demolition has deemed it the "Apartheid Wall," both because it serves to make permanent an apartheid situation between Israelis and Palestinians and also because it rises to a massive concrete wall of eight meters (twenty-six feet) when reaching Palestinian population centers—replete with prison-like watchtowers, gates, security roads, electronic fences, and deadly armaments. While sold to the public as an innocent security device, the Barrier in fact defines the border between Israel (including the areas of the West Bank and East Jerusalem Israel seeks to annex) and the Palestinian mini-state.[61]

In the United States, nearly one million African Americans are incarcerated behind prison walls at a rate nearly six times that of whites. This disparity reflects not a difference in the rate of crimes committed but in conviction rates: African Americans serve virtually as much time in prison for a drug offense (58.7 months) as whites do for a violent offense (61.7 months).[62] The same imprisonment that is claimed as a way to protect society from criminals also reflects and perpetuates racial disparities in the United States.

Julia M. O'Brien

61. Israeli Committee Against House Demolition, "Defining the Palestinian Bantustan. Element #5: The Separation Barrier/Wall," http://www.icahd.org/node/446.

62. NAACP, "Criminal Justice Fact Sheet," http://www.naacp.org/pages/criminal-justice-fact-sheet.

¹⁴Shepherd your people with your staff,
the flock that belongs to you,
which lives alone in a forest
in the midst of a garden land;
let them feed in Bashan and Gilead
as in the days of old.
¹⁵As in the days when you came
out of the land of Egypt,
show us marvelous things.
¹⁶The nations shall see and be ashamed
of all their might;
they shall lay their hands on their mouths;
their ears shall be deaf;
¹⁷they shall lick dust like a snake,
like the crawling things of the earth;
they shall come trembling out of their fortresses;
they shall turn in dread to the Lord our God,
and they shall stand in fear of you.
¹⁸Who is a God like you, pardoning iniquity
and passing over the transgression
of the remnant of your possession?
He does not retain his anger forever,
because he delights in showing clemency.
¹⁹He will again have compassion upon us;
he will tread our iniquities under foot.
You will cast all our sins into the depths of the sea.
²⁰You will show faithfulness to Jacob
and unswerving loyalty to Abraham,
as you have sworn to our ancestors
from the days of old.

I will restore Israel to its pasture, and it shall feed on Carmel and in Bashan, and on the hills of Ephraim and in Gilead its hunger shall be satisfied. (Jer 50:19)

I will bring them home from the land of Egypt, and gather them from Assyria; I will bring them to the land of Gilead and to Lebanon, until there is no room for them. (Zech 10:10)

As discussed in the introduction to this chapter, while the NRSV translation of Mic 7:15 suggests that Daughter Jerusalem continues to speak, the Hebrew text (reflected in the NRSV textual note) reflects a change in speakers. The NIV translation more accurately renders the Hebrew text: "As in the days when you came out of Egypt, I will show them my wonders." Daughter Jerusalem had asked for a return to "the days of old" (7:14) and YHWH complies, promising wonders as dramatic as those surrounding the exodus from Egypt (Exod 3:20; 15:11; Pss 78:12;

EXCURSUS
Shepherd Imagery in the Bible

Within the book of Micah, shepherding imagery is utilized in various ways. In 2:12, the image is menacing, as the people are gathered into a sheepfold for punishment. In 4:8, Daughter Zion is called "tower of the flock." In 5:4 (5:3 MT), the ruler who will come from Bethlehem is envisioned as feeding his flock. Here in 7:14, YHWH is called to act as a gracious shepherd of his people.

Shepherding imagery appears throughout the Hebrew Bible and New Testament, in both positive and negative contexts. The positive images are perhaps the best known. Psalm 23 envisions YHWH as a kind and gentle shepherd, protecting the sheep from harm and allowing them to lie down in safety. John 10 describes Jesus as the good shepherd who lays down his life for his sheep. But negative images also appear. In Zech 11:4-6, YHWH instructs the prophet to oversee a "flock of slaughter," ones designated to be killed. A similar usage is that of Jer 12:3, which asks YHWH to make enemies as sheep destined for slaughter; Ezek 34:3; Ps 44:11, 22; and Isa 53:7 also describe the people as sheep to be slain.

Perhaps because of these associations, all shepherds are traditionally assumed to be male. In Gen 29, however, Rachel is repeatedly described as keeping her father's sheep. The same verb is used for her action (רעה) as for Jacob in Gen 30, for YHWH in Mic 7:14 and Ps 23, and indeed for all the characters who are described as shepherding in the Hebrew Bible. Despite its traditional associations, the image of the deity as "shepherd" is not a gender-specific one.

Julia M. O'Brien

106:7), echoing YHWH's earlier reminder of his favor in delivering the people and sending them Moses, Aaron, and Miriam (Mic 6:4).

Daughter Jerusalem's speech resumes in Mic 7:16 and continues through the end of the book. Her speech of confidence that the nations will be humbled before YHWH echoes the earlier divine promise to destroy the nations (7:13) and depicts in metaphorical terms the nations' pending shame and powerlessness against Judah. They will clamp their hands over their mouths in astonishment (see Job 21:5) and tremble in the presence of Jerusalem. The imagery of licking dust like a snake alludes not only to the curse of the serpent in Gen 3:14 but also to the enemies in Ps 72:9 and Isa 49:23 who lick the dust before YHWH; as in Deut 32:24, snakes crawl in the dust.

The book of Micah closes with Jerusalem's final plea for divine favor. Using the liturgical forms of praise, she bases her appeal on YHWH's character. Because YHWH is forgiving, does not hold anger forever, and is compassionate, Jerusalem trusts that YHWH will honor the promises made to her ancestors. Daughter Jerusalem repeats a credo taught to Israel in the wilderness by YHWH himself:

> The LORD passed before [Moses] and proclaimed,
>   "The LORD, the LORD,
>   a God merciful and gracious,
>   slow to anger,
>   and abounding in steadfast love and faithfulness,
>   keeping steadfast love for the thousandth generation,
>   forgiving iniquity and transgression and sin,
>   yet by no means clearing the guilty,
>   but visiting the iniquity of the parents
>   upon the children
>   and the children's children,
>   to the third and the fourth generation." (Exod 34:6-7)

This credo is repeated various times in the Hebrew Bible in various contexts. In times of crisis, it becomes the promise to which Israel holds YHWH. For example, when YHWH threatens to smite the wilderness generation for their rebellion, Moses reminds the deity of his own character:

> And now, therefore, let the power of the LORD be great in the way that you promised when you spoke, saying,
>   "The LORD is slow to anger,
>   and abounding in steadfast love,
>   forgiving iniquity and transgression,
>   but by no means clearing the guilty,
>   visiting the iniquity of the parents
>   upon the children
>   to the third and the fourth generation."
> Forgive the iniquity of this people according to the greatness of your steadfast love, just as you have pardoned this people, from Egypt even until now. (Num 14:17-19)

In Micah, Jerusalem's praise of YHWH similarly serves to instruct YHWH about his character in an implied appeal for YHWH to be consistent with his own character: be the god we both know you are. Micah 7:18-20 addresses YHWH in the second person ("you") as well as in the third person ("he"). This shift can take place in a single verse, as seen in the Hebrew of 7:18b, reflected in the footnote of the NRSV, and in 7:19.

YHWH's promises to the fathers provide a further basis for appeal and perhaps also an implied critique. By affirming that YHWH *will* honor his promises to Abraham and Isaac, Daughter Jerusalem suggests that YHWH has *not yet* done so. In Ps 105, such recitals serve to *remind the people* of the divine acts of mercy:

> Remember the wonderful works he has done,
>> his miracles, and the judgments he uttered,
> O offspring of his servant Abraham,
>> children of Jacob, his chosen ones.
> He is the Lord our God;
>> his judgments are in all the earth.
> He is mindful of his covenant forever,
>> of the word that he commanded, for a thousand generations,
> the covenant that he made with Abraham,
>> his sworn promise to Isaac,
> which he confirmed to Jacob as a statute,
> to Israel as an everlasting covenant. (Ps 105:5-10)

In Mic 7:18-20, the recital *reminds* YHWH how to treat his people.

The poignant ending of the book of Micah is the key to understanding the theological formulation of the book as a whole. Here, the voice of the Persian-period writer is most transparent, pleading for YHWH to return his favor to Jerusalem, to finally forgive its earlier sin and restore the people. When the book as a whole is read from the vantage point of this concluding plea, we see the judgments of Mic 1–3 and 6 as retrospective explanations of why Jerusalem now suffers. In eighth-century Judah, the Persian-period writer claims, a prophet named Micah announced that YHWH would destroy Israel and Judah as punishment for their corruption—economic dishonesty, land confiscation, and the failure of political and religious leaders. From the same Persian-period vantage point, we can view Mic 4 and 5 as the basis for future hope: the same eighth-century prophet who predicted Jerusalem's punishment, claims this writer, also predicted Jerusalem's exaltation and the rise of a Davidic ruler.

Micah 7 laments the current state of the (Persian-period) community and calls on YHWH to honor the promises such as those recorded in Mic 4–5. Divine punishment has been accomplished; both Samaria and Jerusalem have been destroyed, and the time for restoration is overdue. Now is the time for the rest of the prophet's predications to come true—the humiliation of Jerusalem's enemies and the expansion and glory of the city. The Persian-period author accepts the community's blame for the current state of things but pleads with YHWH to fully forgive and act on the community's behalf. Be the forgiving God that you claim to be, he petitions; honor your promises to the ancestors, and let *today* be *that day* of salvation which you have promised.

In days to come
    the mountain of the LORD's house
shall be established as the highest of the mountains,
    and shall be raised up above the hills.
Peoples shall stream to it,
    and many nations shall come and say:
"Come, let us go up to the mountain of the LORD,
    to the house of the God of Jacob;
that he may teach us his ways
    and that we may walk in his paths."
For out of Zion shall go forth instruction,
    and the word of the LORD from Jerusalem.
He shall judge between many peoples,
    and shall arbitrate between strong nations far away;
they shall beat their swords into plowshares,
    and their spears into pruning hooks;
nation shall not lift up sword against nation,
    neither shall they learn war any more;
    but they shall all sit under their own vines and under their own
        fig trees, and no one shall make them afraid;
    for the mouth of the LORD of hosts has spoken.
For all the peoples walk,
    each in the name of its god,
but we will walk in the name of the LORD our God
    forever and ever.
In that day, says the LORD,
    I will assemble the lame
and gather those who have been driven away,
    and those whom I have afflicted.
The lame I will make the remnant,
    and those who were cast off, a strong nation;
and the LORD will reign over them in Mount Zion
    now and forevermore.
And you, O tower of the flock,
    hill of daughter Zion,
to you it shall come,
    the former dominion shall come,
    the sovereignty of daughter Jerusalem. (Mic 4:1-8)

Daughter Jerusalem who now laments in darkness is ready to be shown marvelous things (7:15).

Conclusion

A Feminist Response to Micah's Theology

The theology of blame that runs through the book of Micah, often called retribution theology, is considered by many modern readers as barbaric. For many religious and secular progressives, such thought is associated with figures such as Pat Robertson, who blamed New Orleans's sinfulness for the devastation wrought by Hurricane Katrina, and Fred Phelps, former pastor of Westboro Baptist Church who picketed military funerals claiming that the US war dead are God's punishment for the country's tolerance of homosexuality. In *God's Problem: How the Bible Fails to Answer Our Most Important Question—Why We Suffer*, even though Bart Ehrman recognizes that the prophets cannot be blamed for ways in which their theology has been applied, he nonetheless claims that the "prophetic view of suffering" raises questions such as, "Is God at fault for the famines in Ethiopia? Does God create military conflict?"[1] Many would share Ehrman's response to such a theology: "I refuse to think that birth defects, massive

---

1. Bart D. Ehrman, *God's Problem: How the Bible Fails to Answer Our Most Important Question—Why We Suffer* (New York: HarperOne, 2008), 54.

starvation, flu epidemics, Alzheimer's disease, and genocides are given by God to make people repent, or to teach them a lesson."[2]

While not disputing the ethical problems of retribution theology, within the past decade an increasing number of biblical scholars has attempted to *understand* the origins and the life situations from which the theology emerged. Many have turned to insights from trauma studies to explore the effect of the violent destruction of Jerusalem on Judah's national identity. Kathleen O'Connor's masterful study *Jeremiah: Pain and Promise*, for example, casts Jeremiah's language of blame, anger, and retribution as the community's response to the trauma of Judah's destruction by Babylonian armies. She claims that, as a provisional attempt at meaning making, Jeremiah's blame of the community for its fate elevates the people from helpless victims to agents of their own future and allows them to continue believing in God and God's promises.[3]

> God is Punisher offers one way, among many in Jeremiah, to integrate the disaster into the long stream of the nation's existence, its long narrative memory. The disaster thus begins to be assimilated into the larger story of their relationship with God from the time of Abraham, Sarah, and Hagar. They are still connected to their past identity as God's people.[4]

Jeremiah's attempts to make sense out of an unspeakable tragedy may not stand the test of *universal* theology, claims O'Connor, but they may have been good news *in their own context*.

Thomas Mann has made a similar argument for the Deuteronomistic History. While he claims that applying a reward-punishment scheme to all of human history is obscene, he recognizes the benefits of the Deuteronomistic understanding of Israel's fate:

> The Former Prophets is a theodicy in that it attempts to show how God is good despite all the evil that has consumed Israel. . . . Both ancient and contemporary history clearly show that the greatest danger is not the nation that sees itself as subject to God's judgment against hubris and injustice, and at times even suffering for that, but rather the nation that sees itself as a completely autonomous power, answerable to no higher authority, for it acknowledges none, responsible for no one's

2. Ibid., 274.

3. Kathleen O'Connor, *Jeremiah: Pain and Promise* (Minneapolis: Fortress Press, 2011).

4. Kathleen O'Connor, "Reclaiming Jeremiah's Violence," in *The Aesthetics of Violence in the Prophets*, ed. Chris Franke and Julia M. O'Brien (New York: T & T Clark, 2010), 47.

welfare other than its Own (or only the elite within it). The greatest failure is the refusal or inability to acknowledge failure.[5]

O'Connor's and Mann's attempts to empathize with, if not approve of, the theology expressed in literature written during the exile are helpful in reminding us of the contextual nature of theology. Theological formulations that are death-dealing in one context might be life-giving in another.

This observation holds true nowhere more tenaciously than in situations that psychologist Judith Herman has deemed "complex trauma," scenarios of long-term systemic suffering such as child abuse at the hands of parents. The abused child, claims Herman,

> must find a way to preserve hope and meaning. The alternative is utter despair, which no child can bear. To preserve her faith in her parents, she must reject the first and most obvious conclusion that something is terribly wrong with them. She will go to any lengths to construct an explanation for her fate that absolves her parents of all blame and responsibility. . . . In the environment of chronic abuse, neither time nor experience provide any corrective for this tendency toward self-blame; rather it is continually reinforced.[6]

David Blumenthal casts the Jewish relationship with its Father God in much this way, suggesting that even after the Holocaust "facing an abusing God" is preferable to staring into the void.[7]

Rather than foregrounding the imagery of the abused child, however, the prophets' gaze turns to the abused woman/wife. As noted previously, feminist scholars have extensively explored the domestic abuse patterns inherent in prophetic descriptions of Israel and Judah and the imbedded patriarchy/misogyny they presuppose. These feminine metaphors suggest how dangerous it was to be a woman in the ancient (and perhaps the modern) world and, in turn, why the authors of the prophetic books might compare their own sense of abjection to the plight of a woman: "The writers of the Bible most certainly 'got the message' of their own vulnerability, even though they chose to understand it as a

5. Thomas W. Mann, *The Book of the Former Prophets* (Eugene, OR: Cascade, 2011), 383.

6. Judith Herman, *Trauma and Recovery: The Aftermath of Violence—from Domestic Abuse to Political Terror* (New York: Basic Books, 1997), 101–3.

7. David Blumenthal, *Facing the Abusing God: A Theology of Protest* (Louisville, KY: Westminster John Knox, 1993).

matter of human sin, and a gendered one at that, instead of divine for-sakenness or the simple fact of being in the way of more ruthless, acqui-sitive powers. . . . A violent god is preferable to an impotent or non-existent one."[8] In her study of Ezekiel, Tamar Kamionkowski ex-plains the psychological function of the horrific violence against women that characterizes Ezek 16 and 23. Operating within the ideology of patriarchy, the masculine anxiety of vulnerability is projected onto meta-phorical women and then "solved" when gender hierarchy and "order" are restored through brutal means.[9]

Interpreting Micah within the framework of trauma studies offers obvious insights, and yet it falls short of addressing the specificity of this book's theological program. The insights emerge from recognizing that its retribution theology might have functioned positively for its writer and his community: because the fall of Jerusalem (and Samaria) was justified, then YHWH's faithfulness need not be questioned. Accepting the *justice* of YHWH allows the writer to depend on the *graciousness* of YHWH. And yet, trauma studies applies less obviously to Micah than it does to Ezekiel and Jeremiah. Micah uses many of same tropes as those books, but exhibits some important differences from them.

The dynamics of blame are complex in Micah. While Mic 1 and 7 do name the sin of Jerusalem as a city, elsewhere in the book Daughter Je-rusalem is more victim than perpetrator. "Heads," prophets, and various leaders are excoriated throughout the book, and the cause of Daughter Jerusalem's dire fate in Mic 4 is not explicitly stated. When Daughter Jerusalem does accept blame in Mic 7 ("I must bear the indignation of the LORD, because I have sinned against him" [7:9]), she is treated as a sympathetic rather than punishable figure. Daughter Jerusalem's first-person speech in Mic 7 elicits compassion rather than accusation.

Moreover, the fragmented, even dissociative, language that O'Connor traces in Jeremiah and the scatological violence that Kamionkowski explores in Ezekiel are missing from Micah, replaced by the *tropes* of lament and abjection rather than their *content*. The book of Micah attri-butes to the prophet the *vocabulary* of lament, but the speeches lack the raw *emotional power* of those that appear in Jer 8; 9; 20; the book of Lam-

---

8. Carole R. Fontaine, *With Eyes of Flesh: The Bible, Gender, and Human Rights*, ed. J. Cheryl Exum, The Bible in the Modern World 10 (Sheffield: Sheffield Phoenix, 2008), 76.

9. S. Tamar Kamionowski, *Gender Reversal and Cosmic Chaos: A Study on the Book of Ezekiel*, JSOTSup 368 (Sheffield: Sheffield Academic Press, 2003), 152.

entations; and the psalms of lament. Of course, trauma affects not only those who experience it directly but also subsequent generations; like guilt, the effects of trauma are visited "upon the children and the children's children, to the third and the fourth generation" (Exod 34:7).[10] Yet, while trauma may linger in Micah's background, it does not stand on bloody display.

Throughout this commentary, I have often turned to postcolonial studies to interpret Micah. Postcolonial studies focuses on the existential realities of communities living under empire, realities that do not exclude the trauma of war yet extend into the ongoing dynamics (external and internal) of what it means to live as a subject people. In conversation with Steed Davidson's provocative article, "Prophets Postcolonially: Initial Insights for a Postcolonial Reading of Prophetic Literature," I have attempted to think about the book of Micah as literature produced in the context of the Persian Empire and explore what such a framework may add to our understanding of the author's analysis of the past and his hopes for the future. Perhaps utlizing literary tropes inherited from parents or grandparents who experienced the Babylonian destruction of Jerusalem, this writer living under empire was working through his own generation's anxieties and concerns.

Davina Lopez insightfully uses postcolonial studies to read the Pauline writings as a response to Roman imperial control. In the Roman imagination, as depicted on its coinage and other artistic productions, conquered nations were women subjected to the superior masculinity of the emperor.[11] By adopting feminine imagery for himself, she claims, the apostle Paul subverts not only such gender expectations but also his community's self-understanding. Lopez also suggests that Paul's comparison of himself to a mother who breastfeeds her children (1 Thess 2:7; 1 Cor 3:1-2) evokes prophetic imagery of Daughter Jerusalem's birth pangs (including that of Micah) and, by extension, the prophets' claims that such pain will inaugurate a new era. Paul thereby subverts Roman ideology by calling for solidarity and a new form of relationship.

10. Psychologists debate about whether the trauma of the Holocaust can affect the survivors' grandchildren—genetically or through family dynamics. See Josh Nathan-Kazis, "Can Holocaust Trauma Affect 'Third Generation'? Studies Debate Impact on Grandchildren of Survivors," *The Jewish Daily Forward*, September 5, 2012, http://forward.com/news/162030/can-holocaust-trauma-affect-third-generation.

11. Davina C. Lopez, *Apostle to the Conquered: Reimaging Paul's Mission* (Minneapolis: Fortress Press, 2008).

Instead of living up to male/female imperial expectations of unequivo-
cal domination and subordination, Paul models uncharacteristic vulnerability. S/he advocates living into an-other world, the new creation,
through inter-national community resistance and nonconformity to the
Roman imperial structure, the metanarrative ordering the world and
helping to keep peace at the time. By turning around and away from
violence toward the outside and lowly, Paul models a masculinity and
femininity that defies the Roman obligation to conquer and promotes
allegiance among the defeated.[12]

I find Lopez's discussion of the destabilizing effects of a male writer
accepting the female subject position intriguing. It helps me to recognize
how even the adoption of stereotypical feminine imagery can be subversive. For example, while in Mic 4 the empowered Jerusalem becomes
masculine, in the book's final chapter the writer does seem to take on
the woman's emotions and position.

Postcolonial studies also recognizes, however, the ways in which cultural productions such as Micah also can reinscribe other forms of power.
The women on whose experiences the prophetic tropes of childbirth,
rape, and dependency rely remain absent from these books—as do the
real lives of men and children. If "the task of liberation hermeneutics—
feminist, queer, black, postcolonial—is to return personhood and agency
to those who have had it taken from them, especially through the literary
personifications of 'nations,' "[13] then the gender of literary figures cannot
be the interpreter's sole concern. The speech of Daughter Jerusalem in
Mic 7 may be in a woman's voice, but it is not necessarily a voice from
a woman's perspective. Our suspicions should be raised when a female
accepts her punishment as justified, even though others—portrayed as
male—are guilty, and when she laments the dissolution of the patriarchal
household despite the subordinate role it grants to her. As elsewhere in
the book, the author offers us no insight into the situations of real women
and men in the author's community—whether they share the author's
theology or find it hopeful.

Feminists have long cautioned us to be suspicious of theological claims
touted as "universal." In 1960, Christian theologian Valerie Saiving argued that the identification of sin with pride and identifying love with
self-sacrifice is a masculine response to the experience of being socialized
to achieve. Women, who regularly sacrifice themselves for children and

12. Ibid., 153.
13. Ibid., 171.

others, face the opposite temptation: to never claim their own worth and needs. A theology based on male experience, she claimed, does not well serve all people.[14] In 2003, the Jewish theologian Melissa Raphael explored the masculine assumptions that have framed much Jewish post-Holocaust theology. Interpreting the Holocaust as a sign of divine impotence or divine indifference, she claims, reflects the masculine value of power and control; the memoirs of female Holocaust survivors do not describe the absence of God at Auschwitz but rather the ways in which the divine was encountered in other women's faces.[15] As Christian theologian Serene Jones claims, women's experience of trauma challenges us to rethink our theologies: "not only about grace, but also about such matters as sin, redemption, hope, community, communion, violence, death, crucifixion, and resurrection."[16]

The historical aspects of my commentary reflect my attempt to contextualize Micah's theology. I have argued that the book emerges from the context of the Persian Empire and have attempted to explore as much as possible women's lives in Persian Yehud. I recognize that this historical reconstruction is not definitive, but it has been motivated by desire to reflect on what theology means for people's real lives. My inclusion of some of the history of Micah's interpretation and the insights of the other contributors has attempted to take this contextualization further, providing concrete testimony to the different things Micah has meant—and can mean—to real-life readers.

The work of contextualization is never complete. It is my hope that these explorations of Micah's articulations of justice and the future will spur yet other readers to discern in community their own hopes and dreams. The details of Micah's moral imagination often differ from my own, and yet this book provokes me to ask the same questions of my community that this writer asks of his. What is justice? What should the future look like? What should we hope for? And Micah reminds me that the past is not only a story of failure but also a story of human actors: Moses, Aaron, Miriam, and a host of unnamed ancient people whose lives have mattered to God.

14. Valerie Saiving, "The Human Situation: A Feminine View," *JR* 40 (1960): 100–112.

15. Melissa Raphael, *The Female Face of God at Auschwitz: A Jewish Feminist Theology of the Holocaust* (New York: Routledge, 2003).

16. Serene Jones, *Trauma and Grace: Theology in a Ruptured World* (Louisville, KY: Westminster John Knox 2009), 11.

Works Cited

Althaus-Reid, Marcella. *Indecent Theology: Theological Perversions in Sex, Gender and Politics*. London and New York: Routledge, 2000.

Anderson, Francis I., and David Noel Freedman. *Micah: A New Translation with Introduction and Commentary*. AB24E. New York: Doubleday, 2000.

Beal, Timothy K. "Opening: Cracking the Binding." In *Reading Bibles, Writing Bodies: Identity and the Book*, edited by Timothy K. Beal and David M. Gunn, 1–12. London: Routledge, 1997.

Ben Zvi, Ehud. *Micah*. The Forms of the Old Testament Literature. Vol. 21B. Grand Rapids, MI: Eerdmans, 2000.

Berry, Wendell. *Bringing It to the Table: Farming and Food*. Berkeley, CA: Counterpoint, 2009.

Bietenhard, Sophia. "Micah: Call for Justice—Hope for All." In *Feminist Biblical Interpretation: A Compendium of Critical Commentary on the Books of the Bible and Related Literature*, edited by Louise Schottroff, Marie-Theres Wacker, and Martin Rusmscheidt, 421–32. Grand Rapids, MI: Eerdmans, 2012.

Blenkinsopp, Joseph. *Ezra–Nehemiah*. Philadelphia: Westminster Press, 1988.

Blumenthal, David. *Facing the Abusing God: A Theology of Protest*. Louisville, KY: Westminster John Knox, 1993.

Boda, Mark J., Carol J. Dempsey, and LeAnn Snow Flesher. *Daughter Zion: Her Portrait, Her Response*. AIL 13. Atlanta, GA: SBL Press, 2012.

Borowski, Oded. *Agriculture in Iron Age Israel*. Winona Lake, IN: Eisenbrauns, 1987.

Bridgeman, Valerie. "Womanist Criticism." In *Oxford Encyclopedia of the Bible and Gender Studies*, vol. 2, edited by Julia M. O'Brien, 431–39. New York: Oxford University Press, 2014.

Brown, Raymond E. *The Birth of the Messiah: A Commentary on the Infancy Narratives in Matthew and Luke*. 2nd ed. ABRL. Garden City, NY: Doubleday, 1993.

Burlein, Ann. *Lift High the Cross: Where White Supremacy and the Religious Right Converge*. Durham, NC: Duke University Press, 2002.

Burns, Rita. *Has the Lord Indeed Only Spoken through Moses? A Study of the Biblical Portrait of Miriam*. SBLDS 84. Atlanta, GA: SBL Press, 1987.

Camp, Claudia V. *Wise, Strange and Holy: The Strange Woman and the Making of the Bible*. JSOTSup 320. Sheffield: Sheffield Academic, 2000.

Carli, Enzo. *Le Sculture Del Duomo Di Orvieto*. Bergano: Instituto Italiano d'Arti Grafiche, 1947.

Cataldo, Jeremiah. "Persian Policy and the Yehud Community During Nehemiah." *JSOT* 28 (2003): 131–43.

———. *A Theocratic Yehud? Issues of Government in a Persian Province*. LHBOTS 498. New York and London: T & T Clark, 2009.

Claassens, L. Juliana M. "Calling the Keeners: The Image of the Wailing Woman as Symbol of Survival in a Traumatized World." *JFSR* 26 (2010): 63–77.

Collins, John J., and Adela Yarbro Collins. *King and Messiah as Son of God: Divine, Human, and Angelic Messianic Figures in Biblical and Related Literature*. Grand Rapids, MI: Eerdmans, 2008.

Cone, James. *The Cross and the Lynching Tree*. Maryknoll, NY: Orbis Books, 2011.

Coomber, Matthew J. M. "Caught in the Crossfire? Economic Injustice and Prophetic Motivation in Eighth-Century Judah." *BibInt* 19 (2011): 396–432.

Copass, B. A., and E. L. Carlson. *A Study of the Prophet Micah: Power by the Spirit*. Grand Rapids, MI: Baker Book House, 1950.

Darr, Katheryn Pfisterer. *Isaiah's Vision and the Family of God*. Louisville, KY: Westminster John Knox, 1994.

Davidson, Steed. "Prophets Postcolonially: Initial Insights for a Postcolonial Reading of Prophetic Literature." *The Bible and Critical Theory* 6, no. 2 (2010): 24-1.13.

Dean, Malcolm. "Margaret Thatcher's Policies Hit the Poor Hardest—and It's Happening Again." *The Guardian* (2013). Published electronically April 9, 2013. http://www.theguardian.com/society/2013/apr/09/margaret-thatcher-policies-poor-society.

Dempsey, Carol J. "Micah 2–3: Literary Artistry, Ethical Message, and Some Considerations about the Image of Yahweh and Micah." *JSOT* 85 (1999): 117–28.

Diamant, Anita. *The Red Tent*. New York: Picador USA, 1997.

Ehrman, Bart D. *God's Problem: How the Bible Fails to Answer Our Most Important Question—Why We Suffer*. New York: HarperOne, 2008.

Diyar. *Diyar: That We Might Have Life and Have It Abundantly*. Diyar Consortium, 2015, http://www.diyar.ps/.

Dodge, Ralph E. *The Revolutionary Bishop: Who Saw God at Work in Africa*. Pasadena, CA: William Carey Library, 1986.

Fantalkin, Alexander, and Oren Tal. "Redating Lachish Level I: Identifying Achaemenid Imperial Policy at the Southern Frontier of the Fifth Satrapy." In

Judah and the Judeans in the Persian Period, edited by Oded Lipshits and Manfred Oeming, 167–97. Winona Lake, IN: Eisenbrauns, 2006.

Farisani, Elelwani B. "Micah." In *The Africana Bible*, edited by Hugh R. Page Jr., 189–93. Minneapolis: Fortress Press, 2010.

Feld, Merle. *A Spiritual Life: Exploring the Heart and Jewish Tradition.* Albany: SUNY Press, 2007.

Fentress-Williams, Judy. "Micah." In *Women's Bible Commentary*, edited by Carol Newsom, Sharon Ringe, and Jacqueline Lapsley, 326–28. 3rd ed. Louisville, KY: Westminster John Knox, 2012.

Fiderer, Anita, and David Finn Moskowitz. *The Facade Reliefs of Orvieto Cathedral.* London and Turnhout: Harvey Miller Publishers, 2009.

Fischer, Irmtraud. "The Authority of Miriam: A Feminist Rereading of Numbers 12 Prompted by Jewish Interpretation." In *A Feminist Companion to Exodus to Deuteronomy*, edited by Athalya Brenner-Idan, 159–73. FCB 6. Sheffield: Sheffield Academic Press, 2000.

Fischer, Shlomo, and Suzanne Last Stone. *Guidelines for Teachers: Tolerance and Principles of Religion.* Sarajevo: International Forum Bosnia, 2004.

Floyd, Michael. *Minor Prophets, Part 2.* Grand Rapids, MI: Eerdmans, 2000.

Fontaine, Carole R. "The Abusive Bible: On the Use of Feminist Method in Pastoral Contexts." In *Feminist Companion to Reading the Bible*, edited by Athalya Brenner and Carole Fontaine, 84–113. Sheffield: Sheffield Academic Press, 1997.

———. *With Eyes of Flesh: The Bible, Gender, and Human Rights.* The Bible in the Modern World 10. Sheffield: Sheffield Phoenix, 2008.

Gafney, Wilda. *Daughters of Miriam: Women Prophets in Ancient Israel.* Philadelphia: Fortress Press, 2008.

Gerstenberger, Erhard S. *Israel in the Persian Period: The Fifth and Fourth Centuries B.C.E.* Atlanta, GA: SBL Press, 2011.

Glass, Zipporah. "Land, Labor, and Law: Viewing Persian Yehud's Economy through Socio-Economic Modeling." PhD diss., Vanderbilt University, 2010.

Grabbe, Lester L. *A History of the Jews and Judaism in the Second Second Period.* Vol. 1. London and New York: T & T Clark, 2004.

———. "Introduction and Overview." In *'Every City Shall Be Forsaken': Urbanism and Prophecy in Ancient Israel and the Near East*, edited by Lester L. Grabbe and Robert D. Haak. JSOTSup 330. Sheffield: Sheffield Academic Press, 2001.

Grant, Jacquelyn. "A Womanist Christology." In *Walk Together Children: Black and Womanist Theologies, Church, and Theological Education*, edited by Dwight N. Hopkins and Linda E. Thomas, 169–80. Eugene, OR: Wipf and Stock, 2010.

Hegewisch, Ariane, and Stephanie Keller Hudiburg. "The Gender Wage Gap by Occupation and by Race and Ethnicity, 2013." *IWPR #C414*. Institute for Women's Policy Research, http://www.iwpr.org/publications/pubs/the-gender-wage-gap-by-occupation-and-by-race-and-ethnicity-2013.

Herman, Judith. *Trauma and Recovery: The Aftermath of Violence—from Domestic Abuse to Political Terror.* New York: Basic Books, 1997.

Hillers, Delbert. *Micah: A Commentary on the Book of the Prophet Micah.* Hermeneia: A Critical and Historical Commentary on the Bible. Philadephia: Fortress Press, 1984.

hooks, bell. "The Oppositional Gaze: Black Female Spectators." In *Feminist Film Theory: A Reader*, edited by Sue Thornham, 307–20. New York: New York University Press, 1999.

Huffmon, Herbert. "The Covenant Lawsuit in the Prophets." *JBL* 78 (1959): 285–95.

IFPRI News. "Report Finds Severe Gender Inequities." *Consultative Group on International Agricultural Reasearch 2*, no. 2, World Bank (1995), http://www-wds.worldbank.org/external/default/WDSContentServer/WDSP/IB/2002/03/29/000094946_0203200402053/Rendered/PDF/multi0page.pdf.

Israeli Committee Against House Demolition. "Defining the Palestinian Bantustan. Element #5: The Separation Barrier/Wall." http://www.icahd.org/node/446.

Jacobs, Mignon R. *The Conceptual Coherence of the Book of Micah.* JSOTSup 322. Sheffield: Sheffield Academic Press, 2001.

James, Elaine. "Miriam and Her Interpreters." In *Women's Bible Commentary*, edited by Carol Newsom, Sharon Ringe, and Jacqueline Lapsley, 67–69. 3rd ed. Louisville, KY: Westminster John Knox, 2012.

Jazairy, Idriss, Mohiuddin Alamgir, Theresa Panuccio, and International Fund for Agricultural Development. *The State of World Rural Poverty: An Inquiry into Its Causes and Consequences.* New York: NYU Press, 1993.

Jeffers, Ann. "Popular Religion and Magic, Subentry Hebrew Bible." In *The Oxford Encyclopedia of the Bible and Gender Studies*, edited by Julia M. O'Brien. Vol. 2. New York: Oxford University Press, 2014.

Jones, Serene. *Trauma and Grace: Theology in a Ruptured World.* Louisville, KY: Westminster John Knox, 2009.

Kamionowski, S. Tamar. *Gender Reversal and Cosmic Chaos: A Study on the Book of Ezekiel.* JSOTSup 368. Sheffield: Sheffield Academic Press, 2003.

Kartzow, Marianne. "Intersectional Studies." In *The Oxford Encyclopedia of the Bible and Gender Studies*, edited by Julia M. O'Brien. Vol. 1. New York: Oxford University Press, 2014.

Kidd, Sue Monk. *The Dance of the Dissident Daughter: A Woman's Journey from Christian Tradition to the Sacred Feminine.* New York: HarperOne, 2006.

Knoppers, Gary. "Revisiting the Samarian Question in the Persian Period." In *Judah and the Judeans in the Persian Period*, edited by Oded Lipschits and Manfred Oeming, 265–89. Winona Lake, IN: Eisebrauns, 2006.

Lichtenstein, Aaron. *The Seven Laws of Noah.* New York: Rabbi Jacob Joseph School Press, 1981.

Lipshits, Oded. "Achaemenid Imperial Policy, Settlement Processes in Palestine, and the Status of Jerusalem in the Middle of the Fifth Century B.C.E." In *Judah and the Judeans in the Persian Period*, edited by Oded Lipschits and Manfred Oeming, 19–52. Winona Lake, IN: Eisenbrauns, 2006.

Lopez, Davina C. *Apostle to the Conquered: Reimaging Paul's Mission.* Minneapolis: Fortress Press, 2008.

MacDonald, Nathan. *What Did the Ancient Israelites Eat? Diet in Biblical Times.* Grand Rapids, MI: Eerdmans, 2008.

MacKay, W. MacKintosh. *The Goodly Fellowship of the Prophets: A Homiletic Study of the Prophetic Literatures of the Old Testament.* New York: Richard R. Smith, Inc., 1929.

Maier, Christl. " 'Daughter Zion' as Gendered Space in the Book of Jeremiah." Paper presented at the Society of Biblical Literature Annual Meeting, 2003.

———. *Daughter Zion, Mother Zion: Gender, Space, and the Sacred in Ancient Israel.* Philadelphia: Fortress Press, 2008.

Mandolfo, Carleen. *Daughter of Zion Talks Back to the Prophets: A Dialogic Theology of the Book of Lamentations.* SemeiaSt 58. Atlanta, GA: SBL Press, 2007.

Mann, Thomas W. *The Book of the Former Prophets.* Eugene, OR: Cascade, 2011.

Mason, Rex. *Micah, Nahum, and Obadiah.* OTG. Sheffield: JSOT Press, 1991.

Mays, James Luther. *Micah: A Commentary.* Philadelphia: Westminster, 1976.

Meir, Tamar. "Miriam: Midrash and Aggadah." *Jewish Women's Archive: Encyclopedia.* March 20, 2009. http://jwa.org/encyclopedia/article/miriam-midrash -and-aggadah.

Meleis, Afaf Ibrahim, Eugenie L. Birch, and Susan M. Wachter. *Women's Health and the World's Cities.* Philadelphia: University of Pennsylvania Press, 2011.

Miriam's Cup. "History: Feminist Rituals in the Passover Seder." Miriam's Cup: A New Ritual for the Passover Seder. http://www.miriamscup.com/History First.htm.

Mitchell, Christine. "1–2 Chronicles." In *Women's Bible Commentary*, edited by Carol Newsom, Sharon Ringe, and Jacqueline Lapsley, 184–90. 3rd ed. Louisville, KY: Westminster John Knox, 2012.

Moskowitz, Anita Fiderer, and David Finn. *The Facade Reliefs of Orvieto Cathedral.* London/Turnhout: Harvey Miller Publishers, 2009.

Moxnes, Halvor. *Putting Jesus in His Place: A Radical Vision of Household and Kingdom.* Louisville, KY: Westminster John Knox, 2003.

Mullen, E. Theodore, Jr. *Ethnic Myths and Pentateuchal Foundations: A New Approach to the Formation of the Pentateuch.* Atlanta, GA: Scholars Press, 1997.

Muzorewa, Abel T. *Rise Up and Walk: An Autobiography.* Nashville, TN: Abingdon, 1978.

Na'aman, Nadav. " 'The House-of-No-Shade Shall Take Away Its Tax from You' (Micah 1:11)." *VT* 45 (1995): 516–67.

———. "Sennacherib's Campaign to Judah and the Date of the *Lmlk* Stamps." *VT* 29 (1979): 61–86.

NAACP. "Criminal Justice Fact Sheet." NAACP.org. http://www.naacp.org/pages /criminal-justice-fact-sheet.

Nathan-Kazis, Josh. "Can Holocaust Trauma Affect 'Third Generation'? Studies Debate Impact on Grandchildren of Survivors." *The Jewish Daily Forward*

(September 5, 2012). http://forward.com/news/162030/can-holocaust
-trauma-affect-third-generation/

Nava, Antonia. "L'albero Di Jesse Nella Cattedrale D'orvieto E La Pittura Bizantina." *Rivista dell'Istituto nazionale d'archeologia e storia dell'arte* 5 (1936): 363–74.

Nissinen, Martti. *Prophets and Prophecy in the Ancient Near East.* Writings from
the Ancient World. Atlanta, GA: SBL Press, 2003.

Nogalski, James. *The Book of the Twelve: Hosea through Jonah.* Macon, GA: Smith
and Helwys, 2011.

———. *Literary Precursors to the Book of the Twelve.* BZAW 217. Berlin and New
York: de Gruyter, 1993.

O'Brien, Julia M. *Challenging Prophetic Metaphor: Theology and Ideology in the
Prophets.* Louisville, KY: Westminster John Knox, 2008.

———. *Nahum.* Sheffield: Sheffield Academic, 2002.

———. "Nahum—Habakkuk—Zephaniah: Reading the 'Former Prophets' in
the Persian Period." *Int* 61 (2007): 168–83.

———. "Once and Future Gender: Gender and the Future in the Twelve." In
Utopia and Dystopia in Prophetic Literature, edited by Ehud Ben Zvi, 144–59.
Helskini: Finnish Exegetical Society, University of Helskini, 2006.

———. "Violent Pictures, Violent Cultures? The 'Aesthetics of Violence' in Contemporary Film and in Ancient Prophetic Texts." In *Aesthetics of Violence in
the Prophets*, edited by Julia M. O'Brien and Chris Franke, 112–30. New York
and London: T & T Clark, 2010.

O'Connor, Kathleen. *Jeremiah: Pain and Promise.* Minneapolis: Fortress Press, 2011.

———. "Reclaiming Jeremiah's Violence." In *The Aesthetics of Violence in the
Prophets*, 37–49: New York: T & T Clark, 2010.

Peterson, Eugene. *The Message: The Bible in Contemporary Language.* Colorado
Springs, CO: NAV Press, 2002.

Petrotta, A. J. "A Closer Look at Matt 2:6 and Its Old Testament Sources." *JETS*
28 (1985): 47–52.

Plaskow, Judith. *Standing Again at Sinai: Judaism from a Feminist Perspective.* Reprint ed. San Francisco, CA: HarperOne 1991.

Premnath, Devadasan N. *Eighth Century Prophets: A Social Analysis.* St. Louis,
MO: Chalice, 2003.

Raphael, Melissa. *The Female Face of God at Auschwitz: A Jewish Feminist Theology
of the Holocaust.* New York: Routledge, 2003.

Rogerson, John. "Micah." In *Eerdmans Commentary on the Bible*, edited by J. D. G.
Dunn and John Rogerson, 703–7. Grand Rapids, MI: Eerdmans, 2003.

Rose, Elizabeth A. "The Meaning of the Reliefs on the Second Pier of the Orvieto
Facade." *The Art Bulletin* 14 (1932): 258–76.

Runions, Erin. *Changing Subjects: Gender, Nation, and Future in Micah.* London
and New York: Sheffield Academic, 2001.

———. "Refusal to Mourn: U.S. National Melancholia and Its Prophetic Precursors." *Postscripts* 1 (2005): 9–45.

————. "Zion Is Burning: 'Gender Fuck' in Micah." *Semeia* 82 (1998): 225–46.

Saiving, Valerie. "The Human Situation: A Feminine View." *JR* 40 (1960): 100–112.

Salonius, Pippa. "Arbor Jesse—Lignum Vitae: The Tree of Jesse, the Tree of Life, and the Mendicants in Late Medieval Orvieto." In *The Tree: Symbol, Allegory, and Mnemonic Device in Medieval Art and Thought*, edited by Pippa Salonius and Andrea Worm, 213–41. Turnhout: Brepols, 2014.

Sanderson, Judith. "Amos." In *The Women's Bible Commentary*, edited by Carol and Sharon H. Ringe Newsom, 205–9. London and Louisville, KY: SPCK and Westminster John Knox, 1992.

————. "Micah." In *Women's Bible Commentary*, edited by Carol Newsom and Sharon H. Ringe, 215–16. Louisville, KY: Westminster John Knox, 1992.

————. "Micah." In *Women's Bible Commentary*, edited by Carol Newsom and Sharon H. Ringe, 229–31. 2nd ed. Louisville, KY: Westminster John Knox, 1998.

Sandoval, Timothy. "Education: Hebrew Bible." In *The Oxford Encyclopedia of the Bible and Gender Studies*, edited by Julia M. O'Brien. Vol. 1. New York: Oxford University Press, 2014.

Schaff, Philip. *The Principal Works of St. Jerome: Nicene and Post-Nicene Fathers, Series 2*. Christian Classics Ethereal Library. Vol. 6. New York: Christian Literature Co., 1893.

————. *Selected Works and Letters of Ambrose: Nicene and Post-Nicene Fathers, Series 2*. Christian Classics Ethereal Library. Vol. 10. New York: Christian Literature Co., 1893.

Schultz, Erika. "Seattle's Landesa Aims to Help Rural Girls in India." *The Seattle Times*, March 16, 2013. http://seattletimes.com/html/picturethis/2020485595_westbeng.html.

Simundson, Daniel. *Hosea, Joel, Amos, Obadiah, Jonah, Micah.* AOTC. Nashville, TN: Abingdon, 2005.

Smith-Christopher, Daniel L. "On the Pleasures of Prophetic Judgment: Reading Micah 1:6 and 3:12 with Stokely Carmichael." In *Aesthetics of Violence in the Prophets*, edited by Julia M. O'Brien and Chris Franke, 72–87. New York: T & T Clark, 2010.

Smith, Daniel L. *The Religion of the Landless: The Social Context of the Babylonian Exile.* Bloomington, IN: Meyer-Stone Books, 1989.

Smith, George Adam. "Micah." In *The Twelve Minor Prophets*, 357–438. New York: George H. Doran Company, 1929.

Steinmetz, Devora. "A Portrait of Miriam in Rabbinic Midrash." *Prooftexts* 8 (1988): 35–65.

Sweeney, Marvin. *The Twelve Prophets.* Vol. 2. Collegeville, MN: Liturgical Press, 2000.

Taylor, Michael D. "Three Local Motifs in Moldavian Trees of Jesse with an Excursus on the Liturgical Basis of the Exterior Mural Programs." *Revue des etudes Sud-Est Europèennes* 12 (1974): 267–75.

————. "The Prophetic Scenes in the Tree of Jesse at Orvieto." *The Art Bulletin* 54 (1972): 403–17.

Trible, Phyllis. "Bringing Miriam out of the Shadows." *BRev* 5 (1989): 14–25, 34.

————. "Bringing Miriam out of the Shadows." In *Feminist Companion to Exodus and Deuteronomy*, edited by Athalya Brenner, 166–86. FCB 6. Sheffield: Sheffield Academic Press, 1994.

van Wolde, Ellen. "The Language of Sentiment." *SBL Forum* , n.p. [cited April 2007]. Online: http://sbl-site.org/Article.aspx?ArticleID=660.

von Ewald, G. H. *Commentary on the Prophets of the Old Testament*. Translated by J. F. Smith. London: Williams & Norgate, 1876.

Waltke, Bruce K. *A Commentary on Micah*. Grand Rapids, MI: Eerdmans, 2007.

Warnock , Raphael G. *The Divided Mind of the Black Church: Theology, Piety, and Public Witness*. New York: New York University Press, 2014.

Washington, Harold. "Sexual Violence, Subentry Hebrew Bible." In *Oxford Encyclopedia of the Bible and Gender Studies*, edited by Julia M. O'Brien. Vol. 2. New York: Oxford University Press, 2014.

————. "The 'Strange Woman' of Proverbs 1–9 and Post-Exilic Judean Society." In *Second Temple Studies 2: Temple and Community in the Persian Period*, edited by Tamara C. Eskenazi and Kent H. Richards, 217–42. Sheffield: JSOT Press, 1994.

Watson, Arthur. "The Imagery of the Tree of Jesse on the West Front of the Orvieto Cathedral." In *Fritz Saxl, 1890–1948: A Volume of Memorial Essays from His Friends in England*, edited by D. J. Gordon, 149–64. London: Thomas Nelson and Sons, 1957.

Williams, Linda. "Film Bodies: Gender, Gender and Excess." In *Feminist Film Theory: A Reader*, edited by Sue Thornham, 267–80. New York: New York University Press, 1999.

Wolff, Hans Walter. *Micah: A Commentary*. Philadelphia: Augsburg Fortress, 1990.

Women-Watch. "Supporting Rural Women to Cope with High Food Prices," *Women Watch: Rural Women and Development*, October 2011, United Nations. http://www.un.org/womenwatch/feature/idrw/.

Yoder, Christine. "The Woman of Substance: A Socioeconomic Reading of Proverbs 31:10-31." *JBL* 122 (2003): 427–47.

Zsolnay, Ilona. "Deity, Subentry Ancient near East." In *The Oxford Encyclopedia of the Bible and Gender Studies*, edited by Julia M. O'Brien. Vol. 1. New York: Oxford University Press, 2014.

Index of Scripture References

Index of Subjects

General Editor

Barbara E. Reid, OP, is a Dominican Sister of Grand Rapids, Michigan. She holds a PhD in biblical studies from The Catholic University of America and is vice president and academic dean and professor of New Testament studies at Catholic Theological Union, Chicago. Her most recent publications are *Wisdom's Feast: An Invitation to Feminist Interpretation of the Scriptures* (Eerdmans, 2016) and *Abiding Word: Sunday Reflections on Year A, B, C* (3 vols.; Liturgical Press, 2011, 2012, 2013). She served as president of the Catholic Biblical Association in 2014–2015.

Volume Editor

Carol J. Dempsey, OP, PhD, is professor of theology (biblical studies) at the University of Portland, Oregon. Her primary research interest is in prophetic literature as it relates to the ancient and contemporary world. Her recent publications include *The Bible and Literature* (Orbis Books, 2015) and *Amos, Hosea, Micah, Nahum, Habakkuk, and Zephaniah: A Commentary* (Liturgical Press, 2013) and numerous articles related to prophets, gender studies, ethics, and environmental concerns. She is a member of the Dominican Order of Caldwell, New Jersey.

Author

Julia M. O'Brien is Paul H. and Grace L. Stern Professor of Hebrew Bible/Old Testament at Lancaster Theological Seminary in Lancaster, Pennsylvania. She is editor in chief of the *Oxford Encyclopedia of the Bible and Gender Studies* (2014), and her other publications include *Challenging Prophetic Metaphor* (Westminster John Knox, 2008); *Nahum through Malachi* (Abingdon Old Testament Commentary series, 2004); *Nahum* (Sheffield Academic Press, 2002; 2nd ed. 2009); and *Priest and Levite in Malachi* (Society of Biblical Literature Dissertation Series, 1990). With Chris Franke, she co-edited *Aesthetics of Violence in the Prophets* (T. & T. Clark, 2010). She holds PhD and MDiv degrees from Duke University and a BA from Wake Forest University.